BHAGAVAD GITA

Praise for *Bhagavad Gita*

'Mani Rao's courageous approach to the Gita not only revitalizes an ancient philosophy but also restores power and majesty to the text's poetry.'

—ARSHIA SATTAR, author of *Maryada*

'My life is so much easier as I don't have to go through maddening archaic prose thanks to Mani Rao's uncluttered, refined poetry.'

—DEVDUTT PATTANAIK, author and mythologist

'Mani Rao brings a felicitous mix of textually informed vigilance and playful irreverence to bear on her translation of the Bhagavad Gita. With its contemporary musicality and relaxed tone, Rao's version opens up this central text of modern Hinduism for a new generation of readers.'

—RANJIT HOSKOTE, author of *Icelight*

'The great virtue of the Bhagavad Gita is courage, and in her luminous new translation, Rao is courageous indeed. Her lines venture to keep pace with the original, stride for stride, revelation for revelation. As Wittgenstein wrote, "Courage is always original." I can avow that Rao's is the first truly original version of this sacred text to appear in decades.'

—DONALD REVELL, poet, and translator of Arthur Rimbaud and Guillaume Apollinaire

'Mani Rao has transformed the most famous spiritual poem in India into a multilayered poem, giving shapes to multiple meanings and sounds to multiple forms. Just as Arjuna saw the universe in Krishna's mouth and like the endless tree, the tree of life, which reveals its roots above and leaves below, Mani Rao has shown us this universe, this endless life with its supporting philosophy, as a poem to be perceived directly, intuitively, cutting through reason and linearity to arrive at the underlying undying poetry and grace of this epic work.'

—FREDERICK M. SMITH, Professor Emeritus, University of Iowa

‘We see [Rao’s] Sanskrit skills shine through in puns that span two languages separated by thousands of years and dozens of isoglosses. Except for the first chapter, almost every word of Rao’s translation has a direct correlate in the Sanskrit text, and yet certain words stand out more than others: they leap from the page, out of their context, rendered visible by the words and spaces around them—or lack thereof. The text is taken apart; Rao does not attempt to give us full, grammatical sentences, but rather, stark fragments of speech. By breaking the rigid confines of the thirty-two syllable anuṣṭubh metre that dominates the Gita, and by isolating and repeating significant words, Rao is burning down the house in order to show what it is made of and to illuminate its surroundings.’

—ERIC GUREVITCH, *Asymptote*

‘Rao negotiates enough room to stretch and move in the semantic and sonic labyrinths of the Gita … Rao’s translation has much else to be celebrated and dwelt over.’

—KALA KRISHNAN, *The Hindu*

‘Rao’s version of the Bhagavad Gita unpacks the original Sanskrit with a range of avant garde techniques—in prosody, diction, mise-en-page and lineation—rendering a new translation of the well-known philosophical text unlike any before it.’

—*The Oxford Companion to Modern Poetry*,
ed. Jeremy Noel-Tod and Ian Hamilton

BHAGAVAD GITA

GOD'S SONG

TRANSLATED FROM THE SANSKRIT BY

MANI RAO

HarperCollins *Publishers* India

First published in India by HarperCollins *Publishers* 2023
4th Floor, Tower A, Building No. 10, DLF Cyber City,
DLF Phase II, Gurugram, Haryana – 122002
www.harpercollins.co.in

2 4 6 8 10 9 7 5 3 1

P-ISBN: 978-93-5699-3730
E-ISBN: 978-93-5699-3747

Typeset in 10.5/14 Times New Roman at
Manipal Technologies Limited, Manipal

Printed and bound at
Thomson Press (India) Ltd

FSC www.fsc.org
MIX
Paper from responsible sources
FSC® C010615

This book is produced from independently certified FSC® paper
to ensure responsible forest management.

a page

a leaf

CONTENTS

Translator's Note
xi

On Reading and Interpretation
xix

Sanskrit Pronunciation
lvi

Bhagavad Gita
1

TRANSLATOR'S NOTE

The Bhagavad Gita—God's Song—is the most revered source of ancient Indian wisdom globally today. Considered a revelation from the divine, the Gita occupies the status of a Hindu scripture. A 700-verse poem, the Gita forms a section within the epic-history Mahabharata's sixth book, 'Bhishma Parva'. When the two opposing armies of the Pandavas and Kauravas are waiting in the battlefield, the Pandava prince Arjuna is filled with self-doubt. Then, the divine Krishna, who is also Arjuna's charioteer, gives Arjuna a response, urging him to do his duty—this is the speech that is called the Gita. It contains expositions about liberation, reincarnation, human nature, duty and devotion, and guidelines for how to live life in a detached and fulfilled manner. In the Gita, Krishna also reveals his own position as the ultimate source of the universe and gives Arjuna a vision of his vast, awe-inspiring divine form.

Through the first and second millennia, the Gita has been the subject of numerous commentaries, including from such saintly and scholarly personalities as Adi Shankaracharya. After the first translation of the Gita into English in 1789 by Charles Wilkins, hundreds of subsequent translations have created a tradition that every new Gita translator inherits and takes forward. None of these efforts are repetitive—each effort is by someone who has been deeply impacted by the Gita and shares that experience with the world. I am one among them.

The Gita is a poem, and in Sanskrit, chanted or read aloud. The shlokas (stanzas) of the Gita do not have end-rhymes but have internal symmetry, including assonant word-pairs. Plain prose translations cannot convey this liveliness. Metrical translations have a more basic challenge—fidelity to meaning. Between prosaic prose translations and straitjacketed metrical translations is the territory of free verse. However, most translations in free verse focus on line breaks; they look like poetry but do not sound like it, and do not attempt to catch the language-play of the Sanskrit Gita. Whether prose or poetry, whether by the letter or by the spirit, translations adhere to the stanza structure.

Studying previous translations, I could not help but feel that the Gita's status as a holy text has held back the translator's hand, making it hesitant to delete even a rhetorical space-filler such as 'indeed', or to shift the order of lines within a stanza. Word-for-word and line-for-line translations create obscurities and retard the pace of communication in English. Available correspondences for the Gita's pivotal concepts such as brahman, atman and karma, prove uncommunicative. 'Atman', for example, is regularly translated as 'soul' or 'self'. 'Soul' is a safe, familiar word, but vague, for we do not know what exactly it refers to; and 'self' is a concept understood in different ways. Sometimes Krishna is referring to *you*, and sometimes to the ungendered, immortal, indestructible *it*, who you really, really are. When Edwin Arnold and Juan Mascaró consistently translate atman as 'soul', they arrive at the idea of how to purify the soul in 6.12, which goes against the grain of the Gita's teaching about the always-pure state of the atman. No wonder then, that Gita translations tend to be accompanied by footnotes and commentary; the reader has to be studious to penetrate the translation. It is also why commentaries prove useful: they achieve communication and integrate subtext and context into the text in a way that word-for-word translations cannot access; however, they take us further away from the poem. My method addresses this gap in the tradition of Gita translations. I follow the order of the text but take the cognitive unit variably as it occurs at each instance in the Gita—in the line, the stanza, or even across a group of stanzas. My lineation style fits the interchangeable word order of Sanskrit syntax. It helps me convey several points at once and keep track of different narrative threads spatially.

I delete nothing except what I regard as overly rhetorical or repetitious. Every verse is numbered to help the reader who chooses to study the details. I do not omit any word that conveys a philosophical point; I may, for instance, ignore 'maharatha', which often seems like a metrical filler, but not 'avyayam', although it comes up suspiciously often. When I comment on (rather than explain) a point, or add a word to link and interpret ideas, I use parentheses. I italicize and explain terms the first time they occur, after which I treat them as a part of the vocabulary. I consider explanation of new terms and concepts imperative; Arjuna's learning depends on understanding what Krishna says, and the reader's learning depends on understanding the translation.

My choices sometimes rely on etymology to bring into play the resonance of the word in Sanskrit: for example, 'sat' (truth) comes from the root 'to be', or what *is*—so truth is 'what is' and untruth is 'what isn't'. The process also works the other way, into English; thus, 'dhyana' translates to 'meditate' and 'samadhi' to 'trans meditate'. Familiar phrases and idiomatic expressions are vibrant modes to help resituate the text in a place where the reader can more easily connect to Krishna. In 10.21 to 10.32, with lists of Hindu deities, I think the specifics will weaken the impact of the concept, so I stack the comparison, and if the reader knows what 'sun' is to 'lights', they can apply that concept to the next line, 'marichi among maruts'. I do not translate epithets for Arjuna and Krishna except when there is an overt logic to their use. As Arjuna, I address Krishna as Krishna, until the revelation in Chapter 11, when I find myself addressing Krishna as God. Krishna uses the masculine pronoun to connect with Arjuna; this is also a convention in ancient texts that either seem to address a male listener, or use the masculine pronoun to cover both men and women. But Arjuna is actually a proxy for the reader. So, as I put myself in Arjuna's shoes, I find that Krishna addresses me, a woman—and in the translation, I make the pronouns feminine. The addressee becomes 'she', and via me, becomes 'herself'.

Stanzas that depart radically from the surface meaning of the original occur when a literal translation would be uncommunicative and when the emotive moment calls for a deeper reading. 1.1 is such an instance. Translated literally, it is: 'In the field of righteousness, in the field of kuru, gathered, eager to fight—my sons, and Pandu's sons, indeed, what did they do, Sanjaya?' 'Dharma' can be translated as 'righteousness', 'virtue', 'truth', 'duty'; 'kshetra', as 'field', 'region'. 'Dharmakshetre', in translatese, is 'in the field of righteousness', and all the gravitas of the Sanskrit word and the import of the scene is lost in the repetitious habit and history of literal translation. When I let 'kshetra' speak to me, I gather: in the area of, in the realm of, in matters of, at, of, context. Dhritarashtra's question equates dharma and kuru. The physical place 'kuru' is not just the scene or setting, it is larger than life, context, situation. What is the situation? The Kauravas cheated in a dice game and ousted the Pandavas, who want revenge, and the only way to resolve the conflict is through a battle. In this verse, place and situation have converged into a point of no return. I translate this as 'when it came to that', placing pressure on 'that'. I note the tension in 'yuyutsavaha': these warriors are keen to have it out. I have a mental image of two sides facing and about to unmask themselves. I take in the words *my sons* and *Pandu's sons* with the full weight of what has gone on in the Mahabharata up until that point: might vs. right. What did they do = who did what, what happened first/next.

> dhritarashtra to sanjaya:
> & when it came to that
> might   right   face-off
> what happened who
> did what?

I use a somewhat different technique for verses 2.22 to 2.25, where Krishna explains 'soul'. The concept: you are not the body, you wear the body, you are the embodied ('dehi', 'this', 'it'). To translate 'dehi', I avoid the usual equivalents 'self' and 'soul', and rely on 'you', allowing its implications to open up along with the text.

> Literally:
>
> Just as, having cast away worn-out garments
> A man takes new ones
> Thus, having cast away worn-out bodies
> The embodied meets/joins other new ones (bodies) (2.22)

My translation collapses this into two lines. I emphasize *you*, and summarize the point in a line. I also imitate the vedantic idea of 'neti' ('not this'), i.e., how discarding reveals the true you. I stack the analogy.

you discard   old clothes for the new
you discard   one worn-out body for another

you are   not your body

In 2.23, there is more information about how the dehi is invulnerable.

Literally:

Weapons pierce not this
Fire burns not this
Waters wet not this
Wind withers not this

The first three lines of 2.24 repeat the content but shift the focus to the dehi.

Literally:

Not-to-be-pierced, this
Not-to-be-burned, this
Not-to-be-wetted, this; Not to be withered, this
Eternal, Everywhere-going, Fixed
Unmoving, this, primordial

I fuse 2.23 and 2.24.

weapons	cannot	pierce	this	unpierceable
fire		burn	who	unburnable
water		wet	you	unwettable
wind		dry	really	undryable
			are	
		forever		
				free
				fixed
		fromever		

In the last two lines, the pairs that resonate with each other are: 'nityah' and 'sanatanah' (eternal, and primordial/ancient/old—time stretching into the past eternal and the future eternal) and 'sarvagatah' and 'sthanuh' ('going everywhere' and 'fixed'). I let these pairs work together. The first set becomes 'forever' and 'fromever'. The next set is absurd in English, for how could anything go everywhere and yet be fixed? The word points to *freedom*; I translate this as 'free'.

Lines 3 and 4 of 2.24 have presented some unfathomable concepts about the embodied, and so it is time for 2.25 to explain why.

Literally:

Unapparent/manifest this, unthinkable this
Unchanging this, it is said
Therefore having known this
Not to mourn you're worthy of

Line 4 of this stanza is similar to Line 4 of 2.26. This is emphatic, and from it, I take as central the contrast between the unfathomable 'embodied', and the limitations of a confused Arjuna. What is reported about the 'embodied' is beyond Arjuna; he cannot grasp the idea. I convert the 'unmanifest' and 'unthinkable' into the tools of apprehension, senses and thoughts. I do so because the next stanza, 2.26, goes further into 'thought'—no matter what you choose to think about the embodied, anyway, you must not mourn. The similarity between Line 4 in 2.25 and Line 4 in 2.26 insists that you do not deserve to, you are not worthy of, mourning the 'embodied'. The stanza puts Arjuna in his place. When you know that the embodied cannot be seen/felt or thought of, you are in no position to mourn for it, and it is not for you to mourn.

understand it
is not for you to mourn

A strategy so varied within itself and from previous translations is only possible because of previous translations, because of the learning of tradition, with interpretive possibilities and bewilderment nicely documented. Previous perspectives, both translations and commentaries, form the thickly layered palimpsest of the Gita tradition that one can, and must, rely on. I refer to, and am grateful to, Shankara's *Gita-Bhashya*, the translations of R.C. Zaehner, Barbara Stoler Miller, Graham M. Schweig, Juan Mascaró, Prabhavanada-Isherwood, Edwin Arnold, P. Lal, and commentaries by Swami Bhaktivedanta and Swami Chinmayananda, Winthrop Sargeant (who, in turn, refers to Ramanujacharya for interpretive notes), and Bhagawan Sathya Sai Baba's discourses. And yet, when on occasion, I have had trouble fathoming a stanza or line, despite—as well as because of—turning to various commentaries, I was helped by recordings of the Gita: I found the recording by Swami Brahmananda especially expressive and clarifying.

I must confess that I never imagined I would care to engage in an intimate and enduring conversation with a text that presents birth-caste as karmic or killing as dharmic. I took consolation in the wider narrative that is not as much about fighting as about detachment—Krishna recommends the sattvic path as the most joyous, and non-violence is part of the sattvic path; Arjuna, though, as a warrior, is a rajasic doer. Besides, the battle is within the clan, the challenge is about standing up for what one believes is 'right', about readiness *even* to oppose one's own kin. Thus, the Gita's recommendation is to take a broader view of humanity and be genuinely impartial. As for caste, I temper my objections with the point Krishna repeatedly makes, that all beings are part of the divine. As I read and reread the Gita, it is Krishna's admission of love for the devotee that most moves me. Other translators tend to present 'bhajami' as 'I serve' or 'I worship' when it refers to devotees, and as 'I reward' when it refers to Krishna (e.g., 4.11); my sense of Krishna's feelings towards the devotee guides me not to differentiate between the two instances. How can Krishna possibly not be in service to the devotee when he plays the role of Arjuna's driver in the story and takes the time (over 700 stanzas) to enlighten Arjuna? Time and time again in the Gita, Krishna declares love for the devotee, and seems to long for the devotee's wisdom and love. The Gita is not only a poem, it is a love poem. May fidelity, then, be deep, complex, and lively.

An army of friends participated in my experience of the Gita and this translation—I only acknowledge here those who were in the thick of it. My father was my first reader: he read every chapter as I drafted it, and his responsiveness vindicated my translation strategy. My mother's sense of humour renewed my energy and kept me grounded—memorably, when I expressed nervousness about confronting the revelation or 'vishvarupam' in Chapter 11, she said, 'Relax, it's just a lot of hands and legs.' My teacher, Dr Sarasvati Mohan, gave me the drill in Sanskrit lessons and pointed me to valuable references. I realized that it was the Gita I would translate in Professor Dr Giuseppe Natale's class on translation theory. An expansive context of Ernest Fenollosa, Henri Michaux, David Slavitt, Marte Werner & c. arrived with translator and poet-professor, Dr Donald Revell. Among numerous Iowa friends who enabled this translation's journey, some have been more directly connected with the publication of this book: the International Writing Program opened doors to a community, editors of *eXchanges* conjured a timely journal debut, and Autumn Hill Books and *91*st *Meridian* booked it. And then it came full circle to India.

My heartfelt thanks to Shinie Antony who placed this book with HarperCollins, and to the brilliant-as-ever Rahul Soni, who took it under his wing and guided its present form. I am grateful to Rinita Banerjee, whose astute and thorough editing was most reassuring. Lokāḥ samastāḥ sukhinoḥ bhavantu.

ON READING AND INTERPRETATION

From time to time over the last century, some content from the Gita has made headlines. In 1945, nuclear physicist J. Robert Oppenheimer compared the totalizing destruction of the atomic bomb with the vision of Krishna as the all-powerful divine in Chapter 11. At the Trinity test site in Los Alamos, New Mexico, looking at the fireball of the atomic bomb explosion, he recalled the Bhagavad Gita: 'Now, I am become Death, the destroyer of worlds.'[1] In the 2012 US elections, Congresswoman Tulsi Gabbard took her oath on the Bhagavad Gita. Gabbard had served with Hawaii's National Guard, and during her time in Iraq, she drew strength from the teachings of the Gita, in particular, about the eternality of the soul.[2] In *The Guardian* in September 2014, musician and rock star Chrissie Hynde called it her favourite book. 'My favourite book is the *Bhagavad Gita*. It's a 700-stanza Hindu scripture and I love the stanza that says your mind can be your best friend or your

---

1 Robert Jungk, *Brighter than a Thousand Suns: A Personal History of the Atomic Scientists*, trans. James Cleugh (London: Victor Gollancz, 1958), p. 8. See also Mani Rao, '"Now, I am become Death, the destroyer of worlds": Truth and Lies in Oppenheimer's Gita Moment', *Scroll.in*, 5 August 2023, accessed on 10 August 2023.

2 See Jaweed Kaleem, 'Tulsi Gabbard, First Hindu in Congress, Uses Bhagavad Gita at Swearing-In', *HuffPost*, 4 January 2013, https://www.huffpost.com/entry/tulsi-gabbard-hindu-bhagavad-gita-swearing-in_n_2410078; and Kaleem, 'Tulsi Gabbard, First Hindu Elected to Congress, Will Swear In on Bhagavad Gita, Sacred Hindu Text', *HuffPost*, 19 November 2012, https://www.huffpost.com/entry/tulsi-gabbard-first-hindu-congress-bhagavad-gita_n_2159249, both accessed on 8 June 2023.

worst enemy. You can either pull yourself down or lift yourself up.'[3] It is through such second-hand reports that people around the world form their first impressions and understandings of the Gita. But such understandings can only be partial at best.

A few shlokas from the Gita are well known and often known by rote. The shloka beginning with 'Karmaṇyevādhikāraste…' tells us to do our work or duty without worrying about the results. The shloka beginning with 'Yadā yadā hi dharmasya glānirbhavati bhārata…' tells us that Krishna/Vishnu incarnates in Bharat (now India) whenever dharma is endangered. The shloka beginning with 'Vāsāṃsi jīrṇāni yathā vihāya…' and those that follow it explain the concept of rebirth. The Gita is typically represented by these few shlokas. As a result, many people do not realize that the Gita covers a wide range of content.

In contemporary India, the peculiar status of the Gita as a generic Hindu source makes it applicable for all sorts of occasions in everyday life—from death ceremonies to birthdays. Whereas the chanting of vedic hymns requires training in the associated tones, the Gita has no such restrictions. The shlokas of the Gita are not mantras, and yet they find their way to any ceremony or event that calls for a blessing, or a flavour of the holy.

The Gita's popularity is easily understood by a quick search on the internet. Amazon lists over 3,000 different entries in just the category of 'books'. These include translations, commentaries, discourses, and even dictionaries. However, buying a copy of the Gita does not mean actually reading it.

The Gita is neither an entertaining read, nor even an easy read. In audio renditions of the Gita, every stanza is sung in the same tune. If it were considered a dramatic poem, the Gita would be called 'dull'—700 stanzas, no real action, no change of scene, the entire text really a monologue posed as a dialogue. No wonder then that in the film *Mahabharata* by Peter Brooks, the subtitle of the Gita section says:

---

3 Chrissie Hynde, '"I don't have to worry like women who were known for their beauty and then get freaked out as they get older"', *The Guardian*, 14 September 2014, https://www.theguardian.com/music/2014/sep/14/chrissie-hynde-this-much-i-know, accessed on 1 May 2023.

'Where's the action?' Arjuna does not get to speak very much in the Gita. He expresses his distress in the first chapter, and after that, his next significant words are in the eleventh chapter, when he is overwhelmed by the vision of Krishna. In many other chapters, he only gets to ask a question, which serves as a prompt for Krishna's response.

The Gita is also difficult to categorize. Some people are attracted to the Gita because they think it is a religious text, while others are put off by just that. Some appreciate it because it is in Sanskrit, others may hate it for that very reason. Some find the Gita open-minded because it presents a multiplicity of paths to God, self-realization, or self-improvement. Others find it indeterminate and confusing.

For one reason or the other, because we think we know it, because it seems offensive, because it seems confusing, because it seems dull, *many people do not read the Gita.* So, the first suggestion in reading the Gita (smile) is—read it.

Upon reading Stanza 4.13, the Gita seems non-egalitarian. In this stanza, Krishna says that the four varnas[4] sorted by traits and tasks were created by him. This seems to put a divine sanction upon social evils and has been misused to justify caste-based oppression. However, across 9.30 to 9.32, Krishna says that not a single one of his devotees is lost, and everyone reaches their goal.

At first glance, it seems as though Krishna asks Arjuna to 'kill' people in the battlefield. But Krishna also specifies non-violence as the highest path.

Which of these is representative of the Gita's message? Only by reading the entire Gita can one get the full picture. *Read all of it.*

THE DISTORTION OF CHAPTERS

Many people study the Gita chapter by chapter. The commentarial tradition reinforces this practice. Often, spiritual leaders give discourses on one chapter this year and another chapter the following year. The chapter divisions are also announced in audio CDs—for instance,

---

4 Varna is actually not translatable as caste. For a discussion on the problem of interpreting and translating this term, see pp. xlix–li of this book.

'athaḥ dvitīyo'dhyāyaḥ' (next, chapter 2). Discussions on the Gita are usually structured around these chapters. To read about karma yoga (the yoga of action), one is expected to go to Chapter 3, or for jnana yoga (knowledge) to Chapter 4, and for bhakti yoga (devotion) to Chapter 12. Can you imagine Krishna taking a pause in the middle of his speech to announce the next chapter? If we really consider the Gita to be a speech or a message from Krishna to Arjuna on a battlefield, we realize that the notes about chapter divisions must be editorial interventions.

When we review the content, we see some repetition and overlap across chapters. If you are only looking for the message of the Gita, you *can* skip Chapter 1 entirely. This chapter, however, is a delightful composition, with onomatopoeic language that impresses upon us the time and place. It is after this that we turn to the other chapters for reflection. Chapter 2 functions as a summary of the key points of the entire Gita, so this is an important part. However, the first ten stanzas of Chapter 2 recapitulate Arjuna's confusion from Chapter 1. The philosophical message of the Gita really begins from Stanza 2.11. Chapters 3, 4 and 5 really ought to be studied together. Even though Chapter 12 has much content about devotion, Chapter 9 has the well-known stanza about how Krishna accepts devotion even in the simple form of a flower, a fruit, water, or a leaf.

Once we recognize the artifice of chapter divisions, we gain the ability to discuss the Gita in terms of chapters without being restricted by the *idea* of chapters. For your first reading, read the Bhagavad Gita from the beginning to the end. This way, you will get an overview of the entire content.

READING IN SCENES AND SECTIONS

Another convention is to study a stanza a day. Sure, some stanzas do stand on their own, and these are the stanzas that have become popular and are often memorized. However, within the narrative and teaching of the Gita, separating a stanza from the stanzas before and after would be like plucking a sentence out of a paragraph. In the Gita, sometimes, the *cognitive unit*—i.e., the unit of comprehension—extends across several stanzas. 12.13 to 12.20 is one section, describing the qualities of a devotee. 10.12 to 10.18 is another section, where Arjuna addresses Krishna's glory. Here is a list of comparisons across twelve stanzas (10.21 to 10.32) that help us understand Krishna's position in the universe.

> vishnu among adityas / sun among lights / marichi among maruts / moon among the night constellations / sama veda among vedas / vasava among deities / mind among senses / awareness among beings / shiva among rudras / kubera among yakshas & rakshasas / pavaka among the vasus / meru among mountains / head priest / priest of the deities / skanda among army chiefs / ocean among water bodies / brighu among sages / om among sounds / chant among yajnas / among the immovable the himalayas / holy fig among the trees / narada among divine sages / chitraratha among gandharvas / kapila among achiever yogis / born from nectar (in oceanchurn) / ucchaishravas among horses / airavat among king elephants / king among people / thunderbolt among weapons / wish-fulfilling cow among cows / kandarpa the begetter / vasuki among serpents / ananta among the naga snakes / varuna among water beings / aryaman among ancestors / death among controllers / prahlada among daityas / time among calculators / king of beasts among beasts / vainateya among birds / wind among purifiers / rama among weaponwielders / makara among sea ferocities / ganga among rivers

All of these lines belong to a single scene, or section. The underlying point is the same in all twelve stanzas. We already know what the sun means in comparison to lights, and we can apply that concept instantaneously to the next line, 'marichi among maruts'. The core message is, 'X is the superlative among its group', and similarly, Krishna is the 'best'. Such an approach helps comprehend the message faster, and we have not spent twelve days over twelve stanzas in the a-shloka-a-day lesson plan. This section may be absorbed—at first reading—as a single idea, and then later become the subject of deeper study.

When you dip later into the Gita (for it takes several dips to soak it in), you can pore over each of the references, and learn about the names and the legends behind them. In this way, you have a general bird's-eye view of the entire Gita at first, and then later, swoop into different sections for a deeper understanding.

The parts or scenes in the Gita are identifiable by having a similar theme, action or form. Often, the form helps us identify small sections within which an action or realization occurs. An example of such a presentation in the Sanskrit Gita is 7.6 to 7.11. The word 'asmi' (I AM) is repeated, dominating Krishna's overall statement in this scene. Noticing this helps us appreciate just how central a position Krishna has in the Gita, and of course, Krishna's omnipresence.

Another example: From 11.15 onwards, Arjuna uses the verb 'see' several times. Noticing this makes one much more aware that this is a spectacle and an extraordinary sight. I have applied such a principle in my own translation of Gita, and reproduce an excerpt from this section below:

i see   in your body   deities
           a gathering of all sorts of beings
           brahma seated on a lotus
           divine serpents & all the sages

i see   you everywhere   infinite form
           myriad eyes arms bellies faces

           no end no middle no beginning

i see   the deity of the universe
           the universe   its form

i see   you   so hard to see
                    in totality

In 11.22, the same sight is also seen by the Adityas, Rudras, Vasus and Sadhyas, and all the deities of the universe. By recognizing the emphasis on 'seeing' we discover how Krishna now becomes the centre of every gaze in the universe. This is not just a description of Krishna's 'vishvarupam' (universal form)—it is a description of 'vishvarupa-darshanam' (the vision of Krishna's universal form).

READING IN SEQUENTIAL ORDER

For your very first reading of the Gita, it is best to read from the beginning to the end, in the expected order. When you follow this sequence, it is easy for you to put yourself in Arjuna's shoes. This way, you listen to Krishna's Gita as though you are Arjuna, and you also understand Arjuna's questions better. There is less chance of misunderstanding the flow of thought and it is less likely that you will have isolated questions that are out of context.

Moreover, the apparent obscurities in particular stanzas are usually clarified by the previous or next few stanzas. An example will help illustrate this point. Consider Stanza 2.16 with the terms 'sat' and 'asat'.

> nāsato vidyate bhāvo nābhāvo vidyate sataḥ |
> ubhayorapi dṛṣṭo'ntastvanayostattvadarśibhiḥ || (2.16)

Here is a word-by-word translation: 'na'—not; 'asataḥ'—of the not-*sat* (translation to be determined); 'vidyate'—it is found; 'bhāvaḥ'—being, becoming; 'na'—not; 'abhāvaḥ'—not being/ not becoming; 'vidyate'—it is found; 'sataḥ'—of the 'sat' (translation to be determined); 'ubhayoḥ'—of both; 'api'—indeed, surely, also, even; 'dṛṣṭaḥ'—seen, perceived; 'antaḥ'—certainty, conclusion; 'tu'—indeed, but; 'anayoḥ'—of these two; 'tattva'—reality, thatness; 'darśibhiḥ'—by the seers/perceivers.

Juan Mascaró's translation:

> The unreal never is: the Real never is not. This truth indeed has been seen by those who can see the true.[5]

5 Juan Mascaró, *The Bhagavad Gita* (1962; New Delhi: Penguin, 1994), p. 49.

Bhaktivedanta's translation:

> Those who are seers have concluded that of the non-existent [the material body] there is no endurance and of the eternal [the soul] there is no change. This they have concluded by studying the nature of both.[6]

Mascaró has translated 'sataḥ' and 'asataḥ' as real/unreal and Bhaktivedanta has translated them as existing/non-existing. More literally, the words refer to 'what is' and 'what is not'. What is real, existing or what 'is' and what 'is not' could refer to anything—living/non-living, animate/inanimate, fact/lie. From the materialist perspective, the physical world 'is' and the 'spiritual' world is conjecture, and may one argue that the Gita ought to be understood as a confirmation of materialism? Besides, it seems unsurprising for that which is non-existent to be non-existent. *But*, if one has paid attention to what was said in Stanza 2.14, Stanza 2.16 is not fuzzy.

> mātrāsparśāstu kaunteya śītoṣṇasukhaduḥkhadāḥ |
> āgamāpāyino'nityāstāṃstitikṣasva bhārata || (2.14)

This translates to: Arjuna, the sensations that cause heat and cold, pleasure and pain, come and go, they are impermanent. Bear them, Arjuna.

This stanza helps us understand 'asat' and 'sat' one verse later in terms of transient and intransient *sensations*. Even though the profound interpretations by commentators are valid, this specific meaning (that sensations are 'asat' due to their transience) is as worthy, if not more, because it is immediately comprehensible!

Does the Gita downplay vedic rituals, or uphold them? Some may say that the Gita scoffs at the veda. Let us review some of the shlokas on this theme before we arrive at a conclusion. In 2.42, Krishna says that ignorant people who relish the word of the veda proclaim with flowery speeches that there is nothing else. In 2.43, he says they

6 A.C. Bhaktivedānta Swami Prabhupāda, *Bhagavad Gītā As It Is* (1989; Bombay: The Bhaktivedanta Book Trust, 1994), p. 95.

conduct many special vedic rituals for pleasure and power; they are full of desires and keen to attain heaven, but the result they obtain is merely rebirth. Two stanzas later, in 2.46, Krishna says that the wise brahmin has as much (i.e., as little) use for the veda as the use(lessness) of a well when surrounded by plenty of water. All three stanzas criticize vedic ritualists and the limited gains from vedic rituals, and are often quoted as examples for the Gita's criticism of veda. However, when we pay attention to the message in the proximate stanzas, we discover that Krishna is specifically criticizing the use of veda for the pursuit of worldly pleasure and fame—Stanza 2.44 clearly specifies veda used for 'bhoga' (pleasure) and 'aishvarya' (power). Next, we discover that *only* selfish rituals are being critiqued—for Stanza 2.47 recommends that one must focus on the work, not on the outcome.

Thus, alertness to the continuity and immediate context of the stanzas helps comprehension.

WHICH GITA COMMENTARY OR TRANSLATION DID YOU READ?

Those who do not know Sanskrit will rely on translations and commentaries to read the Gita. The next step is to choose from the bewildering range of options. Which or whose translation or commentary on the Gita will be most helpful to you? M.K. Gandhi or Balgangadhar Tilak? Swami Bhaktivedanta or Swami Chinmayananda? Juan Mascaró or Rajagopalachari? Mani Rao or George Thompson?

The Gita can convey contrary messages for different groups of people. In the 1930s and '40s, the Indian freedom fighter and national leader M.K. Gandhi made the Gita a regular part of chanting and study in his ashram. For him, the Gita taught detachment in service, and non-violence. Ironically, Gandhi's assassin Nathuram Godse also took inspiration from the Gita, citing it in his Punjab High Court deposition on 8 November 1948:

> Rama killed Ravana in a tumultuous fight and relieved Sita. Krishna killed Kansa to end his wickedness; and Arjuna had to fight and slay quite a number of his friends and relations including the revered Bhishma because the latter was on the

> side of the aggressor. It is my firm belief that in dubbing Rama, Krishna and Arjuna as guilty of violence, the Mahatma betrayed a total ignorance of the springs of human action.[7]

There are other subjects where readers arrive at variant interpretations of the Gita. Followers of advaita (non-dualism) and of dvaita (dualism) both turn to the Gita for guidance and come away satisfied that it supports their views. In short, the translation or commentary you read can skew your understanding of the Gita.

As some of us are aware, there are many Ramayanas generated in the oral tradition, with numerous narrators and versions of the storyline. By contrast, the Gita *seems* an invariable source. In fact, the Gita is a highly mediated source, usually studied with the help of a teacher, commentator, or translator. The Gita is a tradition, a palimpsest, with layers of voices—voices that are lenses. Each commentary and translation becomes a part of the tradition for the next commentary and translation. The Bhagavad Gita is not only 'God's Song', it is also the commentator's song, and the translator's song, and even the reader's song. There is no translation or commentary without interpretation. Instead of being frustrated by these layers of mediators, we can use them to our advantage if we become aware of the interpretive lens of the translator or commentator.

Additionally, even when we (think we) read the original Gita stanzas directly, we already have a lot of preconceptions in our minds, which have been formed by centuries of commentaries and mediation. Even when we embark on a direct study of the Gita stanzas, we deal with our own distortions, for we have our own perspectives and preferences, perceptions and attitudes, that colour our understanding. Commentaries have become a part and parcel of our memories, and we may not even know about it. How can we try to become conscious of our own

---

7 In Nathuram Vinayak Godse and Gopal Vinayak Godse, *May It Please Your Honour: Statement of Nathuram Godse* (Pune: Vitasta Prakashan, 1977), p. 29. E-text from Center for Research Libraries, Chicago, USA, accessed on 27 April 2010.

preconceptions? Techniques of textual analysis and close reading discussed in this book can help in this regard.

Ideological Differences

Some simple techniques will help the reader decipher the translator's or commentator's position. Sometimes even a quick browse will tell us what to expect. Often, the content of the front and back cover, and dedications, give us a basic indication about what to expect. Chances are that a translation dedicated to Bhaktivedanta will give first preference to the path of devotion. Chances are that a commentary published by the Chinmaya Mission will give first preference to the path of knowledge.

Due to the multitude of available books on the Gita, authors tend to explain why they have embarked on yet another translation or commentary. All authors aim to be faithful to what they believe to be the spirit or message of the Gita, and they all believe that their book fills a gap in the library of books on the Gita. Prefaces and prefatory notes can help us gauge if this book will resonate with us. For example, when we read the preface to Mascaró's translation of the Gita, we also understand his target audience. Mascaró explains the concepts in the Gita with the help of references and quotes from the Bible, St John of the Cross, St Teresa, Song of Songs, Mary, Martha, the Gospels, Homer, Socrates, and even Beethoven. He compares Greek philosophy with Indian, and compares the length of the Mahabharata to *Paradise Lost*. Mascaró's translation will be most evocative for a reader familiar with Christian sources. In his 'Notes on the Translation', Mascaró explains how he studied previous translations and interpretations, and ultimately followed his own 'light'. Translating 'dharma' as the 'truth of the universe', he felt vindicated when he came across a similar usage in Rabindranath Tagore.[8] Such notes are very helpful for a reader who wants to understand the translator's lens.

Bhaktivedanta's Gita is called *Gītā As It Is*. We learn something about Bhaktivedanta's perspective just by pondering the book title. It is clear that he considers previous Gita commentaries as distortions, and

8 Mascaró, *The Bhagavad Gita*, p. 37.

believes that he has restored the correct meaning of the Gita, or that he is in a position to do so. Bhaktivedanta is the founder of ISKCON, the international Hare Krishna movement. The preface concludes by presenting a 'disciplic succession', which begins with Krishna as the first guru and ends with the 32nd disciple as A.C. Bhaktivedanta.[9] Such a succession line suggests that Bhaktivedanta is specially positioned and authorized to interpret and explain the Gita; by implication, those who are not a part of his disciplic succession are de-authorized. How will such a position impact the translation and commentary? The reader can expect that this commentary will be dogged in its assertions and promote a sectarian perspective. True to the spirit of an ardent devotee, he translates 'Krishna' as 'the Supreme Personality of Godhead, Kṛṣṇa'.

Consider this line in Stanza 18.66: 'Sarvadharmānparityajya māmekaṃ śaraṇaṃ vraja'. Bhaktivedanta translates: 'Abandon *all varieties of religion* and just surrender unto Me' (italics mine).[10] On the other hand, Mascaró translates this to: 'Leave all things behind and come to me for thy salvation.'[11] Even though Mascaró notes in his preface that he translates 'dharma' as 'truth',[12] he has not translated 'sarvadharmān' as 'all truths' or 'all other truths'—he has translated it as 'all *things*'. Other dharmas or religious paths (as specifically stated in the Gita stanza) are not even given a mention as alternative truths. Also, as a result of dropping the point altogether, Mascaró's interpretation positions Krishna's call as much more all-encompassing. Depending on how the reader interprets 'all', it *may* include anything from other dharmas/religions to job and family.

Conceptual Differences

One of the aims of this chapter is to help readers navigate the thicket of translations, become more aware of a translator's or a commentator's point of view, and know how to expand the scope of their own study

9 Bhaktivedānta, *Bhagavad Gītā As It Is*, p. 34.

10 Ibid., p. 850.

11 Mascaró, *The Bhagavad Gita*, p. 121.

12 Ibid., p. 37.

of the Gita and perhaps arrive at their own conclusions. Towards this objective, here are two examples to illustrate conceptual differences a reader may not catch unless first alerted to the possibility.

Example: Karma

What is 'karma'? In Chapter 2, Krishna has explained a number of points about equanimity, and *seems* to suggest that the path of 'buddhi' (intelligence, discernment) is better than 'karma' (action). Arjuna is confused, and Chapter 3 opens with Arjuna asking Krishna for clarification. Arjuna asks—'If you really think that buddhi is better than karma, why do you urge me to horrible action?' Arjuna is referring to fighting and killing as the horrible actions. Krishna replies:

> śrībhagavānuvāca |
> loke'smindvividhā niṣṭhā purā proktā mayānagha |
> jñānayogena sāṅkhyānāṃ karmayogena yogināṃ || (3.3)

Let us read Bhaktivedanta's translation and commentary to understand Krishna's reply.

> TRANSLATION: The Blessed Lord said: O sinless Arjuna, I have already explained that there are two classes of men who realize the Self. Some are inclined to understand Him by empirical, philosophical speculation, and others are inclined to know Him by devotional work.
>
> PURPORT
> In the Second Chapter, verse 39, the Lord explained two kinds of procedures—namely *sāṅkhya-yoga* and *karma-yoga*, or *buddhi-yoga*. In this verse, the Lord explains the same more clearly. *Sāṅkhya-yoga*, or the analytical study of the nature of spirit and matter, is the subject matter for persons who are inclined to speculate and understand things by experimental knowledge and philosophy. The other class of men work in Kṛṣṇa consciousness, as it is explained in the 61st verse of the Second Chapter. The Lord has explained, also in the 39th

verse, that by working by the principles of *buddhi-yoga*, or Kṛṣṇa consciousness, one can be relieved from the bonds of action; and, furthermore, there is no flaw in the process. The same principle is more clearly explained in the 61st verse—that this *buddhi-yoga* is to depend entirely on the Supreme (or more specifically, on Kṛṣṇa), and in this way all the senses can be brought under control very easily. Therefore, both the yogas are inter-dependent, as religion and philosophy. Religion without philosophy is sentiment, or sometimes fanaticism, while philosophy without religion is mental speculation. The ultimate goal is Kṛṣṇa, because the philosophers who are also sincerely searching after the Absolute Truth come in the end to Kṛṣṇa consciousness. This is also stated in the Bhagavad-gītā. The whole process is to understand the real position of the self in relation to the Superself. The indirect process is philosophical speculation, by which, gradually, one may come to the point of Kṛṣṇa consciousness; and the other process is directly connecting with everything in Kṛṣṇa consciousness. Of these two, the path of Kṛṣṇa consciousness is better because it does not depend on purifying the senses by a philosophical process. Kṛṣṇa consciousness is itself the purifying process, and by the direct method of devotional service it is simultaneously easy and sublime.[13]

In Bhaktivedanta's translation, 'buddhi-yoga' is translated as 'empirical, philosophical speculation' and 'karma' as 'devotional work'. However, his 'purport' moves away from the literal meaning of buddhi yoga and redefines it as 'Kṛṣṇa consciousness'. Now let us read Gandhi's discourse on the same stanza, 3.3.

When Krishna had thus set forth the marks of identification for a *sthitaprajna* person, Arjuna received the impression that one had only to sit quiet in order to attain such a state, as Krishna had not made the slightest reference to any need for

13 Bhaktivedānta, *Bhagavad Gītā As It Is*, pp. 165–66.

action on his part. He therefore asked Krishna, 'It seems as if you hold that knowledge is superior to action. If so, why are you urging me to this terrible deed and thus confusing my mind? Please tell me clearly where my welfare lies.'

Krishna replied: 'O sinless Arjuna, since the beginning of time seekers have taken one or the other of two different paths. In one of these the pride of place is given to knowledge and in the other it is given to action. But you will find that freedom from action cannot be attained without action, that wisdom never comes to a man simply on account of his having ceased to act. Man does not become perfect merely by renouncing everything. Don't you see that every one of us is doing something or other all the time? Our very nature impels us to action. Such being the law of nature, one who sits with folded hands but lets his mind dwell on the objects of sense is a fool and may even be called a hypocrite. Rather than indulge in such senseless inactivity, is it not better that a man should control the senses, overcome his likes and dislikes, and engage himself in some activity or other without fuss and in a spirit of detachment? Do your allotted duty, restraining the organs of sense, for that is better than inaction. An idler will only meet his end the sooner for his idleness. But while acting, remember that action leads to bondage unless it is performed in a spirit of sacrifice. Sacrifice (*yajna*) means exerting oneself for the benefit of others, in a word, service. And where service is rendered for service's sake there is no room for attachment, likes and dislikes. Perform such a sacrifice, render such service. When Brahma created the universe, He created sacrifice along with it, as it were, and said to mankind, "Go forth into the world; serve one another and prosper."'[14]

Even though Gandhi began with translating 'karma' as 'action', and brings in the idea of yajna (sacred fire ritual), he *explains* it as 'service'.

14 M.K. Gandhi, *Discourses on the Gita*, trans. Valji Govindji Desai (1930; Ahmedabad: Navajivan Publishing House, 1960), pp. 18–19.

The two excerpts above illustrate how the word 'karma' means devotion for Bhaktivedanta and service for Gandhi. Similarly, if we look at Yogananda's commentary on the Gita, we find that karma means 'kriya yoga'. *Whose meaning is correct?* One, or none, or all? All these interpretations are valid. Karma does translate into devotional activities for Bhaktivedanta, service for Gandhi, and kriya yoga for Yogananda.

My own methodology has been to trust the Gita for answers and look closer at how the reasoning develops across shlokas. Arjuna had asked Krishna which path is better—knowledge or action. Krishna then speaks at length about karma yoga, and specifically talks about yajna and other ritual karmas. In the Hindu way of life, ritual karmas include both daily and occasional rituals. In 3.4, Krishna sets up a contrast between the person who performs ritual karmas, such as a householder, and an ascetic sanyasi who does not have to perform any rituals. This has a specific context—in Indian culture, a sanyasi is freed of ritual obligations; he is no longer required to perform ritual karmas, including for the death of his father and for his ancestors. Stanzas 3.10 to 3.15 continue this theme of vedic rituals. In the vedic way of life, the yajna is of paramount importance, so much so that the proper functioning of nature and the universe depends on its diligent performance. Krishna presents the case of the renunciant sanyasi who is joyous at his core, content, and not looking for the results of actions. He advocates such a detachment in actions even for those who are not sanyasis. It is by internalizing the meaning of yajna for renunciants that Krishna expands the meaning of karma. Karma includes all daily activities and even bodily functions—even the person who does nothing is actually involuntarily doing something. And therefore, in my assessment, the meaning of karma cannot be limited to devotional acts, service, or kriya yoga.

Example: Atman

The term or the word atman is translated as 'self' or 'soul'. In Sanskrit, 'atman' is a personal pronoun that means 'oneself', and thus, 'self' is closer in meaning to 'atman' than 'soul' with Christian theological associations. However, both 'self' and 'soul' are equally obscure.

'Soul' is an overfamiliar word so diluted by usage that when it is used, one no longer tries to know what is meant precisely by it. As for 'self', you may think of your self as physical, and I may think of it as spiritual. Thus, translating 'atman' as either 'soul' or 'self' does not really solve the problem. Moreover, within the Gita, the word 'atman' seems to carry different meanings in different instances; therefore, a consistent translation of 'self' or 'soul' is not helpful.

Edwin Arnold and Juan Mascaró translate 'atman' as 'soul' regardless of what it refers to in the original. Thus, in Stanza 6.12, both Arnold and Mascaró end up with the idea of how to purify the soul, which goes against the grain of the teaching of the Gita about the always-pure state of atman. In *Bhagavad-Gita: The Song of God*, Swami Prabhavananda and Christopher Isherwood retain the word 'atman' and explain this decision in the preface: '[T]he translator who uses reassuring topical equivalents and twists the meaning of the Sanskrit terms may think he is building a bridge between two systems of thought when actually he is reducing both to nonsense.'[15] Prabhavananda-Isherwood acknowledge that the Gita has its own 'definite picture of the universe' and that the cosmology is unfamiliar to Western thought—therefore, it would be unsuitable to resort to 'reassuring topical equivalents';[16] several key terms in their translation are in Sanskrit transliterations. Despite the decision to retain the original word, they are sensitive enough to translate it in Stanza 6.12 as 'heart'. (Incidentally, Bhaktivedanta is also skillful when translating atman—while he typically translates atman as 'self', in Stanza 6.12, he translates it as 'heart'.)

Graham Schweig has a unique solution for the problem in his *Bhagavad Gita: The Beloved Lord's Secret Love Song*. He translates atman as '[self]', the parenthesis indicating that 'self' is an imperfect translation, a placeholder, a term, rather than a word that conveys meaning. Schweig explains in the appendix that he chooses 'self'

---

15 Swami Prabhavananda and Christopher Isherwood, *Bhagavad-Gita: The Song of God* (1944; New York: Penguin, 2002), p. 9.

16 Ibid.

as the best way to encompass all the meanings 'soul, body, mind or heart'.[17]

When a single word can have so many translations, how may readers navigate the multiple book translations of the Gita? Multiple translations help, and the truth lies somewhere between them. The other option, for the serious student of the Gita, is textual analysis and close reading.

TEXTUAL ANALYSIS

A side-effect of the copious literature on the Gita is that anyone can attempt to unpack the Sanskrit. If you cannot read the Devnagari script, you can still follow a transliteration in roman diacritics, and they are easily found online and in this book. You will also find plenty of Gita dictionaries and sources that give you word-by-word break-up of the stanzas. Winthrop Sargeant's Bhagavad Gita is a good reference, because it not only presents the word breaks, but also gives the grammatical form of each and every word in the stanzas. Bhaktivedanta's Gita is available free online; while this has word breaks only, there is a good interactive menu to help navigate the stanzas. Choose a single shloka that you want to grasp, and go through it, word by word. Then compare two or more translations of the stanza, and you will begin to understand alternative interpretations and get to know the stanza better. Here is an example of textual analysis:

> śrībhagavānuvāca |
> aśocyānanvaśocastvaṃ prajñāvādāṃśca bhāṣase |
> gatāsūnagatāsūṃśca nānuśocanti paṇḍitāḥ || (2.11)

Word-by-word meanings: 'śrībhagavānuvāca'—Sri Bhagavan said; 'aśocyān'—not to be lamented/mourned; 'tvaṃ'—you; 'anvaśocas'—have lamented/mourned; 'prajñāvādāṃś'—wise words; 'ca'—and; 'bhāṣase'—you speak; 'gata'—gone; 'āsūn'—breath; 'agata'—not

17 Graham Schweig, *Bhagavad Gītā: The Beloved Lord's Secret Love Song* (New York: HarperOne, 2007), p. 331.

gone; 'āsūṃś'—breath; 'ca'—and; 'na'—not; 'anuśocanti'—they mourn; 'paṇḍitāḥ'—the wise.

The Sanskrit repeats the word for 'mourn' in different forms, and pairs the dead and the living relative to breath that has gone and not gone—'gatāsūn' and 'agatāsūn'. The living and the dead are similar; the presence of the prefix 'a' makes all the difference. The tone is somewhat mocking. Literally, the words mean: 'those in whom breath/life has gone', and 'those in whom breath/life has not gone'. The person is unaffected, immortal. Here is Mascaró's translation: 'Thy tears are for those beyond tears; and are thy words of wisdom? The wise grieve not for those who live; and they grieve not for those who die—for life and death shall pass away.'[18]

Although Mascaró tries to convey the idea that there is no need to feel sorry for 'those beyond tears' because they do not need the tears, the combination of words makes no sense—it is as if the objects of Arjuna's sympathy have transcended their own tears, rather than them not needing Arjuna's tears. Mascaró achieves some rhythm by repeating 'not for', instead of translating as 'do not grieve for', and this double-negative is not in the original—but it is a shift that helps the meaning. It is towards the end of the stanza that Mascaró nails the content, that the person does not 'pass', it is life and death that are transient.

Here is Bhaktivedanta's translation: 'The Blessed Lord said: While speaking learned words, you are mourning for what is not worthy of grief. Those who are wise lament neither for the living nor the dead.'[19] 'Blessed' and 'Lord' are ways of conveying 'Sri Bhagavan', but blessedness is an obvious addition. '[N]ot worthy of grief' overly reduces the status of those who should not be grieved for; it is as if the people who must not be grieved for deserve to be treated indifferently, rather than that the grief itself is irrelevant. Bhaktivedanta's purport attached to the translation discusses the jibe in Krishna's words, but the translation itself does not capture it. 'While speaking' suggests simultaneity, as if Arjuna was half-lamenting and half-speaking;

18 Mascaró, *The Bhagavad Gita*, p. 49.

19 Bhaktivedānta, *Bhagavad Gītā As It Is*, p. 87.

the accurate construction would have been 'you speak … but'. This translation does not convey the idea of the passage of life and death.

Such a simple textual analysis with the help of a couple of translations not only helps you understand alternative possibilities in meaning but also helps you know the stanza better.

CLOSE READING

Reading closely means focusing on the text to understand what it says and, more importantly, what it does not. A simple example will demonstrate how some of the key messages we believe the Gita contains are the result of layers of interpretations and commentaries rather than direct statements. One such concept is that of the atman, and its evanescence. Another popular notion is that there are three paths: jnana (knowledge), karma (action) and bhakti (devotion).

Example: Are there three 'yogas' in the Gita?

It has become a general understanding that there are three distinct paths to self-realization: karma (action), jnana (knowledge) and bhakti (devotion). In fact, Krishna never presents these as three alternative paths. Even though chapter headings seem to suggest that these topics are different from each other, we find that the content within those chapters does not present three distinct paths. There is even more confusion if the reader is more acquainted with yoga pertaining to pranayama (disciplined breathing) and asanas (disciplined postures)—hatha yoga, raja yoga, kundalini yoga, etc.

When one reads the Gita in Sanskrit, you find that the word 'yoga' is used in a much more generic manner. On the whole, the entire Gita is a 'yoga'. Not only are the chapters on jnana, karma and bhakti titled 'yogas', even the first chapter where Arjuna is disheartened in the middle of a battlefield is called 'Arjuna viṣāda yoga' or 'Yoga of Arjuna's sadness'. In stanzas 4.1 to 4.3, Krishna tells Arjuna that he will reveal to him the secret ancient 'yoga' that has been lost.

Broadly, yoga is the process and the path, as well as the result. Actions must be performed by being firmly established in 'yoga' (2.48).

When one achieves equanimity, it is called yoga—'samatvaṃ yoga ucyate' (2.48); when one achieves skill in action, it is yoga—'yogaḥ karmasu kauśalam' (2.50); and renunciation of selfishness is yoga (6.2)—'yaṃ saṃnyāsamiti'. Chapter 6 of the Gita describes meditation as the method (yoga) followed by the yogi.

Yoga also refers to mastery or capability, and this also applies to Krishna. Thus, Krishna is called 'yogeśvara' or a master of yoga (11.4, 11.9, 18.75, 18.78). It is his 'yogamāyā' (yogic power, illusion due to yogic power) that causes us to be bound to the world.

Example: Does Krishna say 'atman' in 2.13 to 2.27?[20]

In fact, he does not. In stanzas 2.13 to 2.27, Krishna speaks about 'dehin' and 'śarīrin'— i.e., that which has a body. What has a body? Arjuna will find out by and by. Why does Krishna not use the word 'atman' when explaining the concept to Arjuna? Let us take a guess.

Arjuna does not know about atman the way Krishna wants him to understand it. Had Krishna used the word atman, Arjuna might get confused, especially if he already understands the word as a pronoun, referring to his body or personality, and Krishna has to first destabilize these very notions. Arjuna does know what is meant by 'deha' (body). It would be logical, then, for Krishna to begin his persuasive argument with that. And where is Arjuna? On the battlefield—Krishna begins there.

In 2.11, Krishna tells Arjuna that a wise person mourns for neither those whose breath has gone, nor for those whose breath has not gone. In 2.12, Krishna says that there was never a time when he was not, and never a time when he won't be, and then includes Arjuna and the warriors in the statement.

Identity has to be the next topic, logically, because Krishna's statement is grand. It is the 'dehin' that experiences childhood, youth

20 For a more detailed analysis of the topic, see the author's 'The Conjuring of "Ātman" in Gita translations', *Osmania Journal of English Studies*, 2019, pp. 120–28.

and age in the body, and then acquires another body. Krishna uses locative case for body—'dehe' (in/at the body). He positions the body as a site, rather than the experiencer.

In 2.14 we learn something about what happens at this site—sensations come and go, they are transient. 2.15 then advises us that equanimity is the apt response to something transient. It is in the context of 2.15 that we must read 2.16. That which is 'asat'—sensations—has no reality/being/existence. Arjuna can begin to understand what kind of attitude he ought to have towards transient phenomena. 2.17 begins with the word 'avināśi' (indestructible), that (yaḥ, yena) by which the physical world is pervaded and woven. 2.18 continues this contrasting theme: the dehin is 'anāśinaḥ' and 'aprameyaḥ' (indestructible and immeasurable). This stanza is like a summary of the last three stanzas. It tells us the contrasting outcomes of both—the physical body ends; that which has the physical body is indestructible and immeasurable.

2.19 brings the topic back to culpability, framing the discussion in Arjuna's immediate context about the responsibility and potential guilt of participation in war and killing, and notice how Krishna refers to dehin here as 'enam' (this). Again, in 2.20, a well-known stanza, Krishna refers to dehin as 'ayam' (this). Stanza 2.21 has 'enam', 2.22 has 'dehī', 2.23 has 'enam', 2.24 has 'ayam', 2.25 has 'ayam', and 2.26 has 'enam'. From 2.21 onwards, Krishna goes through the parts of the puzzle again. In 2.21, there is a speculation—when a person knows about the nature of dehin, how can they consider themselves the killer?

Stanza 2.22 then presents exactly who is the doer: it is the dehin. There is a parallel established between the person ('naraḥ') and the dehin, but notice the big difference in their personalities. The first line uses the verb for grab, seize, or hold—'gṛhṇāti' and the next line uses the verb for meet, or encounter—'saṃyāti'. People have hands, so they can hold, and the dehin … encounters/meets! This verb does not have sensory or tactile aspects. And with the very next two stanzas, 2.23 and 2.24, we see how nothing sensory occurs to the dehin, how it is out of this range.

At 2.22 we understand how we wear and discard clothes, and we can project a similar action on to what the 'śarīrin' does. In the Sanskrit

Gita, the last part of 2.22 does not actually mention bodies, as the meaning is implied. It is we readers who have to make the connection of equivalence between the 'new ones' of the first couplet and the 'new ones' of the second couplet.

Stanza 2.24 is conclusive on the subject of immutability, and wraps up the point by linking back to Stanza 2.12. Dehin, or you, are also 'nityaḥ' (eternal) and 'sanatanaḥ' (primordial/ancient/old). This repeats the idea of Stanza 2.12. By the time Krishna sings Stanza 2.24, Arjuna has understood that this dehin is who he really is. It means that dehin is not just fixed (sthāṇur) and unmoving (acalaḥ), but also powerful, able to go anywhere (sarvagataḥ). Because line 2 of 2.24 presents some unfathomable concepts about the embodied, it is time for 2.25 to explain why. Also, because it is so potent, Stanza 2.25 explains, there's no need to feel sad. The last part of Stanza 2.25 is repeated across stanzas 2.26 and 2.27; it is a refrain: 'na-śocitumarhasi'. Why the emphasis on 'arhat' (deserving person)? Even though Arjuna is really the dehin, he is nothing compared to the awesome power of the dehin, and it is not his place, or role, or business, to be sentimental and sorry about the dehin. What Krishna reports about the dehin is beyond Arjuna's comprehension. No matter how he thinks about dehin (2.26), anyway he doesn't need to mourn for it. The stanza puts Arjuna in his place. Stanza 2.27 insists that death is only certain for those who are born and rebirth is certain for the dead. Arjuna now knows that neither of these happen to dehin. Mourning becomes irrelevant for dehin; on the other hand, since the deha has to die anyway, mourning is anyway irrelevant. 2.28 asks, again, what's there to cry for? ('tatra kā paridevanā?')

Having heard something so bizarre, we can imagine that perhaps Arjuna wonders, am I the first to know about this? Krishna says everyone's surprised to hear about this, but no one comprehends it, *knows* it (śrutvāpyenaṃ veda). In Stanza 2.30, Krishna repeats, everyone is dehin, so there's no need to mourn at all. In less than twenty stanzas, Krishna has explained two subjects. The first, the physical, is delimited to the world of change. As for the second, we get some inkling that it is ungraspable.

Even up until this point, there is no mention of atman. Here is a synopsis:

2.12 *aham* I / *tvam* you / *ime janādhipāḥ* these leaders (always were and will be)
2.13 *dehin* embodied (takes on infancy youth old age—takes on other bodies)
2.14 (physical—sensations—transient)
2.15 (therefore equanimity in joy and sorrow)
2.16 (*sat* and *asat* or reality and non-reality)
2.17 (imperishable)
2.18 *sarīrin* embodied (eternal)
2.19 *enam* this (doesn't kill can't be killed)
2.20 *ayam* this (never born never dies)
2.21 *enam* this (if you know, who do you kill or cause to)
2.22 *dehin* embodied (old clothes—old bodies)
2.23 *enam* this (weapons don't pierce, etc.)
2.24 *ayam* this (unpierceable, etc.)
2.25 *ayam* this (invisible unthinkable, etc.)
2.26 *enam* this (if born and dies again and again, why lament)
2.27 (death certain for the born, birth for those who die)
2.28 (beginning and ends not manifest, middle manifest)
2.29 *enam* this (surprised some see some hear)
2.30 *dehin* embodied (always un-slayable)

Why must we assume that dehin and śarīrin are equivalent to atman? If atman is only a personal pronoun, then perhaps the point is to understand that the dehin *is* atman. And who or what is dehin? Could it, for instance, be Krishna? Or Brahman? That which has the body does not have to be the self. While we accept the wisdom and guidance of commentaries, we must think about the text based on what it actually says. *Read* the Gita. When atman does come up later in the Gita, Krishna is referring to *you*, and sometimes to the ungendered, immortal, indestructible *it*, who you really, really are.

When does Krishna first use the term 'atman' and what does it mean there? I leave it to you, reader, to discover.

WHY THE GITA?

In Judaeo-Christian traditions, there is *one* 'book' that is considered the authoritative word of God. In Hindu traditions, there is an entire library of revelatory works including Vedas, Tantras, Upanishads, Vedangas, Agamas, Sutras, Itihasas (epics), Puranas and many more. Among these, three works came to be regarded as foundational and were called Prasthana Trayi—Upanishads, Brahmasutras (attributed to Badarayana) and the Bhagavad Gita. Even amongst the Prasthana Trayi, it was the Gita that would become nationally and globally renown as representative of Hindu ideas. One wonders why.

We can take some commonsensical guesses. The Brahmasutras do attempt to reconcile the diverse statements in the various Upanishads and the Gita by placing each teaching in a doctrinal context, but they are terse and incomprehensible without various commentaries. There are over a hundred Upanishads, of which thirteen are considered principal Upanishads. The Upanishads and the Brahmasutras are not as handy as the Gita. In 700 stanzas, the Gita is containable in pocket-sized editions the size of the Bible. The Gita has a single, somewhat coherent narrative. In simple Sanskrit, it is easy to read with a dictionary. The stanzas of the Gita are metrical, employing a couple of basic metres, and enabling easy memorization.

Even though the Gita is not a part of shruti (vedic or tantric revelations), it is treated as one. The important word is the word in the title that prefaces 'Gita': it is 'Bhagavad Gita'—i.e., the Song *of God.* Every time Krishna speaks, the Gita reminds us that Krishna is Bhagavan (god, deity)—'śrībhagavānuvāca'. Some readers find this to be the most compelling aspect of the Gita.

Compare the Gita to vedic and tantric hymns/mantras. Mantras are addressed *to* devatas (gods). Each mantra has a rishi and a devata—the rishi who had the revelation and the devata who presides over the mantra. By contrast, the Gita is addressed to humanity, of which Arjuna is a representative. Arjuna's predicament is humanity's predicament, and we can identify with his dilemma. Thus, the Gita compares well to other early Indian sources that convey spiritual or semi-philosophical ideas; it is much more comprehensible.

Some events in modern history also helped consolidate the Gita's position as the canonical (oral) text and scripture of Hinduism.

A LITTLE HISTORY[21]

The Bhagavad Gita has been influential in Indian thought for many centuries. At first, there were Sanskrit commentaries from each school of thought—Shankaracharya in the eighth century CE, Ramanujacharya in the eleventh century CE and Madhvacharya in the thirteenth century CE. Next, the Gita was rendered into Indian languages, including Marathi, Telugu, Assamese and Malayalam—in Marathi by Gyaneshwara in the thirteenth century CE and Tukaram in the seventeenth century CE, in Telugu by Pedda Thirumalacharya in the fifteenth century CE, etc.

It was the East India company's interest in the Gita that catapulted it to international fame and positioned it as representative of Hinduism. In the late eighteenth century CE, there was a community of Orientalists studying Indian manuscripts, especially Sanskrit, in consultation with Indian pundits. Their ultimate purpose was governance; they thought that one way to understand Indians was to study the literatures that they respected and revered.

The first translator of the Bhagavad Gita into English was a typographer and Orientalist, Charles Wilkins (1749–1836). He spent sixteen years in India, was avidly interested in learning about religions, and became a founding member of The Asiatic Society, together with William Jones. Wilkins went to Varanasi to study Sanskrit, and there, was given a manuscript of the Gita. He was struck by the monotheism of the Gita as contrasting with the polytheism of vedic Hinduism, and translated it into English. The governor of British India, Warren Hastings, recommended publishing this translation under the banner of the East India Company. Ironically, the Gita appealed to the Orientalists because they saw in it an affinity with Christianity. Hastings wrote a letter to Nathaniel Smith, Chairman of the East India Company, in which he applauded this affinity:

---

21 See a longer essay on the topic by the author: 'A Brief History of the Bhagavad Gita's Modern Canonization', *Religion Compass* 7, no. 11 (November 2013). https://doi.org/10.1111/rec3.12075.

> I hesitate not to pronounce the Gēētā a performance of great originality; of a sublimity of conception, reasoning and diction, almost unequaled; and a single exception, among all known religions of mankind, of a theology accurately corresponding with that of the Christian dispensation, and most powerfully illustrating its fundamental doctrines.[22]

Yet another letter, addressed to John Scott on 9 December 1784, articulates his reasons.

> My letter to Mr Smith introducing Mr Wilkin's Translation of the Gheeta is also Business, although began in Play. It is the effect or part of a System which I long since laid down, and supported for reconciling the People of England to the Natives of Hindostan.[23]

This letter reveals the important role given to the Gita, that of bridging cultures. Wilkins' translation was hugely successful in Europe and led to a whole spate of translations across the nineteenth century CE, which in turn were read in America. For instance, August Wilhelm von Schlegel published a Latin translation in 1823, which was read by Ralph Waldo Emerson in America in 1905. American transcendentalists had a romantic idea about a mystical India, and the Gita.

Interestingly, it was these translations that also bridged the gap for Indian freedom fighters with their own culture. Gandhi's first encounter with the Gita was Edwin Arnold's 1896 English translation called *The Song Celestial*. It was after he read this that he read Gujarati translations and then the Sanskrit Gita. Gandhi was deeply impressed, and regarded it to be the source of the quintessential wisdom of Hinduism. In 1929, he wrote: 'If all the other scriptures were reduced to ashes, the seven hundred stanzas of this imperishable booklet are quite enough to tell

---

22 M.J. Franklin and C. Wilkins (eds), *The Bhagvat-Gēētā; the Heetōpdēs of Vishnu Sarmā*, European Discovery of India Series, Vol. 1 of 6 (1785; London: Ganesha Publishing, 2001), p. xxi.

23 Ibid., p. vii.

me what Hinduism is and how one can live up to it.'[24] Gandhi's ideas in the freedom movement included communal readings from the Gita along with fasting. Social theorist Ashis Nandy has pointed out that these activities were pivotal to the consolidation of the Gita's status. 'It was through Gandhi that Gita came closest to being a canonical text in Hindu consciousness.'[25]

The Gita's international reputation found a new milestone in 1944, with a translation published in Hollywood by a guru and a movie star. Swami Prabhavananda–Christopher Isherwood's *Bhagavad-Gita: The Song of God* had an introduction by the renowned thinker, Aldous Huxley. Huxley explained the Gita as 'perennial' and applicable across cultures: 'But under all this confusion of tongues and myths, of local histories and particularist doctrines, there remains a Highest Common Factor, which is the Perennial Philosophy in what may be called its chemically pure state.'[26] According to Huxley, people could follow their own faiths and yet agree on a perennial philosophy, and the Gita was one of the most clear and comprehensive summaries of perennial philosophy ever revealed. At this stage, the Gita became a symbol of Hindu identity within India and a symbol of universal spirituality globally.

RETURN TO THE CONTEXT

The peculiarity of the Gita is how it is repeatedly plucked out of context and treated as a self-contained text/work, available as a holy book and used to represent Hinduism. However, the Gita has a context.

Narrative Context

The Gita is a dialogue that appears before the battle in the sixth parva of the Mahabharata. The Pandavas and Kauravas have become entangled

---

24 In M.K. Gandhi, *The Essence of Hinduism*, compiled and edited by V.B. Kher (1987; Ahmedabad: Navajivan Publishing House, 1996), pp. 126–27.

25 Qtd. by S. Sawhney, *The Modernity of Sanskrit* (Minneapolis: University of Minnesota Press, 2009), p. 86.

26 Prabhavananda and Isherwood, *Bhagavad-Gita*, p. 12.

in a sequence of events that cannot be resolved except by war. By then, the characters of Krishna, Arjuna and all other key figures in the Mahabharata, have been fully developed. Krishna plays a multifaceted role in the epic, including a duplicitous one towards the Kauravas and their allies. Dronacharya's murder is a pivotal moment. When Drona begins to overwhelm the Pandava troops, Krishna advises the Pandavas that Drona will not fight if his son Ashvatthaman is killed and suggests that someone say so. Arjuna dissents. Yudhishtira hesitates but condones, and Bhima acts upon it—killing an elephant whose name happens to be Ashvatthaman. Upon hearing the news, Drona reacts violently and then turns to Yudhishtira for confirmation, because he trusts him to speak the truth. Yudhishtira lies. His chariot, which until then has been in a semi-divine state of being afloat, abruptly touches the ground. When Drona dies, Arjuna declares that he and the entire Pandava army have been condemned to hell.

There is a discrepancy between this personality of Krishna and that of the Gita's Krishna who reveals his true form (in chapters 10 and 11) and declares himself as the source and end of everything. How do we reconcile the two? One way is to consider Krishna as an avatar (incarnation) who employs skillful means in his dealings with the world. When we take this approach, we may also look at the multiple paths recommended in the Gita as multiple tactics to persuade Arjuna to carry on fighting. As the narrative of the Mahabharata shows, Arjuna's moral stance remains full of doubt even after the teaching of the Gita; we, too, are never free of doubt after reading the Gita, and we simply go back to it for repeated reading and reflection (as Arjuna does, again, in the Mahabharata).

Religious Context

It is believed that the battle described in the Mahabharata occurred nearly two millennia ago. Thus, the Gita predates the religion and beliefs we now call Hinduism. In the Gita, Krishna declares himself as the supreme divine, and as an omnipotent, omnipresent, omniscient entity. The backdrop of Vedic practices is clear in the Gita, even as it notes that there are many other ways to win over the divine. The philosophy of Samkhya is mentioned, but the reference is more general—it seems to connote reflection and discernment rather than a categorical school of philosophy. If you consider Krishna a Hindu god, the Gita becomes a Hindu text. If you consider the message of the Gita as transcending religious denominations, that is also valid.

Socio-historical Context

In Chapter 1, when Arjuna discusses his concerns about the consequences of the war, he speaks about the violation of women and the mixing of varnas leading to a neglect of rituals honouring forefathers. Later, Krishna speaks about how each of the varnas has emanated from him. The Mahabharata's social context is far removed from our social context, whether in India or in other parts of the world; and we know that the Gita has also been translated into numerous languages, from Italian to Russian, used predominantly in non-Indic regions of the world. It would be a stretch to expect the relevance of this social system or practice to apply across all cultures and all time.

It helps to be aware of these contexts before reading the Gita because it puts some space and time between us and the text. Instead of approaching it with either ardent devotion or skeptical derision, we can be open-minded and calm, ready to learn what we can from an important source of information and knowledge from the past.

ADMIT YOUR CONCERNS

Despite the divine person of Krishna, despite the revelations about the eternality of the Self and the path to self-realization, some aspects about the Gita continue to be troubling. Over the years, I have come up with 'answers' to these problems, which I duly share with the reader, but this does *not* mean that they are resolved.

Is the Gita Casteist?

In the Gita, Krishna says that he created the four varnas: brahmins, kshatriyas, vaishyas and shudras. In many early sources, there are social roles and tasks assigned and confined to these varnas—brahmins for scholarship and priestly activities, kshatriyas for battle, vaishyas for business activities, and shudras for service. Here is the infamous stanza:

> cāturvarṇyaṃ mayā sṛṣṭaṃ guṇakarmavibhāgaśaḥ |
> tasya kartāramapi māṃ viddhyakartāramavyayam || (4.13)

The meaning: The system of four varnas was created by me as per the distribution of qualities/abilities and activities/roles. Although I am their creator, know that I am a non-doer, imperishable.

The problem in this stanza is obvious: the varna system is directly attributed to God. Krishna takes personal responsibility for it, and that, too, in a tone that could be thought casual, or even boastful. No wonder then that those who belong to privileged varnas can and do seize upon this stanza to claim that they have divine sanction. If the Gita is an authoritative text, privileged varnas can and have built their authority upon its word. Naturally, one way to topple such authoritarianism is to contest the authority of the entire Gita. So, this is the debate: Is the Gita promoting social inequalities, and if it is, should it be rejected? If it is not, what is the explanation or defence for this stanza?

Here is a proposal used by those who are egalitarian but who also want to give credence to the Gita. This proposal would explain or attempt to explain the inner meaning of varna, and problematize the translation of 'varna' as 'caste', and look instead for the ideal meaning of 'brahmin'. 1) 'Varna' is a term not exactly translatable to 'caste'—there are four varnas, but numerous castes. 2) A brahmin is a person who follows brahma—and it is the social application of this that went horribly wrong. 3) When we consider the verbal root of the word 'varṇa', we will understand that it really points at 'tendencies'—'vṛṇute iti varṇaḥ'.

The idea of varna as tendency is problematic, because it seems to claim that varna is inherent, not just based on birth. Yes, we may think of the activity of a doctor or engineer or scholar as a calling; but to think that the activity of a manual labourer or sanitation worker is a calling would be cruel. This is particularly so in a rigid social system where a person born into one caste cannot move into a role/position reserved for or claimed by another caste. If we consider the social system flexible, then translating varna as 'tendencies' *may* solve some of the issues. We only need to go back to the story of the Mahabharata where Dronacharya is a brahmin but fights in the war. The residual problem is that such flexibility does not work the other way around. Is there an instance of a person born into an upper caste who has the tendency of a lower caste and then shifts to this other occupation? If not, even this translation, of 'tendency' or 'caste', is not tenable.

Our next option is to examine the rest of the Gita to discover how to interpret Krishna's statement. Rereading before and after Stanza 4.13 does not add any contextual information to help understand this line. We can then turn to other parts of the Gita, and when we do this, we find many instances of Krishna's equal love or regard for all humanity. Consider stanzas 9.30 to 9.32:

> apicetsudurācāro bhajate māmananyabhāk |
> sādhureva sa mantavyaḥ samyagvyavasito hi saḥ || (9.30)

This translates to: Even if a wrongdoer worships me with undivided attention, he is to be considered good. He is occupied correctly.

> kṣipraṃ bhavati dharmātmā śaśvacchāntiṃ nigacchati |
> kaunteya pratijānīhi na me bhaktaḥ praṇaśyati || (9.31)

This translates to: He quickly becomes an embodiment of dharma, finds eternal peace. Be aware, Arjuna, my devotee is never lost.

> māṃ hi pārtha vyapāśritya ye'pi syuḥ pāpayonayaḥ |
> striyo vaiśyāstathā śūdrāste'pi yānti parāṃ gatim || (9.32)

This translates to: Taking refuge in me, even if they are from sinful wombs, women, vaishyas and even shudras, they too go to the highest place.

That women, vaishyas and shudras are singled out is telling. It underlines the privileged position enjoyed by brahmins and kshatriyas, and the inferior position of *all* women, regardless of varna. I consider this a comment about the social and historical context of the Mahabharata and the Gita. What Krishna says is that *in spite of* hierarchies, anyone who takes refuge in him can reach the ultimate goal. Those who have a tendency to do wrong will be transformed through devotion—thus the crucible is devotion, and it liberates everyone from birth and social hierarchies.

Does the Gita Advocate Violence?

It seems odd to think that Krishna would urge anyone to actually kill people. In the Gita, Krishna tells Arjuna to go ahead and fight, and persuades him that he would not actually be killing anyone, because they are all already dead, and 'that which has the body' is immortal. (Arjuna does not ask: If I am really not killing anyone when I kill them, why kill them at all?) Moreover, Arjuna is asked to fight his friends and relatives, people with whom he has grown up and people he cares about. Arjuna's refusal to fight tells us that he is a sensitive human being who values life and cares for relationships.

The first (and obvious) response to this problem is to recapitulate the narrative context. In the backstory, there has been much injustice. Peace talks having failed, the only way to restore righteousness is to go to war. Arjuna has to fight his own family members—and this is also a way to illustrate that we must stand up for righteousness even if it means going against people who are dear to us. Another response to the problem is to think of the war as an allegory. Gandhi had such a point of view: he saw the war of the Mahabharata as the war between the forces of good and evil in our selves.

My own solution has been to look at what Krishna recommends when he speaks more broadly, and to look for his assessment of violence. What is the sleight of hand that allows Arjuna to fight in battle and yet follow an ideal path? Chapter 16, where Krishna describes divine and demonic natures, provides clues. Stanzas 16.1 to 16.3 are one unit:

śrībhagavānuvāca |
abhayaṃ sattvasaṃśuddhirjñānayogavyavasthitiḥ |
dānaṃ damaśca yajñaśca svādhyāyastapa ārjavam || (16.1)

This translates to: Fearlessness, goodness, purity, steady with knowledge and yoga, charity, self-control and yajnas, self-study, austerity, uprightness…

ahiṃsā satyamakrodhastyāgaḥ śāntirapaiśunam |
dayā bhūteṣvaloluptvaṃ mārdavaṃ hrīracāpalam || (16.2)

This translates to: Non-violence, truth, lack of anger, renunciation, pacifism, non-slander, compassion for all living beings, absence of greed, gentleness, modesty, absence of fickleness…

tejaḥ kṣamā dhṛtiḥ śaucamadrohonātimānitā |
bhavanti saṃpadaṃ daivīmabhijātasya bhārata || (16.3)

This translates to: Radiance, endurance, courage, purity, non-betrayal, not too much pride—these are the assets/wealth of those who are born to a divine destiny.

It is clear from the above stanzas that the Gita considers non-violence divine, and violence, demonic. How, then, is it possible for Arjuna to be asked to go to war? Is he being asked to be demonic? Krishna spells out the duties of each varna, and says that kshatriyas do not flee in battle.

śauryaṃ tejo dhṛtirdākṣyaṃ yuddhe cāpyapalāyanam |
dānamīśvarabhāvaśca kṣātraṃ karma svabhāvajam || (18.43)

This translates to: Heroism, radiance, courage, skill, not fleeing in battle, charity, and the spirit of being in charge—these are the natural duties of kshatriyas. Arjuna is a kshatriya, a warrior, and participating in a war is his duty. However, he is also told *how* to participate in battle. The answer to this is throughout the Gita, in the idea of conducting one's duty without attachment.

> niyataṃ saṅgarahitamarāgadveṣataḥ kṛtam |
> aphalaprepsunā karma yattatsāttvikamucyate || (18.23)

This translates to: The action that is controlled and detached, done without desire or hatred, with no wish for results, that is a sattvic action.

An elaborate system of 'gunas' (qualities) is presented in the Gita. The material world is made of a combination of the qualities of sattva, rajas and tamas. People's characteristics depend on which guna is predominant in them, and everything, from diet preferences to the types of rituals and charities, is governed by these gunas. Among the gunas, sattva leads to happiness. Krishna asks Arjuna to leave aside feelings of hatred and violence, to not seek the fruit of action, and to do his duty. These are sattvic according to Krishna's own exposition, even though Arjuna was born in the kshatriya varna.

A reader may be troubled by these concerns and choose to reject the Gita entirely. However, considering the depth of wisdom and the range of ideas contained in the text, I believe, such a rejection would be a colossal loss. Especially because Krishna says that his message is *not* a commandment or decree.

NOT A DECREE

At a public forum, once, someone in the audience asked me if I thought the Gita was authoritative, and if yes, how did I reconcile the statements about varna. I explained my reasoning, and finally added—if you think God gave us an authoritative Gita, did he also not give us the intelligence to think? Reason has a respectable place in the Gita. There are many words for the mind in Indian conceptions—buddhi, chitta and manas are some of them. 'Buddhi' is typically associated with reason, the rational mind, and with commonsense. The Gita also mentions samkhya, which is one of the schools of Indian philosophy. Stanza 2.39 first introduces the term 'buddhi' as part of 'buddhi-yoga'.

eṣā te'bhihitā sāṅkhye buddhiryoge tvimāṃ śṛṇu |
buddhyā yukto yayā pārtha karmabandhaṃ prahāsyasi ||

This translates to: This is declared in samkhya to you. But listen to this, about buddhi-yoga, Arjuna: When you are joined with buddhi, you avoid the bondage of karma.

Here, the reader may jump to the conclusion that everything that has been said up until then refers to samkhya, and that now Krishna is about to impart something about the path of 'buddhi-yoga'. A quick review of samkhya philosophy, however, reveals that it does not really seem to have much to do with explaining the nature of atman. Instead, it is a dualistic system that explains the material world as the result of the interaction of 'purusha' and 'prakriti'—and this concept is, in fact, covered later in the Gita. Moreover, samkhya does not call for the presence of a divine entity, Ishvara, and that again seems at odds with the Gita. A simple way to understand the reference is that it could have been an early form of samkhya philosophy, or simply a more generic word that means 'philosophy', one which Arjuna would have studied. Understood this way, we are no longer caught up in the specifics of the reference. Instead, we begin to understand it as an official and formal system of philosophy or doctrine, and by contrast, 'buddhi' becomes an active application of Arjuna's own intellect. This also works within the context of the next few stanzas, 2.42 to 2.46, in which Krishna speaks about the limitations of vedic information. This section ends with:

yāvānartha udapāne sarvataḥ samplutodake |
tāvānsarveṣu vedeṣu brāhmaṇasya vijānataḥ || (2.46)

This translates to: As much use there is for a well when water is plentiful everywhere, similarly, in all the vedas, for a brahmin who knows.

'Vijānataḥ' is also derived from 'jñā' (to know), and here, Krishna has pointed out the difference between samkhya and the application of one's own mind, and vedas and the person who already has knowledge. Simply put, Krishna is asking Arjuna to think for himself. Krishna then proceeds to talk instead about a focus on action without the desire for the results of actions. Those who think for themselves ought to figure out that the results are not in their control anyway.

DO AS YOU WISH

Finally, despite all of Krishna's exhortations and recommendations, he gives Arjuna the choice to accept or reject them in 18.63—'yathecchasi tathā kuru' (do as you wish). The Gita is not a decree or a commandment.

SANSKRIT PRONUNCIATION

Sanskrit is a phonetically precise language. A letter can only be pronounced one way (whereas in English, a letter may have different pronunciations in different words). If you know how to pronounce the Sanskrit alphabet, you can read the language accurately. The chart below will help readers who may not know Sanskrit to pronounce the Gīta correctly.

A dash over a vowel makes it a longer syllable. Curl your tongue back when there is a dot under the letter, except for 'ṃ', 'ḥ' and 'ṛ'. An 'h' after consonants calls for aspiration, or an out-breath, and so on. Some transliterated words have an apostrophe in them; this replaces an avagraha, ऽ, and stands for a very slightly pronounced 'a'.

Vowels:

a as in u in cut

ā as in father

i as in bit

ī as in beet

u as in put or foot

ū as in brute or cool

e as in bay or fate

ai as in sigh or aisle

o as in hope

au as in sound or flautist

ṛ (which is a vowel in Sanskrit) similar to brunch, or rig

ṃ where the preceding vowel is nasalized, so oṃ as in the French bon

ḥ softly echoes the preceding vowel

Consonants: as for English except for

v as in wall

ś as in shame (whereas s as in so)

ṣ similar to dish

c as in church or chutney

t as in pasta

ṅ as in sung

ñ as in canyon

ṇ has no equivalent in English, but it is a retroflex, i.e., the tongue needs to curl backwards to touch the palate and then hit the back of the teeth.

d as in the

ḍ as in dart

kh, gh, ch, jh, th, dh, ph, bh are aspirated consonants, i.e., the h is pronounced along with an out-breath. This sound has no exact equivalent in English, but the following examples will help approximate the sound. Thus, k as in skate but kh similar to Khan; g as in gate but gh as in the country, Ghana; ch as in much; and so on.

BHAGAVAD GITA

1.1 धृतराष्ट्र उवाच |
धर्मक्षेत्रे कुरुक्षेत्रे समवेता युयुत्सवः |
मामकाः पाण्डवाश्चैव किमकुर्वत संजय ||

dhṛtarāṣṭra uvāca |
dharmakṣetre kurukṣetre samavetā yuyutsavaḥ |
māmakāḥ pāṇḍavāścaiva kimakurvata saṃjaya ||

1.2 संजय उवाच |
दृष्ट्वा तु पाण्डवानीकं व्यूढं दुर्योधनस्तदा |
आचार्यमुपसङ्गम्य राजा वचनमब्रवीत् ||

saṃjaya uvāca |
dṛṣṭvā tu pāṇḍavānīkaṃ vyūḍhaṃ duryodhanastadā |
ācāryamupasaṃgamya rājā vacanamabravīt ||

1.3 पश्यैतां पाण्डुपुत्राणामाचार्य महतीं चमूम् |
व्यूढां द्रुपदपुत्रेण तव शिष्येण धीमता ||

paśyaitāṃ pāṇḍuputrāṇāmācārya mahatīṃ camūm |
vyūḍhāṃ drupadaputreṇa tava śiṣyeṇa dhīmatā ||

1.4 अत्र शूरा महेष्वासा भीमार्जुनसमा युधि |
युयुधानो विराटश्च द्रुपदश्च महारथः ||

atra śūrā maheṣvāsā bhīmārjunasamā yudhi |
yuyudhāno virāṭaśca drupadaśca mahārathaḥ ||

1.5 धृष्टकेतुश्चेकितानः काशिराजश्च वीर्यवान् |
पुरुजित्कुन्तिभोजश्च शैब्यश्च नरपुङ्गवः ||

dhṛṣṭaketuścekitānaḥ kāśirājaśca vīryavān |
purujitkuntibhojaśca śaibyaśca narapuṅgavaḥ ||

1.6 युधामन्युश्च विक्रान्त उत्तमौजाश्च वीर्यवान् |
सौभद्रो द्रौपदेयाश्च सर्व एव महारथाः ||

yudhāmanyuśca vikrānta uttamaujāśca vīryavān |
saubhadro draupadeyāśca sarva eva mahārathāḥ ||

1.1 dhritarashtra to sanjaya:
& when it came to that
might right face-off
what happened who
did what

1.2 sanjaya to dhritarashtra:
duryodhana took in the
enemy line up & said
to dronacharya:

1.3 no thanks to you prof.
trained by you drishtadyumna
chief of the other side
has put it together

1.4–1.6 a who's who
of heroes each
a bhim
an arjun

yuyudhana – virata – drupada –
dhristaketu – cekitana – & the king of kashi –
purujit – kuntibhoj – bullish saibya
yudhamanyu – uttamaujas – abhimanyu – &
the famous five
sons of draupadi

1.7 अस्माकं तु विशिष्टा ये तान्निबोध द्विजोत्तम |
नायका मम सैन्यस्य संज्ञार्थं तान्ब्रवीमि ते ||

asmākaṃ tu viśiṣṭā ye tānnibodha dvijottama |
nāyakā mama sainyasya saṃjñārthaṃ tānbravīmi te ||

1.8 भवान्भीष्मश्च कर्णश्च कृपश्च समितिञ्जयः |
अश्वत्थामा विकर्णश्च सौमदत्तिस्तथैव च ||

bhavānbhīṣmaśca karṇaśca kṛpaśca samitimñjayaḥ |
aśvatthāmā vikarṇaśca saumadattistathaiva ca ||

1.9 अन्ये च बहवः शूरा मदर्थे त्यक्तजीविताः |
नानाशस्त्रप्रहरणाः सर्वे युद्धविशारदाः ||

anye ca bahavaḥ śūrā madarthe tyaktajīvitāḥ |
nānāśastrapraharaṇāḥ sarve yuddhaviśāradāḥ ||

1.10 अपर्याप्तं तदस्माकं बलं भीष्माभिरक्षितम् |
पर्याप्तं त्विदमेतेषां बलं भीमाभिरक्षितम् ||

aparyāptaṃ tadasmākaṃ balaṃ bhīṣmābhirakṣitam |
paryāptaṃ tvidameteṣāṃ balaṃ bhīmābhirakṣitam ||

1.11 अयनेषु च सर्वेषु यथाभागमवस्थिताः |
भीष्ममेवाभिरक्षन्तु भवन्तः सर्व एव हि ||

ayaneṣu ca sarveṣu yathābhāgamavasthitāḥ |
bhīṣmamevābhirakṣantu bhavantaḥ sarva eva hi ||

1.12 तस्य सञ्जनयन्हर्षं कुरुवृद्धः पितामहः |
सिंहनादं विनद्योच्चैः शङ्खं दध्मौ प्रतापवान् ||

tasya sañjanayanharṣaṃ kuruvṛddhaḥ pitāmahaḥ |
siṃhanādaṃ vinadyoccaiḥ śaṅkhaṃ dadhmau pratāpavān ||

1.13 ततः शङ्खाश्च भेर्यश्च पणवानकगोमुखाः |
सहसैवाभ्यहन्यन्त स शब्दस्तुमुलोऽभवत् ||

tataḥ śaṅkhāśca bheryaśca paṇavānakagomukhāḥ |
sahasaivābhyahanyanta sa śabdastumulo'bhavat ||

1.7–1.8 not that we're less
prepped

we've got bhishma
& karna
& kripacharya
& asvatthama
& vikarna
& the somadatta sons
&

1.9 all sorts of weapons
at their fingertips
for my sake their
life on the line

1.10 & yet it's not
enough
our might guarded by bhishma
to their might guarded by bhima

1.11 in every move
stick to your roles
keep your head   bhishma
safe

1.12–1.13 grandlion bhishma
bellowed
    yeaarrghh
& blew his

conch erupt his
troops took it up
on drums & cymbals
& trumpets

what a riot

1.14 ततः श्वेतैर्हयैर्युक्ते महति स्यन्दने स्थितौ |
माधवः पाण्डवश्चैव दिव्यौ शङ्खौ प्रदध्मतुः ||

tataḥ śvetairhayairyukte mahati syandane sthitau |
mādhavaḥ pāṇḍavaścaiva divyau śaṅkhau pradadhmatuḥ ||

1.15 पाञ्चजन्यं हृषीकेशो देवदत्तं धनंजयः |
पौण्ड्रं दध्मौ महाशङ्खं भीमकर्मा वृकोदरः ||

pāñcajanyaṃ hṛṣīkeśo devadattaṃ dhanaṃjayaḥ |
pauṇḍraṃ dadhmau mahāśaṅkhaṃ bhīmakarmā vṛkodaraḥ ||

1.16 अनन्तविजयं राजा कुन्तीपुत्रो युधिष्ठिरः |
नकुलः सहदेवश्च सुघोषमणिपुष्पकौ ||

anaṃtavijayaṃ rājā kuntīputro yudhiṣṭhiraḥ |
nakulaḥ sahadevaśca sughoṣamaṇipuṣpakau ||

1.17 काश्यश्च परमेष्वासः शिखण्डी च महारथः |
धृष्टद्युम्नो विराटश्च सात्यकिश्चापराजितः ||

kāśyaśca parameṣvāsaḥ śikhaṇḍī ca mahārathaḥ |
dhṛṣṭadyumno virāṭaśca sātyakiścāparājitaḥ ||

1.18 द्रुपदो द्रौपदेयाश्च सर्वशः पृथिवीपते |
सौभद्रश्च महाबाहुः शङ्खान्दध्मुः पृथक् पृथक् ||

drupado draupadeyāśca sarvaśaḥ pṛthivīpate |
saubhadraśca mahābāhuḥ śaṅkhāndadhmuḥ pṛthak pṛthak ||

1.19 स घोषो धार्तराष्ट्राणां हृदयानि व्यदारयत् |
नभश्च पृथिवीं चैव तुमुलोव्यनुनादयन् ||

sa ghoṣo dhārtarāṣṭrāṇāṃ hṛdayāni vyadārayat |
nabhaśca pṛthivīṃ caiva tumulovyanunādayan ||

1.20 अथ व्यवस्थितान्दृष्ट्वा धार्तराष्ट्रान् कपिध्वजः |
प्रवृत्ते शस्त्रसम्पाते धनुरुद्यम्य पाण्डवः ||

atha vyavasthitāndṛṣṭvā dhārtarāṣṭrān kapidhvajaḥ |
pravṛtte śastrasampāte dhanurudyamya pāṇḍavaḥ ||

1.14 then

from a sleek chariot
on two white steeds leapt
unearthly sound

1.15–1.18 krishna's panchajanya &
arjuna's devadatta

then bhima's hungry paundra –
king yudhishtira's victory call –
nakula's nice tone –
sahadeva's gembloom – each

announced himself
unique

king of kashi – sikhandin – drishtadyumna –
virata – unbeatable satyaki – drupada – his
sons in law the five pandavas –

& powerarm abhimanyu
revved

1.19 shook earth & sky
busted your sons'
hearts

1.20 armies all set
weapons about to clash

under the hero-hanuman banner
arjuna reached for his bow
& paused

1.21 हृषीकेशं तदा वाक्यमिदमाह महीपते |
सेनयोरुभयोर्मध्ये रथं स्थापय मेऽच्युत ||

hṛṣīkeśaṃ tadā vākyamidamāha mahīpate |
senayorubhayormadhye rathaṃ sthāpaya me'cyuta ||

1.22 यावदेतान्निरीक्षेऽहं योद्धुकामानवस्थितान् |
कैर्मया सह योद्धव्यमस्मिन् रणसमुद्यमे ||

yāvadetānnirikṣe'haṃ yoddhukāmānavasthitān |
kairmayā saha yoddhavyamasmin raṇasamudyame ||

1.23 योत्स्यमानानवेक्षेऽहं य एतेऽत्र समागताः |
धार्तराष्ट्रस्य दुर्बुद्धेर्युद्धे प्रियचिकीर्षवः ||

yotsyamānānavekṣe'haṃ ya ete'tra samāgatāḥ |
dhārtarāṣṭrasya durbuddheryuddhe priyacikīrṣavaḥ ||

1.24 एवमुक्तो हृषीकेशो गुडाकेशेन भारत |
सेनयोरुभयोर्मध्ये स्थापयित्वा रथोत्तमम् ||

evamukto hṛṣīkeśo guḍākeśena bhārata |
senayorubhayormadhye sthāpayitvā rathottamam ||

1.25 भीष्मद्रोणप्रमुखतः सर्वेषां च महीक्षिताम् |
उवाच पार्थ पश्यैतान्समवेतान्कुरूनिति ||

bhīṣmadroṇapramukhataḥ sarveṣāṃ ca mahīkṣitām |
uvāca pārtha paśyaitānsamavetānkurūniti ||

1.21 to krishna:

sir can we go
to a vantage point
between armies

1.22–1.25 who's there   who's
to fight for evil   sweet on evil
duryodhana

chariot parked
in no man's land

in front of bhishma & drona & all the chiefs
arjuna said   see
& saw

1.26 तत्रापश्यत्स्थितान् पार्थः पितॄनथ पितामहान् |
आचार्यान्मातुलान्भ्रातॄन्पुत्रान्पौत्रान्सखींस्तथा ||

tatrāpaśyatsthitān pārthaḥ pitṛnatha pitāmahān |
ācāryānmātulānbhrātṛnputrānpautrānsakhīṃstathā ||

1.27 श्वशुरान्सुहृदश्चैव सेनयोरुभयोरपि |
तान्समीक्ष्य स कौन्तेयः सर्वान्बन्धूनवस्थितान् ||

śvaśurānsuhṛdaścaiva senayorubhayorapi |
tānsamīkṣya sa kaunteyaḥ sarvānbandhūnavasthitān ||

1.28 कृपया परयाविष्टो विषीदन्निदमब्रवीत् |
दृष्ट्वेमं स्वजनं कृष्ण युयुत्सुं समुपस्थितम् ||

kṛpayā parayāviṣṭo viṣīdannidamabravīt |
dṛṣṭvemaṃ svajanaṃ kṛṣṇa yuyutsuṃ samupasthitam ||

1.29 सीदन्ति मम गात्राणि मुखं च परिशुष्यति |
वेपथुश्च शरीरे मे रोमहर्षश्च जायते ||

sīdanti mama gātrāṇi mukhaṃ ca pariśuṣyati |
vepathuśca śarīre me romaharṣaśca jāyate ||

1.30 गाण्डीवं स्रंसते हस्तात्त्वक्चैव परिदह्यते |
न च शक्नोम्यवस्थातुं भ्रमतीव च मे मनः ||

gāṇḍīvaṃ sraṃsate hastāttvakcaiva paridahyate |
na ca śaknomyavasthātuṃ bhramatīva ca me manaḥ ||

1.31 निमित्तानि च पश्यामि विपरीतानि केशव |
न च श्रेयोऽनुपश्यामि हत्वा स्वजनमाहवे ||

nimittāni ca paśyāmi viparītāni keśava |
na ca śreyo'nupaśyāmi hatvā svajanamāhave ||

1.26–1.27	familiars	foster fathers &
		fathers' fathers &
		fathers
		in law & uncles &
		teachers &
		brothers & friends
		& sons &
		grandsons
1.28–1.30	& said	
	pitiful	
	these people	war urgent
	are	
	my people	i feel
	drained	my
	mouth's dry	my
	tremble	is me my every
	hair in shock	my
	bow slips	i'm
	feverish	i can barely
	stand	my mind
	wheels	
1.31	all the signs are grave	
	no good can come	
	from killing my own	

1.32 न काङ्क्षे विजयं कृष्ण न च राज्यं सुखानि च |
किं नो राज्येन गोविन्द किं भोगैर्जीवितेन वा ||

na kāṅkṣe vijayaṃ kṛṣṇa na ca rājyaṃ sukhāni ca |
kiṃ no rājyena govinda kiṃ bhogairjīvitena vā ||

1.33 येषामर्थे काङ्क्षितं नो राज्यं भोगाः सुखानि च |
त इमेऽवस्थिता युद्धे प्राणांस्त्यक्त्वा धनानि च ||

yeṣāmarthe kāṅkṣitaṃ no rājyaṃ bhogāḥ sukhāni ca |
ta ime'vasthitā yuddhe prāṇāṃstyaktvā dhanāni ca ||

1.34 आचार्याः पितरः पुत्रास्तथैव च पितामहाः |
मातुलाः श्वशुराः पौत्राः श्यालाः सम्बन्धिनस्तथा ||

ācāryāḥ pitaraḥ putrāstathaiva ca pitāmahāḥ |
mātulāḥ śvaśurāḥ pautrāḥ śyālāḥ sambandhinastathā ||

1.35 एतान्न हन्तुमिच्छामि घ्नतोऽपि मधुसूदन |
अपि त्रैलोक्यराज्यस्य हेतोः किं नु महीकृते ||

etānna hantumicchāmi ghnato'pi madhusūdana |
api trailokyarājyasya hetoḥ kiṃ nu mahīkṛte ||

1.36 निहत्य धार्तराष्ट्रान्नः का प्रीतिः स्याज्जनार्दन |
पापमेवाश्रयेदस्मान हत्वैतानाततायिनः ||

nihatya dhārtarāṣṭrānnaḥ kā prītiḥ syājjanārdana |
pāpamevāśrayedasmān hatvaitānātatāyinaḥ ||

1.37 तस्मान्नार्हा वयं हन्तुं धार्तराष्ट्रान्स्वबान्धवान् |
स्वजनं हि कथं हत्वा सुखिनः स्याम माधव ||

tasmānnārhā vayaṃ hantuṃ dhārtarāṣṭrānsvabāndhavān |
svajanaṃ hi kathaṃ hatvā sukhinaḥ syāma mādhava ||

1.38 यद्यप्येते न पश्यन्ति लोभोपहतचेतसः |
कुलक्षयकृतं दोषं मित्रद्रोहे च पातकम् ||

yadyapyete na paśyanti lobhopahatacetasaḥ |
kulakṣayakṛtaṃ doṣaṃ mitradrohe ca pātakam ||

1.32 don't wanna be a hero
don't need no empire
what's there to enjoy
what's the point of it all

1.33 all those
for whom i'd want
to live it up
are here to die

1.34 fathers & fathers' fathers & fathers
in law & brothers in law &
sons & sons' sons & teachers
& uncles & others

1.35 i'm not into
this they-kill-so-i-kill

not if i was paid three
worlds as for mere earth
pah!

1.36 what kind of fun's
in murdering the sons
of dhritarashtra
the sin will do us in

1.37 dhritarashtra's sons are
family how can we
happily
slaughter our own

1.38 they don't know greed won't let them
think
how blind it is this
fratricide

1.39 कथं न ज्ञेयमस्माभिः पापादस्मान्निवर्तितुम् |
कुलक्षयकृतं दोषं प्रपश्यद्भिर्जनार्दन ||

kathaṃ na jñeyamasmābhiḥ pāpādasmānnivartitum |
kulakṣayakṛtaṃ doṣaṃ prapaśyadbhirjanārdana ||

1.40 कुलक्षये प्रणश्यन्ति कुलधर्माः सनातनाः |
धर्मे नष्टे कुलं कृत्स्नमधर्मोऽभिभवत्युत ||

kulakṣaye praṇaśyanti kuladharmāḥ sanātanāḥ |
dharme naṣṭe kulaṃ kṛtsnamadharmo'bhibhavatyuta ||

1.41 अधर्माभिभवात्कृष्ण प्रदुष्यन्ति कुलस्त्रियः |
स्त्रीषु दुष्टासु वार्ष्णेय जायते वर्णसङ्करः ||

adharmābhibhavātkṛṣṇa praduṣyanti kulastriyaḥ |
strīṣu duṣṭāsu vārṣṇeya jāyate varṇasaṅkaraḥ ||

1.42 सङ्करो नरकायैव कुलघ्नानां कुलस्य च |
पतन्ति पितरो ह्येषां लुप्तपिण्डोदकक्रियाः ||

saṅkaro narakāyaiva kulaghnānāṃ kulasya ca |
patanti pitaro hyeṣāṃ luptapiṇḍodakakriyāḥ ||

1.43 दोषैरेतैः कुलघ्नानां वर्णसङ्करकारकैः |
उत्साद्यन्ते जातिधर्माः कुलधर्माश्च शाश्वताः ||

doṣairetaiḥ kulaghnānāṃ varṇasaṅkarakārakaiḥ |
utsādyante jātidharmāḥ kuladharmāśca śāśvatāḥ ||

1.44 उत्सन्नकुलधर्माणां मनुष्याणां जनार्दन |
नरकेऽनियतं वासो भवतीत्यनुशुश्रुम ||

utsannakuladharmāṇāṃ manuṣyāṇāṃ janārdana |
narake'niyataṃ vāso bhavatītyanuśuśruma ||

1.45 अहो बत महत्पापं कर्तुं व्यवसिता वयम् |
यद्राज्यसुखलोभेन हन्तुं स्वजनमुद्यताः ||

aho bata mahatpāpaṃ kartuṃ vyavasitā vayam |
yadrājyasukhalobhena hantuṃ svajanamudyatāḥ ||

1.39 but we can see shall we not say no
devastation
of the clan

1.40–1.44 family = values
de structing → chaos

when lawlessness
= law
our women violated
roles confused
rites undone
ancestors let down

that totally ruins the family
& destroyers of the family HELL!

1.45 & yet we seem intent
we greedy powermongers

1.46 यदि मामप्रतीकारमशस्त्रं शस्त्रपाणयः |
धार्तराष्ट्रा रणे हन्युस्तन्मे क्षेमतरं भवेत् ||

yadi māmapratīkāramaśastraṃ śastrapāṇayaḥ |
dhārtarāṣṭrā raṇe hanyustanme kṣemataraṃ bhavet ||

1.47 एवमुक्त्वार्जुनः सङ्ख्ये रथोपस्थ उपाविशत् |
विसृज्य सशरं चापं शोकसंविग्नमानसः ||

evamuktvārjunaḥ saṅkhye rathopastha upāviśat |
visṛjya saśaraṃ cāpaṃ śokasaṃvignamānasaḥ ||

2.1 संजय उवाच |
तं तथा कृपयाविष्टमश्रुपूर्णाकुलेक्षणम् |
विषीदन्तमिदं वाक्यमुवाच मधुसूदनः ||

saṃjaya uvāca |
taṃ tathā kṛpayāviṣṭamaśrupūrṇākulekṣaṇam |
viṣīdantamidaṃ vākyamuvāca madhusūdanaḥ ||

2.2 श्रीभगवानुवाच |
कुतस्त्वा कश्मलमिदं विषमे समुपस्थितम् |
अनार्यजुष्टमस्वर्ग्यमकीर्तिकरमर्जुन ||

śrībhagavānuvāca |
kutastvā kaśmalamidaṃ viṣame samupasthitam |
anāryajuṣṭamasvargyamakīrtikaramarjuna ||

2.3 क्लैब्यं मा स्म गमः पार्थ नैतत्त्वय्युपपद्यते |
क्षुद्रं हृदयदौर्बल्यं त्यक्त्वोत्तिष्ठ परंतप ||

klaibyaṃ mā sma gamaḥ pārtha naitattvayyupapadyate |
kṣudraṃ hṛdayadaurbalyaṃ tyaktvottiṣṭha paraṃtapa ||

1.46 i'd be better off if they kill me
unarmed
unresistant

1.47 sad as a sack
arjuna flopped
flung bow
& arrow

2.1 sanjaya:
to him (arjuna)
pitiful
teary-eyed depressed
this is what
krishna said

2.2–2.3 krishna:

why such a muddle
just for a spot of trouble

don't be a coward
it does not become you

drop this pathetic
faint-heartedness

stand up! arjuna

2.4 अर्जुन उवाच |
कथं भीष्ममहं सङ्ख्ये द्रोणं च मधुसूदन |
इषुभि: प्रतियोत्स्यामि पूजार्हावरिसूदन ||

arjuna uvāca |
kathaṃ bhīṣmamahaṃ saṅkhye droṇaṃ ca madhusūdana |
iṣubhiḥ pratiyotsyāmi pūjārhāvarisūdana ||

2.5 गुरूनहत्वा हि महानुभावान् श्रयो भोक्तुं भैक्ष्यमपीह लोके |
हत्वार्थकामांस्तु गुरूनिहैव भुञ्जीय भोगान् रुधिरप्रदिग्धान् ||

gurūnahatvā hi mahānubhāvān
śreyo bhoktuṃ bhaikṣyamapīha loke |
hatvārthakāmāṃstu gurūnihaiva
bhuñjīya bhogān rudhirapradigdhān ||

2.6 न चैतद्विद्म: कतरन्नो गरीयो यद्वा जयेम यदि वा नो जयेयु: |
यानेव हत्वा न जिजीविषाम: तेऽवस्थिता: प्रमुखे धार्तराष्ट्रा: ||

na caitadvidmaḥ kataranno garīyo
yadvā jayema yadi vā no jayeyuḥ |
yāneva hatvā na jijīviṣāmaḥ
te'vasthitāḥ pramukhe dhārtarāṣṭrāḥ ||

2.7 कार्पण्यदोषोपहत स्वभाव: पृच्छामि त्वां धर्मसम्मूढचेता: |
यच्छ्रेय: स्यान्निश्चितं ब्रूहि तन्मे शिष्यस्तेऽहं शाधिमां त्वांप्रपन्नम् ||

kārpaṇyadoṣopahata svabhāvaḥ
pṛcchāmi tvāṃ dharmasaṃmūḍhacetāḥ |
yacchreyaḥ syānniścitaṃ brūhi tanme
śiṣyaste'haṃ śādhimāṃ tvāṃprapannam ||

2.4–2.5 arjuna:

krishna how can i fight
bhishma and drona
    attack with arrows
those worthy
    of my worship

    better to eat alms
    than kill
great gurus in this world

killing gurus for gain

the pleasures i enjoy
will be bloody

2.6 nor do we know
    what's better
should we conquer them
or they us

we will no longer want to live
if we kill

the sons of dhritarashtra
who stand before us

2.7 my spirit is weak
i'm confused
what's right

    i ask you
    what's better for sure
        tell me

    i'm your student
    correct me
        i beseech you

2.8 न हि प्रपश्यामि ममापनुद्याद् यच्छोकमुच्छोषणम् इन्द्रियाणाम् |
अवाप्य भूमावसपत्नमृद्धम् राज्यंसुराणामपिचाधिपत्यम् ||

na hi prapaśyāmi mamāpanudyād
yacchokamucchoṣaṇam indriyāṇām |
avāpya bhūmāvasapatnamṛddhaṃ
rājyaṃsurāṇāmapicādhipatyam ||

2.9 संजय उवाच |
एवमुक्त्वा हृषीकेशं गुडाकेश: परंतप |
न योत्स्य इति गोविन्दमुक्त्वा तूष्णीं बभूव ह ||

saṃjaya uvāca |
evamuktvā hṛṣīkeśaṃ guḍākeśaḥ paraṃtapa |
na yotsya iti govindamuktvā tūṣṇīṃ babhūva ha ||

2.10 तमुवाच हृषीकेश: प्रहसन्निव भारत |
सेनयोरुभयोर्मध्ये विषीदन्तमिदं वच: ||

tamuvāca hṛṣīkeśaḥ prahasanniva bhārata |
senayorubhayormadhye viṣīdantamidaṃ vacaḥ ||

2.11 श्रीभगवानुवाच |
अशोच्यानन्वशोचस्त्वं प्रज्ञावादांश्च भाषसे |
गतासूनगतासूंश्च नानुशोचन्ति पण्डिता: ||

śrībhagavānuvāca |
aśocyānanvaśocastvaṃ prajñāvādāṃśca bhāṣase |
gatāsūnagatāsūṃśca nānuśocanti paṇḍitāḥ ||

2.8 nor do I understand
even if I attain
unrivalled fortune in this world
kingship of the gods

what will remove this
my sadness
dries my senses

2.9 sanjaya:

having said so
arjuna said to krishna

i will not fight
and was silent

2.10 o' dhritarashtra

in the middle of two armies
krishna smiled

spoke this to sad arjuna

2.11 krishna:
nice speech arjuna but

the truly wise
know better

than to be sad
over life that's gone
or not

life & death pass

2.12 न त्वेवाहं जातु नासं न त्वं नेमे जनाधिपाः |
न चैव न भविष्यामः सर्वे वयमतः परम् ||

na tvevāhaṃ jātu nāsaṃ na tvaṃ neme janādhipāḥ |
na caiva na bhaviṣyāmaḥ sarve vayamataḥ param ||

2.13 देहिनोऽस्मिन्यथा देहे कौमारं यौवनं जरा |
तथा देहान्तरप्राप्तिर्धीरस्तत्र न मुह्यति ||

dehino'sminyathā dehe kaumāraṃ yauvanaṃ jarā |
tathā dehāntaraprāptirdhīrastatra na muhyati ||

2.14 मात्रास्पर्शास्तु कौन्तेय शीतोष्णसुखदुःखदाः |
आगमापायिनोऽनित्यास्तांस्तितिक्षस्व भारत ||

mātrāsparśāstu kaunteya śītoṣṇasukhaduḥkhadāḥ |
āgamāpāyino'nityāstāṃstitikṣasva bhārata ||

2.15 यं हि न व्यथयन्त्येते पुरुषं पुरुषर्षभ |
समदुःखसुखं धीरं सोऽमृतत्वाय कल्पते ||

yaṃ hi na vyathayantyete puruṣaṃ puruṣarṣabha |
samaduḥkhasukhaṃ dhīraṃ so'mṛtatvāya kalpate ||

2.16 नासतो विद्यते भावो नाभावो विद्यते सतः |
उभयोरपि दृष्टोऽन्तस्त्वनयोस्तत्त्वदर्शिभिः ||

nāsato vidyate bhāvo nābhāvo vidyate sataḥ |
ubhayorapi dṛṣṭo'ntastvanayostattvadarśibhiḥ ||

2.12 i was never not
& never won't be

you too
& them

2.13 you
change in this body from child to adult
& decrepit
& you
change into another body again

2.14–2.15 sensations cold heat
pleasure pain
are mortal they come & go

stay
unruffled by them get ready
for immortality

2.16 if it isn't it isn't
true real

what you call reality
is really virtual
reality

your reality's materiality
(material = changeable = mortal = untrue = immaterial)

it seems as if but
there's no
truth in fiction

what is what is
clear to a seer

2.17 अविनाशि तु तद्विद्धि येन सर्वमिदं ततम् |
विनाशमव्ययस्यास्य न कश्चित्कर्तुमर्हति ||

avināśi tu tadviddhi yena sarvamidaṃ tatam |
vināśamavyayasyāsya na kaścitkartumarhati ||

2.18 अन्तवन्त इमे देहा नित्यस्योक्ताः शरीरिणः |
अनाशिनोऽप्रमेयस्य तस्माद्युध्यस्व भारत ||

antavanta ime dehā nityasyoktāḥ śarīriṇaḥ |
anāśino'prameyasya tasmādyudhyasva bhārata ||

2.19 य एनं वेत्ति हन्तारं यश्चैनं मन्यते हतम् |
उभौ तौ न विजानीतो नायं हन्ति न हन्यते ||

ya enaṃ vetti hantāraṃ yaścainaṃ manyate hatam |
ubhau tau na vijānīto nāyaṃ hanti na hanyate ||

2.20 न जायते म्रियते वा कदाचित् नायं भूत्वा भविता वा न भूयः |
अजो नित्यः शाश्वतोऽयं पुराणो न हन्यते हन्यमाने शरीरे ||

na jāyate mriyate vā kadācit
nāyaṃ bhūtvā bhavitā vā na bhūyaḥ |
ajo nityaḥ śāśvato'yaṃ purāṇo
na hanyate hanyamāne śarīre ||

2.17–2.18 that by which this
immaterial matter
is permeated
is permanent

bodies end
the embodied timeless (let's call it 'it')
can not be measured destroyed

so fight arjuna

2.19 she who thinks it kills &
she who thinks it is killed

don't get
it
is neither

it is who you really are

2.20 never was it born
never will it die
nor ever having been will ever not be

for ever
from ever
unchanging in the changing body

2.21 वेदाविनाशिनं नित्यं य एनमजमव्ययम् |
कथं स पुरुषः पार्थ कं घातयति हन्ति कम् ||

vedāvināśinaṃ nityaṃ ya enamajamavyayam |
kathaṃ sa puruṣaḥ pārtha kaṃ ghātayati hanti kam ||

2.22 वासांसि जीर्णानि यथा विहाय नवानि गृह्णाति नरोऽपराणि |
तथा शरीराणि विहाय जीर्णान्यन्यानि संयाति नवानि देही ||

vāsāṃsi jīrṇāni yathā vihāya navāni gṛhṇāti naro'parāṇi |
tathā śarīrāṇi vihāya jīrṇānyanyāni saṃyāti navāni dehī ||

2.23 नैनं छिन्दन्ति शस्त्राणि नैनं दहति पावकः |
न चैनं क्लेदयन्त्यापो न शोषयति मारुतः ||

nainaṃ chindanti śastrāṇi nainaṃ dahati pāvakaḥ |
na cainaṃ kledayantyāpo na śoṣayati mārutaḥ ||

2.24 अच्छेद्योऽयमदाह्योऽयमक्लेद्योऽशोष्य एव च |
नित्यः सर्वगतः स्थाणुरचलोऽयं सनातनः ||

acchedyo'yamadāhyo'yamakledyo'śoṣya eva ca |
nityaḥ sarvagataḥ sthāṇuracalo'yaṃ sanātanaḥ ||

2.25 अव्यक्तोऽयमचिन्त्योऽयमविकार्योऽयमुच्यते |
तस्मादेवं विदित्वैनं नानुशोचितुमर्हसि ||

avyakto'yamacintyo'yamavikāryo'yamucyate |
tasmādevaṃ viditvainaṃ nānuśocitumarhasi ||

2.26 अथ चैनं नित्यजातं नित्यं वा मन्यसे मृतम् |
तथापि त्वं महाबाहो नैवं शोचितुमर्हसि ||

atha cainaṃ nityajātaṃ nityaṃ vā manyase mṛtam |
tathāpi tvaṃ mahābāho naivaṃ śocitumarhasi ||

2.21 if you know you
are indestructible   eternal   birthless   changeless
for instance

how can you believe you
are the one to kill
& whom do you kill

2.22 you discard   old clothes for the new
you discard   one worn-out body for another

you are   not your body

2.23–2.24 weapons   cannot   pierce | this | unpierceable
fire   burn | who | unburnable
water   wet | you | unwettable
wind   dry | really | undryable
| are |
forever
free
fixed
fromever

2.25 can not be felt by the senses
can not be grasped by thought

beyond the variable

understand it
is not for you to mourn

2.26 even if you imagine it
birthing dying
recurring
still not your place to mourn

2.27 जातस्य हि ध्रुवो मृत्युर्ध्रुवं जन्म मृतस्य च |
तस्मादपरिहार्येऽर्थे न त्वं शोचितुमर्हसि ||

jātasya hi dhruvo mṛtyurdhruvaṃ janma mṛtasya ca |
tasmādaparihārye'rthe na tvaṃ śocitumarhasi ||

2.28 अव्यक्तादीनि भूतानि व्यक्तमध्यानि भारत |
अव्यक्तनिधनान्येव तत्र का परिदेवना ||

avyaktādīni bhūtāni vyaktamadhyāni bhārata |
avyaktanidhanānyeva tatra kā paridevanā ||

2.29 आश्चर्यवत्पश्यति कश्चिदेनम् आश्चर्यवद्वदति तथैव चान्यः |
आश्चर्यवच्चैनमन्यः शृणोति श्रुत्वाप्येनं वेद न चैव कश्चित् ||

āścaryavatpaśyati kaścidenam
āścaryavadvadati tathaiva cānyaḥ |
āścaryavaccainamanyaḥ śṛṇoti
śrutvāpyenaṃ veda na caiva kaścit ||

2.30 देही नित्यमवध्योऽयं देहे सर्वस्य भारत |
तस्मात्सर्वाणि भूतानि न त्वं शोचितुमर्हसि ||

dehī nityamavadhyo'yaṃ dehe sarvasya bhārata |
tasmātsarvāṇi bhūtāni na tvaṃ śocitumarhasi ||

2.31 स्वधर्ममपि चावेक्ष्य न विकम्पितुमर्हसि |
धर्म्याद्धि युद्धाच्छ्रेयोऽन्यत्क्षत्रियस्य न विद्यते ||

svadharmamapi cāvekṣya na vikampitumarhasi |
dharmyāddhi yuddhācchreyo'nyatkṣatriyasya na vidyate ||

2.32 यदृच्छया चोपपन्नं स्वर्गद्वारमपावृतम् |
सुखिनः क्षत्रियाः पार्थ लभन्ते युद्धमीदृशम् ||

yadṛcchayā copapannaṃ svargadvāramapāvṛtam |
sukhinaḥ kṣatriyāḥ pārtha labhante yuddhamīdṛśam ||

2.27 it's the 'born' who are guaranteed to 'die'
it's the 'dead' who are 'reborn'
pointless for you to mourn

2.28 & birth to death
is the obvious part
the middle part

your true beginning & end
is hidden
so what

2.29 the truth is
so awesome that

some visualize it
some talk about it
some hear about it

all awed
none the wiser

2.30 this – it – (some call it 'soul')
is indestructible in
everyone's body
so no need to mourn

2.31 war = warrior's duty
= your duty
fear not

2.32 happy the warriors what luck!
to get a war like this open heaven gates

2.33 अथ चेत्त्वमिमं धर्म्यं संग्रामं न करिष्यसि |
ततः स्वधर्मं कीर्तिं च हित्वा पापमवाप्स्यसि ||

atha cettvamimaṃ dharmyaṃ saṃgrāmaṃ na kariṣyasi |
tataḥ svadharmaṃ kīrtiṃ ca hitvā pāpamavāpsyasi ||

2.34 अकीर्तिं चापि भूतानि कथयिष्यन्ति तेऽव्ययाम् |
सम्भावितस्य चाकीर्तिर्मरणादतिरिच्यते ||

akīrtiṃ cāpi bhūtāni kathayiṣyanti te'vyayām |
sambhāvitasya cākīrtirmaraṇādatiricyate ||

2.35 भयाद्रणादुपरतं मंस्यन्ते त्वां महारथाः |
येषां च त्वं बहुमतो भूत्वा यास्यसि लाघवम् ||

bhayādraṇāduparataṃ maṃsyante tvāṃ mahārathāḥ |
yeṣāṃ ca tvaṃ bahumato bhūtvā yāsyasi lāghavam ||

2.36 अवाच्यवादांश्च बहून्वदिष्यन्ति तवाहिताः |
निन्दन्तस्तव सामर्थ्यं ततो दुःखतरं नु किम् ||

avācyavādāṃśca bahūnvadiṣyanti tavāhitāḥ |
nindantastava sāmarthyaṃ tato duḥkhataraṃ nu kim ||

2.37 हतो वा प्राप्स्यसि स्वर्गं जित्वा वा भोक्ष्यसे महीम् |
तस्मादुत्तिष्ठ कौन्तेय युद्धाय कृतनिश्चयः ||

hato vā prāpsyasi svargaṃ jitvā vā bhokṣyase mahīm |
tasmāduttiṣṭha kaunteya yuddhāya kṛtaniścayaḥ ||

2.38 सुखदुःखे समे कृत्वा लाभालाभौ जयाजयौ |
ततो युद्धाय युज्यस्व नैवं पापमवाप्स्यसि ||

sukhaduḥkhe same kṛtvā lābhālābhau jayājayau |
tato yuddhāya yujyasva naivaṃ pāpamavāpsyasi ||

2.39 एषा तेऽभिहिता साङ्ख्ये बुद्धिर्योगे त्विमां शृणु |
बुद्ध्या युक्तो यया पार्थ कर्मबन्धं प्रहास्यसि ||

eṣā te'bhihitā sāṅkhye buddhiryoge tvimāṃ śṛṇu |
buddhyā yukto yayā pārtha karmabandhaṃ prahāsyasi ||

2.33 to not do what's
right your duty
this war
your glory
that's wrong

2.34 disgraceful
people will talk
the talk won't die
better to die

2.35 you'll be seen as a wimp among warriors
be littled among your fans

2.36 unspeakable the way your enemies will mock you
what's more awful than that

2.37 if you die you'll get to heaven
if you live you'll enjoy yourself

get up get
ready to fight

2.38 do the math
happiness = sorrow
gain = loss
then take on the war you can't lose

2.39 now all that's explained in theory samkhya
philosophy
now think
how to practise

to lose karma's braces

2.40 नेहाभिक्रमनाशोऽस्ति प्रत्यवायो न विद्यते |
स्वल्पमप्यस्य धर्मस्य त्रायते महतो भयात् ||

nehābhikramanāśo'sti pratyavāyo na vidyate |
svalpamapyasya dharmasya trāyate mahato bhayāt ||

2.41 व्यवसायात्मिका बुद्धिरेकेह कुरुनन्दन |
बहुशाखा ह्यनन्ताश्च बुद्धयोऽव्यवसायिनाम् ||

vyavasāyātmikā buddhirekeha kurunandana |
bahuśākhā hyanantāśca buddhayo'vyavasāyinām ||

2.42 यामिमां पुष्पितां वाचं प्रवदन्त्यविपश्चितः |
वेदवादरताः पार्थ नान्यदस्तीति वादिनः ||

yāmimāṃ puṣpitāṃ vācaṃ pravadantyavipaścitaḥ |
vedavādaratāḥ pārtha nānyadastīti vādinaḥ ||

2.43 कामात्मानः स्वर्गपरा जन्मकर्मफलप्रदाम् |
क्रियाविशेषबहुलां भोगैश्वर्यगतिं प्रति ||

kāmātmānaḥ svargaparā janmakarmaphalapradām |
kriyāviśeṣabahulāṃ bhogaiśvaryagatiṃ prati ||

2.44 भोगैश्वर्यप्रसक्तानां तयापहृतचेतसाम् |
व्यवसायात्मिका बुद्धिः समाधौ न विधीयते ||

bhogaiśvaryaprasaktānāṃ tayāpahṛtacetasām |
vyavasāyātmikā buddhiḥ samādhau na vidhīyate ||

2.45 त्रैगुण्यविषया वेदा निस्त्रैगुण्यो भवार्जुन |
निर्द्वन्द्वो नित्यसत्त्वस्थो निर्योगक्षेम आत्मवान् ||

traiguṇyaviṣayā vedā nistraiguṇyo bhavārjuna |
nirdvandvo nityasattvastho niryogakṣema ātmavān ||

2.40 there is a path

no effort's wasted
even a little bit of practice
helps you fear less

2.41–2.44 the smart ones are singleminded
clear about it

ignoramuses have endless opinions
give flowery speeches & swear by the veda
gazillion ritual pleas for pleasure / power

they want nothing less than heaven
get nothing more than rebirth

stuck distracted
their minds can't stay still
to trans meditate

2.45 the world of the veda
is made of qualities three (i'll explain more later)

without them be free
without swinging between opposites
pairs extremes
(heat / cold – yin / yang –
pain / pleasure)

without playing the getting & keeping
game

be anchored in yourself
(not in the vedic rulebook)

2.46 यावानर्थ उदपाने सर्वतः सम्प्लुतोदके |
तावान्सर्वेषु वेदेषु ब्राह्मणस्य विजानतः ||

yāvānartha udapāne sarvataḥ samplutodake |
tāvānsarveṣu vedeṣu brāhmaṇasya vijānataḥ ||

2.47 कर्मण्येवाधिकारस्ते मा फलेषु कदाचन |
मा कर्मफलहेतुर्भूर्मा ते सङ्गोऽस्त्वकर्मणि ||

karmaṇyevādhikāraste mā phaleṣu kadācana |
mā karmaphalaheturbhūrmā te saṅgo'stvakarmaṇi ||

2.48 योगस्थः कुरु कर्माणि सङ्गं त्यक्त्वा धनंजय |
सिद्ध्यसिद्ध्योः समो भूत्वा समत्वं योग उच्यते ||

yogasthaḥ kuru karmāṇi saṅgaṃ tyaktvā dhanaṃjaya |
siddhyasiddhyoḥ samo bhūtvā samatvaṃ yoga ucyate ||

2.46 vedic rituals
like a well surrounded by water

useless
when you have
knowledge

2.47 (back to the path of activity karma yoga
every action   work
has an equal reaction   result
we call it 'fruit of action')

you've got to do what you've got to do
not get hung up on the outcome

work for work's sake
have no agenda

which doesn't mean you
sulk from the world
action

2.48 steady   do what must be done
without differences
be the same   undifferent
in success
in failure

practise level headedness
level headedness = yoga

2.49 दूरेण ह्यवरं कर्म बुद्धियोगाद्धनंजय |
बुद्धौ शरणमन्विच्छ कृपणाः फलहेतवः ||

dūreṇa hyavaraṃ karma buddhiyogāddhanaṃjaya |
buddhau śaraṇamanviccha kṛpaṇāḥ phalahetavaḥ ||

2.50 बुद्धियुक्तो जहातीह उभे सुकृतदुष्कृते |
तस्माद्योगाय युज्यस्व योगः कर्मसु कौशलम् ||

buddhiyukto jahātīha ubhe sukṛtaduṣkṛte |
tasmādyogāya yujyasva yogaḥ karmasu kauśalam ||

2.51 कर्मजं बुद्धियुक्ता हि फलं त्यक्त्वा मनीषिणः |
जन्मबन्धविनिर्मुक्ताः पदं गच्छन्त्यनामयम् ||

karmajaṃ buddhiyuktā hi phalaṃ tyaktvā manīṣiṇaḥ |
janmabandhavinirmuktāḥ padaṃ gacchantyanāmayam ||

2.52 यदा ते मोहकलिलं बुद्धिर्व्यतितरिष्यति |
तदा गन्तासि निर्वेदं श्रोतव्यस्य श्रुतस्य च ||

yadā te mohakalilaṃ buddhirvyatitariṣyati |
tadā gantāsi nirvedaṃ śrotavyasya śrutasya ca ||

2.53 श्रुतिविप्रतिपन्ना ते यदा स्थास्यति निश्चला |
समाधावचला बुद्धिस्तदा योगमवाप्स्यसि ||

śrutivipratipannā te yadā sthāsyati niścalā |
samādhāvacalā buddhistadā yogamavāpsyasi ||

2.49 action is nowhere near
thoughtful action

rely on reason
& you'll understand what makes
the agenda-seeker so
wretched

2.50 think about it
drop the notion
of 'good' & 'bad' actions

get a fix on yoga

yoga = skill
doing something well

2.51 the wise let go
of fruit of action
& they're let go
from the birth-decay chain
reincarnation

2.52 when your wisdom cuts through delusion
you won't care for the official revelations

2.53 transcending scriptures when you
transcend in meditation totally still

you'll get there
the ultimate yoga
united
with it who you really are

2.54 अर्जुन उवाच |
स्थितप्रज्ञस्य का भाषा समाधिस्थस्य केशव |
स्थितधीः किं प्रभाषेत किमासीत व्रजेत किम् ||

arjuna uvāca |
sthitaprajñasya kā bhāṣā samādhisthasya keśava |
sthitadhīḥ kiṃ prabhāṣeta kimāsīta vrajeta kim ||

2.55 श्रीभगवानुवाच |
प्रजहाति यदा कामान्सर्वान्पार्थ मनोगतान् |
आत्मन्येवात्मना तुष्टः स्थितप्रज्ञस्तदोच्यते ||

śrībhagavānuvāca |
prajahāti yadā kāmānsarvānpārtha manogatān |
ātmanyevātmanā tuṣṭaḥ sthitaprajñastadocyate ||

2.56 दुःखेष्वनुद्विग्नमनाः सुखेषु विगतस्पृहः |
वीतरागभयक्रोधः स्थितधीर्मुनिरुच्यते ||

duḥkheṣvanudvignamanāḥ sukheṣu vigataspṛhaḥ |
vītarāgabhayakrodhaḥ sthitadhīrmunirucyate ||

2.57 यः सर्वत्रानभिस्नेहस्तत्तत्प्राप्य शुभाशुभम् |
नाभिनन्दति न द्वेष्टि तस्य प्रज्ञा प्रतिष्ठिता ||

yaḥ sarvatrānabhisnehastattatprāpya śubhāśubham |
nābhinandati na dveṣṭi tasya prajñā pratiṣṭhitā ||

2.58 यदा संहरते चायं कूर्मोऽङ्गानीव सर्वशः |
इन्द्रियाणीन्द्रियार्थेभ्यस्तस्य प्रज्ञा प्रतिष्ठिता ||

yadā saṃharate cāyaṃ kūrmo'ṅgānīva sarvaśaḥ |
indriyāṇīndriyārthebhyastasya prajñā pratiṣṭhitā ||

2.54 arjuna:

this wise and steady type
who can deep meditate

what's she like how does she
walk talk sit

2.55 krishna:

she ignores desires
they come & go

with self
is happy to simply be

2.56 in bad times not down
in good times not up

passion fear anger gone

2.57 in everything wants
nothing

pleasant & unpleasant alike

neither salutes nor dislikes

2.58 can disengage sense organs
from sensuous things
completely as a tortoise
withdraws into shell its limbs

2.59 विषया विनिवर्तन्ते निराहारस्य देहिनः |
रसवर्जं रसोऽप्यस्य परं दृष्ट्वा निवर्तते ||

viṣayā vinivartante nirāhārasya dehinaḥ |
rasavarjaṃ raso'pyasya paraṃ dṛṣṭvā nivartate ||

2.60 यततो ह्यपि कौन्तेय पुरुषस्य विपश्चितः |
इन्द्रियाणि प्रमाथीनि हरन्ति प्रसभं मनः ||

yatato hyapi kaunteya puruṣasya vipaścitaḥ |
indriyāṇi pramāthīni haranti prasabhaṃ manaḥ ||

2.61 तानि सर्वाणि संयम्य युक्त आसीत मत्परः |
वशे हि यस्येन्द्रियाणि तस्य प्रज्ञा प्रतिष्ठिता ||

tāni sarvāṇi saṃyamya yukta āsīta matparaḥ |
vaśe hi yasyendriyāṇi tasya prajñā pratiṣṭhitā ||

2.62 ध्यायतो विषयान्पुंसः सङ्गस्तेषूपजायते |
सङ्गात्संजायते कामः कामात्क्रोधोऽभिजायते ||

dhyāyato viṣayānpuṃsaḥ saṅgasteṣūpajāyate |
saṅgātsaṃjāyate kāmaḥ kāmātkrodho'bhijāyate ||

2.63 क्रोधाद्भवति सम्मोहः सम्मोहात्स्मृतिविभ्रमः |
स्मृतिभ्रंशाद् बुद्धिनाशो बुद्धिनाशात्प्रणश्यति ||

krodhādbhavati saṃmohaḥ saṃmohātsmṛtivibhramaḥ |
smṛtibhraṃśād buddhināśo buddhināśātpraṇaśyati ||

2.59 when you don't feed on them
temptations drop off

it takes more time to
lose the taste
for pleasure

but after the ultimate experience
liberation

that too is a non issue

2.60 wild the senses run away
with the mind
even of the earnest seeker

2.61 so the wise and steady has
senses under control
sits in deep thought of me

2.62 instead of meditating on me if you
meditate on indulgences you

feel fond
& then you want

then frustrated
fury

2.63 fury clouds
send memory for a spin
intelligence for a toss
you'll be lost

2.64 रागद्वेषवियुक्तस्तु विषयानिन्द्रियैश्चरन् |
आत्मवश्यैर्विधेयात्मा प्रसादमधिगच्छति ||

rāgadveṣaviyuktastu viṣayānindriyaiścaran |
ātmavaśyairvidheyātmā prasādamadhigacchati ||

2.65 प्रसादे सर्वदुःखानां हानिरस्योपजायते |
प्रसन्नचेतसो ह्याशु बुद्धिः पर्यवतिष्ठते ||

prasāde sarvaduḥkhānāṃ hānirasyopajāyate |
prasannacetaso hyāśu buddhiḥ paryavatiṣṭhate ||

2.66 नास्ति बुद्धिरयुक्तस्य न चायुक्तस्य भावना |
न चाभावयतः शान्तिरशान्तस्य कुतः सुखम् ||

nāsti buddhirayuktasya na cāyuktasya bhāvanā |
na cābhāvayataḥ śāntiraśāntasya kutaḥ sukham ||

2.67 इन्द्रियाणां हि चरतां यन्मनोऽनुविधीयते |
तदस्य हरति प्रज्ञां वायुर्नावमिवाम्भसि ||

indriyāṇāṃ hi caratāṃ yanmano'nuvidhīyate |
tadasya harati prajñāṃ vāyurnāvamivāmbhasi ||

2.68 तस्माद्यस्य महाबाहो निगृहीतानि सर्वशः |
इन्द्रियाणीन्द्रियार्थेभ्यस्तस्य प्रज्ञा प्रतिष्ठिता ||

tasmādyasya mahābāho nigṛhītāni sarvaśaḥ |
indriyāṇīndriyārthebhyastasya prajñā pratiṣṭhitā ||

2.69 या निशा सर्वभूतानां तस्यां जागर्ति संयमी |
यस्यां जाग्रति भूतानि सा निशा पश्यतो मुनेः ||

yā niśā sarvabhūtānāṃ tasyāṃ jāgarti saṃyamī |
yasyāṃ jāgrati bhūtāni sā niśā paśyato muneḥ ||

2.64 the self-controlled has no
likes & dislikes

can be mobbed by temptations
& be serene

2.65 & in this serene
sorrows vanish
mind steadies

2.66 by contrast
the undisciplined seeker has
no understanding no focus no peace
so no happiness

2.67 when mind chases senses
understanding's swept away

wind-tossed ship

2.68 (summary)
the wise and steady =
she who has self-control
withdraws senses from temptations

2.69 the difference (between her & others)
day & night
    different worlds

she's awake to
what the worldly cannot see

she finds nothing
in what the worldly see
    material things

2.70 आपूर्यमाणमचलप्रतिष्ठं समुद्रमापः प्रविशन्ति यद्वत् |
तद्वत्कामा यंप्रविशन्ति सर्वे स शान्तिमाप्नोति न कामकामी ||

āpūryamāṇamacalapratiṣṭhaṃ
samudramāpaḥ praviśanti yadvat |
tadvatkāmā yaṃpraviśanti sarve
sa śāntimāpnoti na kāmakāmī ||

2.71 विहाय कामान्यः सर्वान्पुमांश्चरति निःस्पृहः |
निर्ममो निरहङ्कारः स शान्तिमधिगच्छति ||

vihāya kāmānyaḥ sarvānpumāṃścarati niḥspṛhaḥ |
nirmamo nirahaṅkāraḥ sa śāntimadhigacchati ||

2.72 एषा ब्राह्मी स्थितिः पार्थ नैनां प्राप्य विमुह्यति |
स्थित्वास्यामन्तकालेऽपि ब्रह्मनिर्वाणमृच्छति ||

eṣā brāhmī sthitiḥ pārtha naināṃ prāpya vimuhyati |
sthitvāsyāmantakāle'pi brahmanirvāṇamṛcchati ||

3.1 अर्जुन उवाच |
ज्यायसी चेत्कर्मणस्ते मता बुद्धिर्जनार्दन |
तत्किं कर्मणि घोरे मां नियोजयसि केशव ||

arjuna uvāca |
jyāyasī cetkarmaṇaste matā buddhirjanārdana |
tatkiṃ karmaṇi ghore māṃ niyojayasi keśava ||

3.2 व्यामिश्रेणेव वाक्येन बुद्धिं मोहयसीव मे |
तदेकं वद निश्चित्य येन श्रेयोऽहमाप्नुयाम् ||

vyāmiśreṇeva vākyena buddhiṃ mohayasīva me |
tadekaṃ vada niścitya yena śreyo'hamāpnuyām ||

2.70 she's oceanlike exposed to desire rivers
any which way
yet
steadydeep
peace full

2.71 she has dropped all 'i want'
'me' 'my'
egoism
goes freely
in peace

2.72 this is it

once here never fooled again
stays here right to the end

then bliss blown
uberliberation brahman = ultimate = capital g o d
brahmanirvana

3.1 arjuna:
if the life of the mind thought is
better than the life of
activity

why drive me
to gory acts

3.2 your mixed messages confuse
please tell me one thing straight

what will take me further

3.3 श्रीभगवानुवाच ।
लोकेऽस्मिन्द्विविधा निष्ठा पुरा प्रोक्ता मयानघ ।
ज्ञानयोगेन साङ्ख्यानां कर्मयोगेन योगिनाम् ॥

śrībhagavānuvāca |
loke'smindvividhā niṣṭhā purā proktā mayānagha |
jñānayogena sāṅkhyānāṃ karmayogena yoginām ||

3.4 न कर्मणामनारम्भान्नैष्कर्म्यं पुरुषोऽश्नुते ।
न च संन्यसनादेव सिद्धिं समधिगच्छति

na karmaṇāmanārambhānnaiṣkarmyaṃ puruṣo'śnute |
na ca saṃnyasanādeva siddhiṃ samadhigacchati ||

3.5 न हि कश्चित्क्षणमपि जातु तिष्ठत्यकर्मकृत् ।
कार्यते ह्यवशः कर्म सर्वः प्रकृतिजैर्गुणैः ॥

na hi kaścitkṣaṇamapi jātu tiṣṭhatyakarmakṛt |
kāryate hyavaśaḥ karma sarvaḥ prakṛtijairguṇaiḥ ||

3.6 कर्मेन्द्रियाणि संयम्य य आस्ते मनसा स्मरन् ।
इन्द्रियार्थान्विमूढात्मा मिथ्याचारः स उच्यते ॥

karmendriyāṇi saṃyamya ya āste manasā smaran |
indriyārthānvimūḍhātmā mithyācāraḥ sa ucyate ||

3.7 यस्त्विन्द्रियाणि मनसा नियम्यारभतेऽर्जुन ।
कर्मेन्द्रियैः कर्मयोगमसक्तः स विशिष्यते ॥

yastvindriyāṇi manasā niyamyārabhate'rjuna |
karmendriyaiḥ karmayogamasaktaḥ sa viśiṣyate ||

3.3 krishna:
as i said ages ago
two paths:
knowledge (samkhya)
action (karma yoga)

3.4 but
doing nothing doesn't mean
you're free from karma

nor does renunciation mean
you're anywhere
near enlightenment

3.5 because in fact
not for a moment
do you do
nothing

doing is what you're made to do
not in your control

by nature
inborn

3.6 she who represses senses organs
while mind fondles pleasures
hypocrite!
fools herself

3.7 but she who's detached &
harnesses senses actions organs
with the mind

is better

3.8 नियतं कुरु कर्म त्वं कर्म ज्यायो ह्यकर्मण: |
शरीरयात्रापि च ते न प्रसिद्ध्येदकर्मण: ||

niyataṃ kuru karma tvaṃ karma jyāyo hyakarmaṇaḥ |
śarīrayātrāpi ca te na prasiddhyedakarmaṇaḥ ||

3.9 यज्ञार्थात्कर्मणोऽन्यत्र लोकोऽयं कर्मबन्धन: |
तदर्थं कर्म कौन्तेय मुक्तसङ्ग: समाचर ||

yajñārthātkarmaṇo’nyatra loko’yaṃ karmabandhanaḥ |
tadarthaṃ karma kaunteya muktasaṅgaḥ samācara ||

3.10 सहयज्ञा: प्रजा: सृष्ट्वा पुरोवाच प्रजापति: |
अनेन प्रसविष्यध्वमेष वोऽस्त्विष्टकामधुक् ||

sahayajñāḥ prajāḥ sṛṣṭvā purovāca prajāpatiḥ |
anena prasaviṣyadhvameṣa vo’stviṣṭakāmadhuk ||

3.11 देवान्भावयतानेन ते देवा भावयन्तु व: |
परस्परं भावयन्त: श्रेय: परमवाप्स्यथ ||

devānbhāvayatānena te devā bhāvayantu vaḥ |
parasparaṃ bhāvayantaḥ śreyaḥ paramavāpsyatha ||

3.8 do what you have to do
rather than not

if nothing's done
even the body won't run

3.9 in this world
all activity except yajna (sacred fire ritual
oblation to the divine
but you'll soon see
it's a way of living)

creates a chain cycle of karma

so that's how you've got to do it

so do duties rituals
detached

3.10 way back after
creating humans
via yajna

said prajapati
(a creator mentioned in the vedas)

by yajna may you flourish
let yajna be your wishing cow

3.11 by yajna
may you nourish the deities
may the deities nourish you

being together for each other
you'll get there all's well

3.12 इष्टान्भोगान्हि वो देवा दास्यन्ते यज्ञभाविताः |
तैर्दत्तानप्रदायैभ्यो यो भुङ्क्ते स्तेन एव सः ||

iṣṭānbhogānhi vo devā dāsyante yajñabhāvitāḥ |
tairdattānapradāyaibhyo yo bhuṅkte stena eva saḥ ||

3.13 यज्ञशिष्टाशिनः सन्तो मुच्यन्ते सर्वकिल्बिषैः |
भुञ्जते ते त्वघं पापा ये पचन्त्यात्मकारणात् ||

yajñaśiṣṭāśinaḥ santo mucyante sarvakilbiṣaiḥ |
bhuñjate te tvaghaṃ pāpā ye pacantyātmakāraṇāt ||

3.14 अन्नाद्भवन्ति भूतानि पर्जन्यादन्नसंभवः |
यज्ञाद्भवति पर्जन्यो यज्ञः कर्मसमुद्भवः ||

annādbhavanti bhūtāni parjanyādannasaṃbhavaḥ |
yajñādbhavati parjanyo yajñaḥ karmasamudbhavaḥ ||

3.15 कर्म ब्रह्मोद्भवं विद्धि ब्रह्माक्षरसमुद्भवम् |
तस्मात्सर्वगतं ब्रह्म नित्यं यज्ञे प्रतिष्ठितम् ||

karma brahmodbhavaṃ viddhi brahmākṣarasamudbhavam |
tasmātsarvagataṃ brahma nityaṃ yajñe pratiṣṭhitam ||

3.12 pleased by the yajna the
deities will give you
what you like

(caution:) she who enjoys their gifts
without reciprocating
is a thief

3.13 those who are wise
eat leftovers (after offering the yajna)
they're freed from problems

the wretched cook for their own sake
feed on misery

3.14 living beings
↓ from
food
↓
rain
↓
yajna
↓
action / duties

(life's based on action)

3.15 the first rites action arose
from brahman

brahman
arose as om (the undying sound
in akasha ether)
& spread so

the omnipresent is ever
rooted in yajna

3.16 एवं प्रवर्तितं चक्रं नानुवर्तयतीह यः |
अघायुरिन्द्रियारामो मोघं पार्थ स जीवति ||

evaṃ pravartitaṃ cakraṃ nānuvartayatīha yaḥ |
aghāyurindriyārāmo moghaṃ pārtha sa jīvati ||

3.17 यस्त्वात्मरतिरेव स्यादात्मतृप्तश्च मानवः |
आत्मन्येव च सन्तुष्टस्तस्य कार्यं न विद्यते ||

yastvātmaratireva syādātmatṛptaśca mānavaḥ |
ātmanyeva ca saṃtuṣṭastasya kāryaṃ na vidyate ||

3.18 नैव तस्य कृतेनार्थो नाकृतेनेह कश्चन |
न चास्य सर्वभूतेषु कश्चिदर्थव्यपाश्रयः ||

naiva tasya kṛtenārtho nākṛteneha kaścana |
na cāsya sarvabhūteṣu kaścidarthavyapāśrayaḥ ||

3.19 तस्मादसक्तः सततं कार्यं कर्म समाचर |
असक्तो ह्याचरन्कर्म परमाप्नोति पूरुषः ||

tasmādasaktaḥ satataṃ kāryaṃ karma samācara |
asakto hyācarankarma paramāpnoti pūruṣaḥ ||

3.20 कर्मणैव हि संसिद्धिमास्थिता जनकादयः |
लोकसंग्रहमेवापि संपश्यन्कर्तुमर्हसि ||

karmaṇaiva hi saṃsiddhimāsthitā janakādayaḥ |
lokasaṃgrahamevāpi saṃpaśyankartumarhasi ||

3.16 thus arjuna the wheel
was set in motion

those who don't move it along
hedonists
troublemakers
live in vain but

3.17 she whose joy is
her divine self (the embodied timeless 'atman')
satisfied
content
doesn't feel the pressure

3.18 the question
to do or not to do
doesn't come up

she doesn't have
an agenda
or need anyone

3.19 so do what has to be done
always detached that's
how you'll get
to the ultimate goal

3.20 king janaka (for instance)
made it to perfection
through work

if only for the sake of
the world to keep it running
you're to work

3.21 यद्यदाचरति श्रेष्ठस्तत्तदेवेतरो जनः |
स यत्प्रमाणं कुरुते लोकस्तदनुवर्तते ||

yadyadācarati śreṣṭhastattadevetaro janaḥ |
sa yatpramāṇaṃ kurute lokastadanuvartate ||

3.22 न मे पार्थास्ति कर्तव्यं त्रिषु लोकेषु किंचन |
नानवाप्तमवाप्तव्यं वर्त एव च कर्मणि ||

na me pārthāsti kartavyaṃ triṣu lokeṣu kiṃcana |
nānavāptamavāptavyaṃ varta eva ca karmaṇi ||

3.23 यदि ह्यहं न वर्तेयं जातु कर्मण्यतन्द्रितः |
मम वर्त्मानुवर्तन्ते मनुष्याः पार्थ सर्वशः ||

yadi hyahaṃ na varteyaṃ jātu karmaṇyatandritaḥ |
mama vartmānuvartante manuṣyāḥ pārtha sarvaśaḥ ||

3.24 उत्सीदेयुरिमे लोका न कुर्यां कर्म चेदहम् |
सङ्करस्य च कर्ता स्यामुपहन्यामिमाः प्रजाः ||

utsīdeyurime lokā na kuryāṃ karma cedaham |
saṅkarasya ca kartā syāmupahanyāmimāḥ prajāḥ ||

3.25 सक्ताः कर्मण्यविद्वांसो यथा कुर्वन्ति भारत |
कुर्याद्विद्वांस्तथासक्तश्चिकीर्षुर्लोकसंग्रहम् ||

saktāḥ karmaṇyavidvāṃso yathā kurvanti bhārata |
kuryādvidvāṃstathāsaktaścikīrṣurlokasaṃgraham ||

3.21 a leader sets the standard

whatever she does
everyone follows

3.22 there's nothing for me
to do in the three worlds

no unfinished business
to be done

yet i keep at it i work

3.23 if i did not carry on
tireless

neither would anyone o' arjuna

3.24 if i did not do my bit
these worlds would collapse

i would be the cause of
chaos
these people destroyed

3.25 the ignorant cling
  to what they do

the wise must work detached
for the sake of the world collective

3.26 न बुद्धिभेदं जनयेदज्ञानां कर्मसङ्गिनाम् |
जोषयेत्सर्वकर्माणि विद्वान्युक्तः समाचरन् ||

na buddhibhedaṃ janayedajñānāṃ karmasaṅginām |
joṣayetsarvakarmāṇi vidvānyuktaḥ samācaran ||

3.27 प्रकृतेः क्रियमाणानि गुणैः कर्माणि सर्वशः |
अहङ्कारविमूढात्मा कर्ताहमिति मन्यते ||

prakṛteḥ kriyamāṇāni guṇaiḥ karmāṇi sarvaśaḥ |
ahaṅkāravimūḍhātmā kartāhamiti manyate ||

3.28 तत्त्ववित्तु महाबाहो गुणकर्मविभागयोः |
गुणा गुणेषु वर्तन्त इति मत्वा न सज्जते ||

tattvavittu mahābāho guṇakarmavibhāgayoḥ |
guṇā guṇeṣu vartanta iti matvā na sajjate ||

3.29 प्रकृतेर्गुणसम्मूढाः सज्जन्ते गुणकर्मसु |
तानकृत्स्नविदो मन्दान्कृत्स्नविन्न विचालयेत् ||

prakṛterguṇasaṃmūḍhāḥ sajjante guṇakarmasu |
tānakṛtsnavido mandānkṛtsnavinna vicālayet ||

3.26 don't mess with the minds
of ignoramuses
entangled in their work

in fact help them let them
enjoy all that they do
& you stay on course

3.27 nature is the work of
the properties of matter nature is
the nature
of nature

the egoist (literally 'i am the doer')
takes the credit

3.28 arjuna
she who knows
how it works
nature & events roleplay
how properties inhere in matter
natura naturans

is not attached

3.29 those fooled by the ways of nature
are attached to its actions
let them be

those who know it all
must not disturb the dull
who don't know the whole story

3.30 मयि सर्वाणि कर्माणि संन्यस्याध्यात्मचेतसा |
निराशीर्निर्ममो भूत्वा युध्यस्व विगतज्वरः ||

mayi sarvāṇi karmāṇi saṃnyasyādhyātmacetasā |
nirāśīrnirmamo bhūtvā yudhyasva vigatajvaraḥ ||

3.31 ये मे मतमिदं नित्यमनुतिष्ठन्ति मानवाः |
श्रद्धावन्तोऽनसूयन्तो मुच्यन्ते तेऽपि कर्मभिः ||

ye me matamidaṃ nityamanutiṣṭhanti mānavāḥ |
śraddhāvanto'nasūyanto mucyante te'pi karmabhiḥ ||

3.32 ये त्वेतदभ्यसूयन्तो नानुतिष्ठन्ति मे मतम् |
सर्वज्ञानविमूढांस्तान्विद्धि नष्टानचेतसः ||

ye tvetadabhyasūyanto nānutiṣṭhanti me matam |
sarvajñānavimūḍhāṃstānviddhi naṣṭānacetasaḥ ||

3.33 सदृशं चेष्टते स्वस्याः प्रकृतेर्ज्ञानवानपि |
प्रकृतिं यान्ति भूतानि निग्रहः किं करिष्यति ||

sadṛśaṃ ceṣṭate svasyāḥ prakṛterjñānavānapi |
prakṛtiṃ yānti bhūtāni nigrahaḥ kiṃ kariṣyati ||

3.34 इन्द्रियस्येन्द्रियस्यार्थे रागद्वेषौ व्यवस्थितौ |
तयोर्न वशमागच्छेत्तौ ह्यस्य परिपन्थिनौ ||

indriyasyendriyasyārthe rāgadveṣau vyavasthitau |
tayorna vaśamāgacchettau hyasya paripanthinau ||

3.30 just leave it all up to me
mind inward
desireless
undifferent to possession
unfrenzied
fight!

3.31 those who practise this my teaching
in earnest
without cynicism
are free from karma

3.32 but note
those who don't
cynical
confused by any knowledge
thoughtless
are ruined

3.33 so each even the wise
acts according to nature

living beings
follow their nature

what good will repression do

3.34 a sense organ's
attraction
aversion
hooked
to its object

don't be seduced by them
they're obstacles
in your way

3.35 श्रेयान्स्वधर्मो विगुण: परधर्मात्स्वनुष्ठितात् |
स्वधर्मे निधनं श्रेय: परधर्मो भयावह: ||

śreyānsvadharmo viguṇaḥ paradharmātsvanuṣṭhitāt |
svadharme nidhanaṃ śreyaḥ paradharmo bhayāvahaḥ ||

3.36 अर्जुन उवाच |
अथ केन प्रयुक्तोऽयं पापं चरति पूरुष: |
अनिच्छन्नपि वार्ष्णेय बलादिव नियोजित: ||

arjuna uvāca |
atha kena prayukto'yaṃ pāpaṃ carati pūruṣaḥ |
anicchannapi vārṣṇeya balādiva niyojitaḥ ||

3.37 श्रीभगवानुवाच |
काम एष क्रोध एष रजोगुणसमुद्भव: ||
महाशनो महापाप्मा विद्ध्येनमिह वैरिणम् ||

śrībhagavānuvāca |
kāma eṣa krodha eṣa rajoguṇasamudbhavaḥ |
mahāśano mahāpāpmā viddhyenamiha vairiṇam ||

3.38 धूमेनाव्रियते वह्निर्यथादर्शो मलेन च |
यथोल्बेनावृतो गर्भस्तथा तेनेदमावृतम् ||

dhūmenāvriyate vahniryathādarśo malena ca |
yatholbenāvṛto garbhastathā tenedamāvṛtam ||

3.39 आवृतं ज्ञानमेतेन ज्ञानिनो नित्यवैरिणा |
कामरूपेण कौन्तेय दुष्पूरेणानलेन च ||

āvṛtaṃ jñānametena jñānino nityavairiṇā |
kāmarūpeṇa kaunteya duṣpūreṇānalena ca ||

3.35 take responsibility
do your duty   even if it isn't nice
rather than another's role well done

better to die
in your own work
than to risk danger
in another's

3.36 arjuna:
then why does one go wrong   krishna
although unwilling
& even as if coerced

3.37 krishna:
this 'anger'
this 'desire'
comes from rajas
(pleasure-loving nature explained
in detail later)
note   voracious & heinous
this   here   is enemy

3.38 as fire enveloped by smoke
mirror by dust
embryo by womb

this
is masked by
that

3.39 knowledge   even in the wise
is obscured
by desire … lust

fire insatiable
ever enemy o' arjuna

3.40 इन्द्रियाणि मनो बुद्धिरस्याधिष्ठानमुच्यते |
एतैर्विमोहयत्येष ज्ञानमावृत्य देहिनम् ||

indriyāṇi mano buddhirasyādhiṣṭhānamucyate |
etairvimohayatyeṣa jñānamāvṛtya dehinam ||

3.41 तस्मात्त्वमिन्द्रियाण्यादौ नियम्य भरतर्षभ |
पाप्मानं प्रजहि ह्येनं ज्ञानविज्ञाननाशनम् ||

tasmāttvamindriyāṇyādau niyamya bharatarṣabha |
pāpmānaṃ prajahi hyenaṃ jñānavijñānanāśanam ||

3.42 इन्द्रियाणि पराण्याहुरिन्द्रियेभ्यः परं मनः |
मनसस्तु परा बुद्धिर्यो बुद्धेः परतस्तु सः ||

indriyāṇi parāṇyāhurindriyebhyaḥ paraṃ manaḥ |
manasastu parā buddhiryo buddheḥ paratastu saḥ ||

3.43 एवं बुद्धेः परं बुद्ध्वा संस्तभ्यात्मानमात्मना |
जहि शत्रुं महाबाहो कामरूपं दुरासदम् ||

evaṃ buddheḥ paraṃ buddhvā saṃstabhyātmānamātmanā |
jahi śatruṃ mahābāho kāmarūpaṃ durāsadam ||

3.40 & its address?
the senses mind intellect!

by using them it
blocks your knowledge
confuses seduces you
who are in a body
and encased in them

3.41 restraining your senses arjuna
determined as a bull

destroy desire the wretch
it destroys
knowledge wisdom

3.42 they call sense organs great but

mind is greater than senses
intellect is greater than mind

& you
even greater than intellect

3.43 so
knowing who
tops the intellect

support your self
by yourself

as for this enemy in the guise of desire
hard to face

arjuna
destroy it!

4.1 श्रीभगवानुवाच |
इमं विवस्वते योगं प्रोक्तवानहमव्ययम् |
विवस्वान्मनवे प्राह मनुरिक्ष्वाकवेऽब्रवीत् ||

śrībhagavānuvāca |
imaṃ vivasvate yogaṃ proktavānahamavyayam |
vivasvānmanave prāha manurikṣvākave'bravīt ||

4.2 एवं परम्पराप्राप्तमिमं राजर्षयो विदुः |
स कालेनेह महता योगो नष्टः परंतप ||

evaṃ paramparāprāptamimaṃ rājarṣayo viduḥ |
sa kāleneha mahatā yogo naṣṭaḥ paraṃtapa ||

4.3 स एवायं मया तेऽद्य योगः प्रोक्तः पुरातनः |
भक्तोऽसि मे सखा चेति रहस्यं ह्येतदुत्तमम् ||

sa evāyaṃ mayā te'dya yogaḥ proktaḥ purātanaḥ |
bhakto'si me sakhā ceti rahasyaṃ hyetaduttamam ||

4.4 अर्जुन उवाच |
अपरं भवतो जन्म परं जन्म विवस्वतः |
कथमेतद्विजानीयां त्वमादौ प्रोक्तवानिति ||

arjuna uvāca |
aparaṃ bhavato janma paraṃ janma vivasvataḥ |
kathametadvijānīyāṃ tvamādau proktavāniti ||

4.5 श्रीभगवानुवाच |
बहूनि मे व्यतीतानि जन्मानि तव चार्जुन |
तान्यहं वेद सर्वाणि न त्वं वेत्थ परंतप ||

śrībhagavānuvāca |
bahūni me vyatītāni janmāni tava cārjuna |
tānyahaṃ veda sarvāṇi na tvaṃ vettha paraṃtapa ||

4.1 krishna:

about this method   everlasting yoga
i told vivasvat (sun) who
told manu (first human) who
told ikshvaku (his son)

4.2 passed on this way   that's how
the best of seers knew of it

by time   on earth
vast
was lost arjuna

4.3 this ancient yoga
is top secret

i only told you
as my devotee
& friend

4.4 arjuna:

but
your birth was later
vivasvat's earlier

how can i believe
you said it first

4.5 krishna:

many my past lives
yours too

i know them
you don't

4.6 अजोऽपि सन्नव्ययात्मा भूतानामीश्वरोऽपि सन् |
प्रकृतिं स्वामधिष्ठाय संभवाम्यात्ममायया ||

ajo'pi sannavyayātmā bhūtānāmīśvaro'pi san |
prakṛtiṃ svāmadhiṣṭhāya saṃbhavāmyātmamāyayā ||

4.7 यदा यदा हि धर्मस्य ग्लानिर्भवति भारत |
अभ्युत्थानमधर्मस्य तदात्मानं सृजाम्यहम् ||

yadā yadā hi dharmasya glānirbhavati bhārata |
abhyutthānamadharmasya tadātmānaṃ sṛjāmyaham ||

4.8 परित्राणाय साधूनां विनाशाय च दुष्कृताम् |
धर्मसंस्थापनार्थाय संभवामि युगे युगे ||

paritrāṇāya sādhūnāṃ vināśāya ca duṣkṛtām |
dharmasaṃsthāpanārthāya saṃbhavāmi yuge yuge ||

4.9 जन्म कर्म च मे दिव्यमेवं यो वेत्ति तत्त्वतः |
त्यक्त्वा देहं पुनर्जन्म नैति मामेति सोऽर्जुन ||

janma karma ca me divyamevaṃ yo vetti tattvataḥ |
tyaktvā dehaṃ punarjanma naiti māmeti so'rjuna ||

4.10 वीतरागभयक्रोधा मन्मया मामुपाश्रिताः |
बहवो ज्ञानतपसा पूता मद्भावमागताः ||

vītarāgabhayakrodhā manmayā māmupāśritāḥ |
bahavo jñānatapasā pūtā madbhāvamāgatāḥ ||

4.6 although
i am birthless deathless
god of all

by my creativity
i direct my own nature &
lo here i wholly am

4.7 arjuna
when the correct fades
incorrect rises

i procreate myself

4.8 full on
i am
from time to time to
save good people
crackdown on evil
settle what's right

4.9 she who realizes
my divinity in birth & action
when she leaves body
comes to me
not to rebirth

4.10 mind full of me
depending fully on me

by the practice of wisdom
purified

passionangerfearless

many have become
one with me

4.11 ये यथा मां प्रपद्यन्ते तांस्तथैव भजाम्यहम् |
मम वर्त्मानुवर्तन्ते मनुष्याः पार्थ सर्वशः ||

ye yathā māṃ prapadyante tāṃstathaiva bhajāmyaham |
mama vartmānuvartante manuṣyāḥ pārtha sarvaśaḥ ||

4.12 काङ्क्षन्तः कर्मणां सिद्धिं यजन्त इह देवताः |
क्षिप्रं हि मानुषे लोके सिद्धिर्भवति कर्मजा ||

kāṅkṣantaḥ karmaṇāṃ siddhiṃ yajanta iha devatāḥ |
kṣipraṃ hi mānuṣe loke siddhirbhavati karmajā ||

4.13 चातुर्वर्ण्यं मया सृष्टं गुणकर्मविभागशः |
तस्य कर्तारमपि मां विद्ध्यकर्तारमव्ययम् ||

cāturvarṇyaṃ mayā sṛṣṭaṃ guṇakarmavibhāgaśaḥ |
tasya kartāramapi māṃ viddhyakartāramavyayam ||

4.14 न मां कर्माणि लिम्पन्ति न मे कर्मफले स्पृहा |
इति मां योऽभिजानाति कर्मभिर्न स बध्यते ||

na māṃ karmāṇi limpanti na me karmaphale spṛhā |
iti māṃ yo'bhijānāti karmabhirna sa badhyate ||

4.15 एवं ज्ञात्वा कृतं कर्म पूर्वैरपि मुमुक्षुभिः |
कुरु कर्मैव तस्मात्त्वं पूर्वैः पूर्वतरं कृतम् ||

evaṃ jñātvā kṛtaṃ karma pūrvairapi mumukṣubhiḥ |
kuru karmaiva tasmāttvaṃ pūrvaiḥ pūrvataraṃ kṛtam ||

4.11 who what they ask
them that i serve
you get what you ask for
all ways are mine
regardless of what path
you follow
me

4.12 wanting success
in what they do

people
make offerings
to deities

worldly success comes quick
from these activities

4.13 the four varnas
were issued by me
yet note
i am a constant my energy infinite everlasting
a non doer

4.14 what i do does not stain me
for i have no desire
for the fruit of action

she who knows just this of me
is as free

4.15 bygone seekers
knew this &
followed my example

so should you

4.16 किं कर्म किमकर्मेति कवयोऽप्यत्र मोहिताः |
तत्ते कर्म प्रवक्ष्यामि यज्ज्ञात्वा मोक्ष्यसेऽशुभात् ||

kiṃ karma kimakarmeti kavayo'pyatra mohitāḥ |
tatte karma pravakṣyāmi yajjñātvā mokṣyase'śubhāt ||

4.17 कर्मणो ह्यपि बोद्धव्यं बोद्धव्यं च विकर्मणः |
अकर्मणश्च बोद्धव्यं गहना कर्मणो गतिः ||

karmaṇo hyapi boddhavyaṃ boddhavyaṃ ca vikarmaṇaḥ |
akarmaṇaśca boddhavyaṃ gahanā karmaṇo gatiḥ ||

4.18 कर्मण्यकर्म यः पश्येदकर्मणि च कर्म यः |
स बुद्धिमान्मनुष्येषु स युक्तः कृत्स्नकर्मकृत् ||

karmaṇyakarma yaḥ paśyedakarmaṇi ca karma yaḥ |
sa buddhimānmanuṣyeṣu sa yuktaḥ kṛtsnakarmakṛt ||

4.19 यस्य सर्वे समारम्भाः कामसङ्कल्पवर्जिताः |
ज्ञानाग्निदग्धकर्माणं तमाहुः पण्डितं बुधाः ||

yasya sarve samārambhāḥ kāmasaṅkalpavarjitāḥ |
jñānāgnidagdhakarmāṇaṃ tamāhuḥ paṇḍitaṃ budhāḥ ||

4.16 what is &
what isn't action
even poets
are perplexed

i'll explain

knowing better
you'll be free from dullness

4.17 you've got to know
what is action   what is
incorrect action what is
non action
    the ways of action are
    hard to fathom

4.18 she who spots
non action in
what looks like action

action in
what looks like not

is by far smarter
connected   yogi
in everything she does

4.19 she whose
projects are without
greedy motives

work primed
in knowledge-fire

the wise call pundit

4.20 त्यक्त्वा कर्मफलासङ्गं नित्यतृप्तो निराश्रय: |
कर्मण्यभिप्रवृत्तोऽपि नैव किंचित्करोति स: ||

tyaktvā karmaphalāsaṅgaṃ nityatṛpto nirāśrayaḥ |
karmaṇyabhipravṛtto'pi naiva kiṃcitkaroti saḥ ||

4.21 निराशीर्यतचित्तात्मा त्यक्तसर्वपरिग्रह: |
शारीरं केवलं कर्म कुर्वन्नाप्नोति किल्बिषम् ||

nirāśīryatacittātmā tyaktasarvaparigrahaḥ |
śārīraṃ kevalaṃ karma kurvannāpnoti kilbiṣam ||

4.22 यदृच्छालाभसंतुष्टो द्वन्द्वातीतो विमत्सर: |
सम: सिद्धावसिद्धौ च कृत्वापि न निबध्यते ||

yadṛcchālābhasaṃtuṣṭo dvandvātīto vimatsaraḥ |
samaḥ siddhāvasiddhau ca kṛtvāpi na nibadhyate ||

4.23 गतसङ्गस्य मुक्तस्य ज्ञानावस्थितचेतस: |
यज्ञायाचरत: कर्म समग्रं प्रविलीयते ||

gatasaṅgasya muktasya jñānāvasthitacetasaḥ |
yajñāyācarataḥ karma samagraṃ pravilīyate ||

4.20 she who

giving up the clinging
to profit

content
undependent

even when busy   in fact
accrues no karma

4.21 she who
wishlessly
    mind self under control
    giving up acquisition
works only with body
is not culpable

4.22 content   whatever the gain

not swinging to opposites   pleasure pain

envyfree

in success unsuccess
equanimous

although working
is unbound   no karma

4.23 she whose
    work is free from expectations
    mind anchored in knowledge
work = yajna
karma dissolves

4.24 ब्रह्मार्पणं ब्रह्म हविर्ब्रह्माग्नौ ब्रह्मणा हुतम् |
ब्रह्मैव तेन गन्तव्यं ब्रह्मकर्मसमाधिना ||

brahmārpaṇaṃ brahma havirbrahmāgnau brahmaṇā hutam |
brahmaiva tena gantavyaṃ brahmakarmasamādhinā ||

4.25 दैवमेवापरे यज्ञं योगिनः पर्युपासते |
ब्रह्माग्नावपरे यज्ञं यज्ञेनैवोपजुह्वति ||

daivamevāpare yajñaṃ yoginaḥ paryupāsate |
brahmāgnāvapare yajñaṃ yajñenaivopajuhvati ||

4.26 श्रोत्रादीनीन्द्रियाण्यन्ये संयमाग्निषु जुह्वति |
शब्दादीन्विषयानन्य इन्द्रियाग्निषु जुह्वति ||

śrotrādīnīndriyāṇyanye saṃyamāgniṣu juhvati |
śabdādīnviṣayānanya indriyāgniṣu juhvati ||

4.27 सर्वाणीन्द्रियकर्माणि प्राणकर्माणि चापरे |
आत्मसंयमयोगाग्नौ जुह्वति ज्ञानदीपिते ||

sarvāṇīndriyakarmāṇi prāṇakarmāṇi cāpare |
ātmasaṃyamayogāgnau juhvati jñānadīpite ||

4.24 she whose actions are absorbed in brahman

food = brahman / offering / god
eating = brahman / process / god
digesting fire = brahman / fire / god
eater = brahman / god

goes to brahman

4.25 some yogis do the ritual yajna
to a deity

others offer
to this fire of brahman

4.26 some offer sense pleasures
hearing etcetera
to discipline-fires
(burn pleasures in discipline
= giving them up)

others offer sense objects sound etcetera
to sense-fires
(senses consume objects
so senses are like fires)

4.27 some offer all actions of the senses
& of the prana (qi energy breath of life)

into the fire of self discipline
kindled by wisdom
(however you live
your life is yajna
if you make it so)

4.28 द्रव्ययज्ञास्तपोयज्ञा योगयज्ञास्तथापरे |
स्वाध्यायज्ञानयज्ञाश्च यतयः संशितव्रताः ||

dravyayajñāstapoyajñā yogayajñāstathāpare |
svādhyāyajñānayajñāśca yatayaḥ saṃśitavratāḥ ||

4.29 अपाने जुह्वति प्राणं प्राणेऽपानं तथापरे |
प्राणापानगती रुद्ध्वा प्राणायामपरायणाः ||

apāne juhvati prāṇaṃ prāṇe'pānaṃ tathāpare |
prāṇāpānagatī ruddhvā prāṇāyāmaparāyaṇāḥ ||

4.30 अपरे नियताहाराः प्राणान्प्राणेषु जुह्वति |
सर्वेऽप्येते यज्ञविदो यज्ञक्षपितकल्मषाः ||

apare niyatāhārāḥ prāṇānprāṇeṣu juhvati |
sarve'pyete yajñavido yajñakṣapitakalmaṣāḥ ||

4.31 यज्ञशिष्टामृतभुजो यान्ति ब्रह्म सनातनम् |
नायं लोकोऽस्त्ययज्ञस्य कुतोऽन्यः कुरुसत्तम ||

yajñaśiṣṭāmṛtabhujo yānti brahma sanātanam |
nāyaṃ loko'styayajñasya kuto'nyaḥ kurusattama ||

4.28 yajnas galore:
material things
austerities
yogic practices

& for ascetics with strict vows
self study
knowledge

4.29 controlling breath   keen to
control prana

some cycle
inhalation into exhalation
exhalation into inhalation
(yogic breathing practices)

4.30 those who restrict diet
burn breath in prana   (body ... to spirit)

all these ways work
& their errors are destroyed by yajna

4.31 those who eat leftovers   manna
(after offering food to deities)
go to brahman

those who offer nothing
don't even get by in this world
where's the question
of another world

4.32 एवं बहुविधा यज्ञा वितता ब्रह्मणो मुखे |
कर्मजान्विद्धि तान्सर्वानेवं ज्ञात्वा विमोक्ष्यसे ||

evaṃ bahuvidhā yajñā vitatā brahmaṇo mukhe |
karmajānviddhi tānsarvānevaṃ jñātvā vimokṣyase ||

4.33 श्रेयान्द्रव्यमयाद्यज्ञाज्ज्ञानयज्ञः परंतप |
सर्वं कर्माखिलं पार्थ ज्ञाने परिसमाप्यते ||

śreyāndravyamayādyajñājjñānayajñaḥ paraṃtapa |
sarvaṃ karmākhilaṃ pārtha jñāne parisamāpyate ||

4.34 तद्विद्धि प्रणिपातेन परिप्रश्नेन सेवया |
उपदेक्ष्यन्ति ते ज्ञानं ज्ञानिनस्तत्त्वदर्शिनः ||

tadviddhi praṇipātena paripraśnena sevayā |
upadekṣyanti te jñānaṃ jñāninastattvadarśinaḥ ||

4.35 यज्ज्ञात्वा न पुनर्मोहमेवं यास्यसि पाण्डव |
येन भूतान्यशेषेण द्रक्ष्यस्यात्मन्यथो मयि ||

yajjñātvā na punarmohamevaṃ yāsyasi pāṇḍava |
yena bhūtānyaśeṣeṇa drakṣyasyātmanyatho mayi ||

4.36 अपि चेदसि पापेभ्यः सर्वेभ्यः पापकृत्तमः |
सर्वं ज्ञानप्लवेनैव वृजिनं संतरिष्यसि ||

api cedasi pāpebhyaḥ sarvebhyaḥ pāpakṛttamaḥ |
sarvaṃ jñānaplavenaiva vṛjinaṃ saṃtariṣyasi ||

4.37 यथैधांसि समिद्धोऽग्निर्भस्मसात्कुरुतेऽर्जुन |
ज्ञानाग्निः सर्वकर्माणि भस्मसात्कुरुते तथा ||

yathaidhāṃsi samiddho'gnirbhasmasātkurute'rjuna |
jñānāgniḥ sarvakarmāṇi bhasmasātkurute tathā ||

4.32 different yajnas are thus
laid at the mouth of brahman

they all come from activity

note that
& you will be liberated

4.33 dedicating knowledge to brahman
is better than giving up material things

all actions none excluded
are included in knowledge

4.34 knowers seers of truth
will give you knowledge so
submit humbly
interrogate
serve

4.35 you won't get
confused again

you'll see without exception
all beings in yourself
& then in me

4.36 even if you are
the worst of evildoers

you'll cross evil
with knowledge-plank

4.37 fire ignited turns wood to ash
knowledge-fire turns karma to ash

4.38 न हि ज्ञानेन सदृशं पवित्रमिह विद्यते |
तत्स्वयं योगसंसिद्धः कालेनात्मनि विन्दति ||

na hi jñānena sadṛśaṃ pavitramiha vidyate |
tatsvayaṃ yogasaṃsiddhaḥ kālenātmani vindati ||

4.39 श्रद्धावान् लभते ज्ञानं तत्परः संयतेन्द्रियः |
ज्ञानं लब्ध्वा परां शान्तिमचिरेणाधिगच्छति ||

śraddhāvān labhate jñānaṃ tatparaḥ saṃyatendriyaḥ |
jñānaṃ labdhvā parāṃ śāntimacireṇādhigacchati ||

4.40 अज्ञश्चाश्रद्दधानश्च संशयात्मा विनश्यति |
नायं लोकोऽस्ति न परो न सुखं संशयात्मनः ||

ajñaścāśraddadhānaśca saṃśayātmā vinaśyati |
nāyaṃ loko'sti na paro na sukhaṃ saṃśayātmanaḥ ||

4.41 योगसंन्यस्तकर्माणं ज्ञानसंछिन्नसंशयम् |
आत्मवन्तं न कर्माणि निबध्नन्ति धनंजय ||

yogasaṃnyastakarmāṇaṃ jñānasaṃchinnasaṃśayam |
ātmavantaṃ na karmāṇi nibadhnanti dhanaṃjaya ||

4.38 there's nothing in this world as
pure as knowledge

one who is perfected in yoga   in time
knows knowledge in oneself

4.39 the faithful one gets knowledge
    holding it as highest
    & restraining sense organs
having got it goes
to super peace without delay

4.40 the ignorant
the faithless
the doubter   is lost

    neither this world nor
    the beyond nor
    happiness

(to sum up)

4.41 she whose
actions renounced in yoga
doubt severed by knowledge
self possessed

actions don't bind

4.42 तस्मादज्ञानसंभूतं हृत्स्थं ज्ञानासिनात्मनः |
छित्त्वैनं संशयं योगमातिष्ठोत्तिष्ठ भारत ||

tasmādajñānasaṃbhūtaṃ hṛtsthaṃ jñānāsinātmanaḥ |
chittvainaṃ saṃśayaṃ yogamātiṣṭhottiṣṭha bhārata ||

5.1 अर्जुन उवाच |
संन्यासं कर्मणां कृष्ण पुनर्योगं च शंससि |
यच्छ्रेय एतयोरेकं तन्मे ब्रूहि सुनिश्चितम् ||

arjuna uvāca |
saṃnyāsaṃ karmaṇāṃ kṛṣṇa punaryogaṃ ca śaṃsasi |
yacchreya etayorekaṃ tanme brūhi suniścitam ||

5.2 श्रीभगवानुवाच |
संन्यासः कर्मयोगश्च निःश्रेयसकरावुभौ |
तयोस्तु कर्मसंन्यासात्कर्मयोगो विशिष्यते ||

śrībhagavānuvāca |
saṃnyāsaḥ karmayogaśca niḥśreyasakarāvubhau |
tayostu karmasaṃnyāsātkarmayogo viśiṣyate ||

5.3 ज्ञेयः स नित्यसंन्यासी यो न द्वेष्टि न काङ्क्षति |
निर्द्वन्द्वो हि महाबाहो सुखं बन्धात्प्रमुच्यते ||

jñeyaḥ sa nityasaṃnyāsī yo na dveṣṭi na kāṅkṣati |
nirdvandvo hi mahābāho sukhaṃ bandhātpramucyate ||

4.42 therefore
sever the doubt in your heart
originating in ignorance
with knowledge-sword
& having cut away this doubt

go yoga!
stand up! arjuna

5.1 arjuna:
krishna first you say
renunciation of activity then
you say activity

what's better which one
tell me for sure

5.2 krishna:
both are best causes of the
nothing's-better-than-this
state
especially
the path of activity

5.3 she who
beyond opposites
neither desires nor hates

is ever the yogi
freed easy from
ties responsibilities

5.4 साङ्ख्ययोगौ पृथग्बालाः प्रवदन्ति न पण्डिताः |
एकमप्यास्थितः सम्यगुभयोर्विन्दते फलम् ||

sāṅkhyayogau pṛthagbālāḥ pravadanti na paṇḍitāḥ |
ekamapyāsthitaḥ samyagubhayorvindate phalam ||

5.5 यत्साङ्ख्यैः प्राप्यते स्थानं तद्योगैरपि गम्यते |
एकं साङ्ख्यं च योगं च यः पश्यति स पश्यति ||

yatsāṅkhyaiḥ prāpyate sthānaṃ tadyogairapi gamyate |
ekaṃ sāṅkhyaṃ ca yogaṃ ca yaḥ paśyati sa paśyati ||

5.6 संन्यासस्तु महाबाहो दुःखमाप्तुमयोगतः |
योगयुक्तो मुनिर्ब्रह्म नचिरेणाधिगच्छति ||

saṃnyāsastu mahābāho duḥkhamāptumayogataḥ |
yogayukto munirbrahma nacireṇādhigacchati ||

5.7 योगयुक्तो विशुद्धात्मा विजितात्मा जितेन्द्रियः |
सर्वभूतात्मभूतात्मा कुर्वन्नपि न लिप्यते ||

yogayukto viśuddhātmā vijitātmā jitendriyaḥ |
sarvabhūtātmabhūtātmā kurvannapi na lipyate ||

5.4 the inexperienced   not wise
call these
two paths two
different directions but

either followed well
finds the same results

5.5 karma yoga goes
where samkhya
does

the two are one

she who can see that
has insight

5.6 renunciation is hard to get to
without first training in
karma yoga
    but arjuna
the yogi who's fastened
to karma yoga
gets there fast   to brahman

5.7 dedicated to
purified by   karma yoga

in command   of oneself
                  of sense organs

seeing one self
in everyone

although working
is untainted   no karma

5.8 नैव किंचित्करोमीति युक्तो मन्येत तत्त्ववित् |
पश्यञ्शृण्वन्स्पृशञ्जिघ्रन्नश्नन्गच्छन्स्वपञ्श्वसन् ||

naiva kiṃcitkaromīti yukto manyeta tattvavit |
paśyañśruṇvanspṛśañjighrannaśnangacchansvapañśvasan ||

5.9 प्रलपन्विसृजन्गृह्णन्नुन्मिषन्निमिषन्नपि |
इन्द्रियाणीन्द्रियार्थेषु वर्तन्त इति धारयन् ||

pralapanvisṛjangṛhṇannunmiṣannimiṣannapi |
indriyāṇīndriyārtheṣu vartanta iti dhārayan ||

5.10 ब्रह्मण्याधाय कर्माणि सङ्गं त्यक्त्वा करोति यः |
लिप्यते न स पापेन पद्मपत्रमिवाम्भसा ||

brahmaṇyādhāya karmāṇi saṅgaṃ tyaktvā karoti yaḥ |
lipyate na sa pāpena padmapatramivāmbhasā ||

5.11 कायेन मनसा बुद्ध्या केवलैरिन्द्रियैरपि |
योगिनः कर्म कुर्वन्ति सङ्गं त्यक्त्वात्मशुद्धये ||

kāyena manasā buddhyā kevalairindriyairapi |
yoginaḥ karma kurvanti saṅgaṃ tyaktvātmaśuddhaye ||

5.12 युक्तः कर्मफलं त्यक्त्वा शान्तिमाप्नोति नैष्ठिकीम् |
अयुक्तः कामकारेण फले सक्तो निबध्यते ||

yuktaḥkarmaphalaṃ tyaktvā śāntimāpnoti naiṣṭhikīm |
ayuktaḥ kāmakāreṇa phale sakto nibadhyate ||

5.8 i do nothing   thinks
the attuned yogi when

seeinghearingtouchingsmelling
eatingwalkingsleepingbreathing

5.9 talkingexcretingcatching&
openingclosingeyes

certain that senses organs
only exist in their objects

5.10 she who offers
all activities to brahman
giving up attachment is

unmarked by negativity
like a lotus leaf   by water

5.11–5.12 the yogi works with body mind intellect
or only with senses
forsaking attachment & results
for self purification
reaches peace

due to selfish desires
the non yogi is bound
to be attached
to consequences

5.13 सर्वकर्माणि मनसा संन्यस्यास्ते सुखं वशी |
नवद्वारे पुरे देही नैव कुर्वन्न कारयन् ||

sarvakarmāṇi manasā saṃnyasyāste sukhaṃ vaśī |
navadvāre pure dehī naiva kurvanna kārayan ||

5.14 न कर्तृत्वं न कर्माणि लोकस्य सृजति प्रभुः |
न कर्मफलसंयोगं स्वभावस्तु प्रवर्तते ||

na kartṛtvaṃ na karmāṇi lokasya sṛjati prabhuḥ |
na karmaphalasaṃyogaṃ svabhāvastu pravartate ||

5.15 नादत्ते कस्यचित्पापं न चैव सुकृतं विभुः |
अज्ञानेनावृतं ज्ञानं तेन मुह्यन्ति जन्तवः ||

nādatte kasyacitpāpaṃ na caiva sukṛtaṃ vibhuḥ |
ajñānenāvṛtaṃ jñānaṃ tena muhyanti jantavaḥ ||

5.16 ज्ञानेन तु तदज्ञानं येषां नाशितमात्मनः |
तेषामादित्यवज्ज्ञानं प्रकाशयति तत्परम् ||

jñānena tu tadajñānaṃ yeṣāṃ nāśitamātmanaḥ |
teṣāmādityavajjñānaṃ prakāśayati tatparam ||

5.13 forsaking ownership of all actions
with the mind

in command of oneself

sits relaxed in her place (body)
of nine gates (2 ears 2 eyes 2 nostrils
1 mouth 1 anus 1 genital)

neither does
nor causes to be done

5.14 (but let's be clear)
i'm no agent (either) for
actions
& consequences

come together
by nature

5.15 i do not receive
'bad' & 'good'

knowledge is hidden
by lack of knowledge
that's why people get confused

5.16 knowledge sun
removes lack of illuminates
knowledge ultimate
reality

5.17 तद्बुद्धयस्तदात्मानस्तन्निष्ठास्तत्परायणाः |
गच्छन्त्यपुनरावृत्तिं ज्ञाननिर्धूतकल्मषाः ||

tadbuddhayastadātmānastanniṣṭhāstatparāyaṇāḥ |
gacchantyapunarāvṛttiṃ jñānanirdhūtakalmaṣāḥ ||

5.18 विद्याविनयसंपन्ने ब्राह्मणे गवि हस्तिनि |
शुनि चैव श्वपाके च पण्डिताः समदर्शिनः ||

vidyāvinayasaṃpanne brāhmaṇe gavi hastini |
śuni caiva śvapāke ca paṇḍitāḥ samadarśinaḥ ||

5.19 इहैव तैर्जितः सर्गो येषां साम्ये स्थितं मनः |
निर्दोषं हि समं ब्रह्म तस्माद् ब्रह्मणि ते स्थिताः ||

ihaiva tairjitaḥ sargo yeṣāṃ sāmye sthitaṃ manaḥ |
nirdoṣaṃ hi samaṃ brahma tasmād brahmaṇi te sthitāḥ ||

5.20 न प्रहृष्येत्प्रियं प्राप्य नोद्विजेत्प्राप्य चाप्रियम् |
स्थिरबुद्धिरसम्मूढो ब्रह्मविद् ब्रह्मणि स्थितः ||

na prahṛṣyetpriyaṃ prāpya nodvijetprāpya cāpriyam |
sthirabuddhirasaṃmūḍho brahmavid brahmaṇi sthitaḥ ||

5.17 mind set on this
as both foundation & goal

faults dusted off by knowledge

no return to rebirth

5.18 pundits see unity in all:
    a humble scholar priest
    a cow an elephant
    a dog & a dog-
    cooking outcaste

5.19 she whose mind
    is fixed in unity
is with brahman
    perfect unity
& conquers rebirth
right here

5.20 don't rejoice   when you get what you like
don't shudder   when you don't

    firm in thought
    unshakeable
the brahman-knower's
    rooted
in brahman

5.21 बाह्यस्पर्शेष्वसक्तात्मा विन्दत्यात्मनि यत्सुखम् |
स ब्रह्मयोगयुक्तात्मा सुखमक्षयमश्नुते ||

bāhyasparśeṣvasaktātmā vindatyātmani yatsukham |
sa brahmayogayuktātmā sukhamakṣayamaśnute ||

5.22 ये हि संस्पर्शजा भोगा दुःखयोनय एव ते |
आद्यन्तवन्तः कौन्तेय न तेषु रमते बुधः ||

ye hi saṃsparśajā bhogā duḥkhayonaya eva te |
ādyantavantaḥ kaunteya na teṣu ramate budhaḥ ||

5.23 शक्नोतीहैव यः सोढुं प्राक्शरीरविमोक्षणात् |
कामक्रोधोद्भवं वेगं स युक्तः स सुखी नरः ||

śaknotīhaiva yaḥ soḍhuṃ prākṣarīravimokṣaṇāt |
kāmakrodhodbhavaṃ vegaṃ sa yuktaḥ sa sukhī naraḥ ||

5.24 योऽन्तःसुखोऽन्तरारामस्तथान्तर्ज्योतिरेव यः |
स योगी ब्रह्मनिर्वाणं ब्रह्मभूतोऽधिगच्छति ||

yo'ntaḥsukho'ntarārāmastathāntarjyotireva yaḥ |
sa yogī brahmanirvāṇaṃ brahmabhūto'dhigacchati ||

5.25 लभन्ते ब्रह्मनिर्वाणमृषयः क्षीणकल्मषाः |
छिन्नद्वैधा यतात्मानः सर्वभूतहिते रताः ||

labhante brahmanirvāṇamṛṣayaḥ kṣīṇakalmaṣāḥ |
chinnadvaidhā yatātmānaḥ sarvabhūtahite ratāḥ ||

5.21 she who knows happiness
within herself

undependent
on external things

attached to brahman
via yoga she
reaches joy everlasting

5.22 pleasures born of contact
are wombs of pain o' arjuna
son of kunti

begin
& end

the wise person doesn't
enjoy them

5.23 only she
who can endure
the stirrings of lust & anger right here when
in the body

is an attuned
happy person

5.24 in joy with in overjoy with in light with in brahman
the yogi reaches brahmanirvana

5.25 errorless
doubtfree
oneself under control
sages who rejoice
in the welfare of all beings
attain brahmanirvana

5.26 कामक्रोधवियुक्तानां यतीनां यतचेतसाम् |
अभितो ब्रह्मनिर्वाणं वर्तते विदितात्मनाम् ||

kāmakrodhaviyuktānāṃ yatīnāṃ yatacetasām |
abhito brahmanirvāṇaṃ vartate viditātmanām ||

5.27 स्पर्शान्कृत्वा बहिर्बाह्यांश्चक्षुश्चैवान्तरे भ्रुवोः |
प्राणापानौ समौ कृत्वा नासाभ्यन्तरचारिणौ ||

sparśānkṛtvā bahirbāhyāṃścakṣuścaivāntare bhruvoḥ |
prāṇāpānau samau kṛtvā nāsābhyantaracāriṇau ||

5.28 यतेन्द्रियमनोबुद्धिर्मुनिर्मोक्षपरायणः |
विगतेच्छाभयक्रोधो यः सदा मुक्त एव सः ||

yatendriyamanobuddhirmunirmokṣaparāyaṇaḥ |
vigatecchābhayakrodho yaḥ sadā mukta eva saḥ ||

5.29 भोक्तारं यज्ञतपसां सर्वलोकमहेश्वरम् |
सुहृदं सर्वभूतानां ज्ञात्वा मां शान्तिमृच्छति ||

bhoktāraṃ yajñatapasāṃ sarvalokamaheśvaram |
suhṛdaṃ sarvabhūtānāṃ jñātvā māṃ śāntimṛcchati ||

6.1 श्रीभगवानुवाच |
अनाश्रितः कर्मफलं कार्यं कर्म करोति यः |
स संन्यासी च योगी च न निरग्निर्न चाक्रियः ||

śrībhagavānuvāca |
anāśritaḥ karmaphalaṃ kāryaṃ karma karoti yaḥ |
sa saṃnyāsī ca yogī ca na niragnirna cākriyaḥ ||

5.26 the lustfree angerfree
self controlled thought controlled
self knower's
brahmanirvana
is at hand

5.27 ousting worldly contact

gaze in between eyebrows

inbreath & outbreath
regulated in the nostrils (yogic breathing
pranayama)

5.28 the seeker with the highest goal liberation
without desire fear anger
mind thought senses reined in
is everfree

5.29 knowing me vast god of all worlds
a friend in the heart
of all beings
eater receiver
of offerings in yajnas & penances
reaches peace

6.1 krishna:
she who
does duties rituals
without banking on the results
is a sanyasi a yogi

doesn't
isn't

6.2 यं संन्यासमिति प्राहुर्योगं तं विद्धि पाण्डव |
न ह्यसंन्यस्तसङ्कल्पो योगी भवति कश्चन ||

yaṃ saṃnyāsamiti prāhuryogaṃ taṃ viddhi pāṇḍava |
na hyasaṃnyastasaṅkalpo yogī bhavati kaścana ||

6.3 आरुरुक्षोर्मुनेर्योगं कर्म कारणमुच्यते |
योगारूढस्य तस्यैव शमः कारणमुच्यते ||

ārurukṣormuneryogaṃ karma kāraṇamucyate |
yogārūḍhasya tasyaiva śamaḥ kāraṇamucyate ||

6.4 यदा हि नेन्द्रियार्थेषु न कर्मस्वनुषज्जते |
सर्वसङ्कल्पसंन्यासी योगारूढस्तदोच्यते ||

yadā hi nendriyārtheṣu na karmasvanuṣajjate |
sarvasaṅkalpasaṃnyāsī yogārūḍhastadocyate ||

6.5 उद्धरेदात्मनात्मानं नात्मानमवसादयेत् |
आत्मैव ह्यात्मनो बन्धुरात्मैव रिपुरात्मनः ||

uddharedātmanātmānaṃ nātmānamavasādayet |
ātmaiva hyātmano bandhurātmaiva ripurātmanaḥ ||

6.6 बन्धुरात्मात्मनस्तस्य येनात्मैवात्मना जितः |
अनात्मनस्तु शत्रुत्वे वर्तेतात्मैव शत्रुवत् ||

bandhurātmātmanastasya yenātmaivātmanā jitaḥ |
anātmanastu śatrutve vartetātmaiva śatruvat ||

6.2 ‘renunciation’
is yoga

no one’s a yogi
without renouncing
self interest

6.3 for the seeker
who wants to advance   be yogi
karma yoga   selfless activity
is the way

for the advanced yogi
equanimity is the way

6.4 when she isn’t attached   to actions
sense objects
has renounced self interest

she’s said to have
stepped up to
yoga

6.5–6.6 you’ve got to
help yourself up   not   put yourself down

you are your own   you are your own
friend   enemy

she who has   she who hasn’t
self mastery is her   is her
own friend   own enemy

6.7 जितात्मनः प्रशान्तस्य परमात्मा समाहितः |
शीतोष्णसुखदुःखेषु तथा मानापमानयोः ||

jitātmanaḥ praśāntasya paramātmā samāhitaḥ |
śītoṣṇasukhaduḥkheṣu tathā mānāpamānayoḥ ||

6.8 ज्ञानविज्ञानतृप्तात्मा कूटस्थो विजितेन्द्रियः |
युक्त इत्युच्यते योगी समलोष्टाश्मकाञ्चनः ||

jñānavijñānatṛptātmā kūṭastho vijitendriyaḥ |
yukta ityucyate yogī samaloṣṭāśmakāñcanaḥ ||

6.9 सुहृन्मित्रार्युदासीनमध्यस्थद्वेष्यबन्धुषु |
साधुष्वपि च पापेषु समबुद्धिर्विशिष्यते ||

suhṛnmitrāryudāsīnamadhyasthadveṣyabandhuṣu |
sādhuṣvapi ca pāpeṣu samabuddhirviśiṣyate ||

6.10 योगी युञ्जीत सततमात्मानं रहसि स्थितः |
एकाकी यतचित्तात्मा निराशीरपरिग्रहः ||

yogī yuñjīta satatamātmānaṃ rahasi sthitaḥ |
ekākī yatacittātmā nirāśīraparigrahaḥ ||

6.7 for the self mastered peaceful you
the divine (literally, the ultimate you)
is immediate accessible
in cold heat
happiness unhappiness
honour dishonour

6.8–6.9 she who is content
in knowledge understanding
who's on top of things controlling senses
attuned to her inner self

yoked = yogi

for her dirt = stone = gold
it's all the same
she's the same to friend ~ foe
relative ~ enemy
good ~ bad

6.10 a yogi must always be yoked to focused on
her inner self

keep to herself

alone
self controlled (even) in thought

wanting nothing ↔ having nothing

6.11 शुचौ देशे प्रतिष्ठाप्य स्थिरमासनमात्मनः |
नात्युच्छ्रितं नातिनीचं चैलाजिनकुशोत्तरम् ||

śucau deśe pratiṣṭhāpya sthiramāsanamātmanaḥ |
nātyucchritaṃ nātinīcaṃ cailājinakuśottaram ||

6.12 तत्रैकाग्रं मनः कृत्वा यतचित्तेन्द्रियक्रियः |
उपविश्यासने युञ्ज्याद्योगमात्मविशुद्धये ||

tatraikāgraṃ manaḥ kṛtvā yatacittendriyakriyaḥ |
upaviśyāsane yuñjyādyogamātmaviśuddhaye ||

6.13 समं कायशिरोग्रीवं धारयन्नचलं स्थिरः |
सम्प्रेक्ष्य नासिकाग्रं स्वं दिशश्चानवलोकयन् ||

samaṃ kāyaśirogrīvaṃ dhārayannacalaṃ sthiraḥ |
saṃprekṣya nāsikāgraṃ svaṃ diśaścānavalokayan ||

6.14 प्रशान्तात्मा विगतभीर्ब्रह्मचारिव्रते स्थितः |
मनः संयम्य मच्चित्तो युक्त आसीत मत्परः ||

praśāntātmā vigatabhīrbrahmacārivrate sthitaḥ |
manaḥ saṃyamya maccitto yukta āsīta matparaḥ ||

6.11 founding a clean place
a steady seat

not too high
not too low

(layers)
cloth
antelope skin
kusha holy grass

6.12 sitting there mind focused
thought & senses arrested

practise yoga for self purification

6.13 | neck
| head
| back in line
steady no motion
(inwardly) gazing

at your nose
(where your eyebrows meet)
nowhere else

6.14 quiet fearless
firmly celibate

yoked controlling mind
thinking of me as ideal

sit

6.15 युञ्जन्नेवं सदात्मानं योगी नियतमानसः |
शान्तिं निर्वाणपरमां मत्संस्थामधिगच्छति ||

yuñjannevaṃ sadātmānaṃ yogī niyatamānasaḥ |
śāntiṃ nirvāṇaparamāṃ matsaṃsthāmadhigacchati ||

6.16 नात्यश्नतस्तु योगोऽस्ति न चैकान्तमनश्नतः |
न चातिस्वप्नशीलस्य जाग्रतो नैव चार्जुन ||

nātyaśnatastu yogo'sti na caikāntamanaśnataḥ |
na cātisvapnaśīlasya jāgrato naiva cārjuna ||

6.17 युक्ताहारविहारस्य युक्तचेष्टस्य कर्मसु |
युक्तस्वप्नावबोधस्य योगो भवति दुःखहा ||

yuktāhāravihārasya yuktaceṣṭasya karmasu |
yuktasvapnāvabodhasya yogo bhavati duḥkhahā ||

6.18 यदा विनियतं चित्तमात्मन्येवावतिष्ठते |
निःस्पृहः सर्वकामेभ्यो युक्त इत्युच्यते तदा ||

yadā viniyataṃ cittamātmanyevāvatiṣṭhate |
niḥspṛhaḥ sarvakāmebhyo yukta ityucyate tadā ||

6.19 यथा दीपो निवातस्थो नेङ्गते सोपमा स्मृता |
योगिनो यतचित्तस्य युञ्जतो योगमात्मनः ||

yathā dīpo nivātastho neṅgate sopamā smṛtā |
yogino yatacittasya yuñjato yogamātmanaḥ ||

6.15 ever disciplined
mind controlled

the yogi arrives
at peace   nirvana

is one with me

6.16 yoga's not possible
for one who   overeats
fasts
oversleeps or
stays up all night

6.17 balanced yoked in   food 'n entertainment
activities
sleeping waking
yoga kills depression

6.18 when she's

mind controlled
innerself absorbed
desireless to all desires

she's said to be yoked disciplined

6.19 there's a simile
for a mindcontrolled yogi
focused on yoga:

a lamp unflickering
a windless place

6.20 यत्रोपरमते चित्तं निरुद्धं योगसेवया |
यत्र चैवात्मनात्मानं पश्यन्नात्मनि तुष्यति ||

yatroparamate cittaṃ niruddhaṃ yogasevayā |
yatra caivātmanātmānaṃ paśyannātmani tuṣyati ||

6.21 सुखमात्यन्तिकं यत्तद्बुद्धिग्राह्यमतीन्द्रियम् |
वेत्ति यत्र न चैवायं स्थितश्चलति तत्त्वतः ||

sukhamātyantikaṃ yattadbuddhigrāhyamatīndriyam |
vetti yatra na caivāyaṃ sthitaścalati tattvataḥ ||

6.22 यं लब्ध्वा चापरं लाभं मन्यते नाधिकं ततः |
यस्मिन्स्थितो न दुःखेन गुरुणापि विचाल्यते ||

yaṃ labdhvā cāparaṃ lābhaṃ manyate nādhikaṃ tataḥ |
yasminsthito na duḥkhena guruṇāpi vicālyate ||

6.23 तं विद्याद् दुःखसंयोगवियोगं योगसंज्ञितम् |
स निश्चयेन योक्तव्यो योगोऽनिर्विण्णचेतसा ||

taṃ vidyād duḥkhasaṃyogaviyogaṃ yogasaṃjñitam |
sa niścayena yoktavyo yogo'nirviṇṇacetasā ||

6.24 सङ्कल्पप्रभवान्कामांस्त्यक्त्वा सर्वानशेषतः |
मनसैवेन्द्रियग्रामं विनियम्य समन्ततः ||

saṅkalpaprabhavānkāmāṃstyaktvā sarvānaśeṣataḥ |
manasaivendriyagrāmaṃ viniyamya samantataḥ ||

6.20 when the mind stops roaming
checked by yoga

& when you see yourself thus
ohhappy!

6.21 that infinite joy
that's understood by intelligence
that's beyond the senses

she knows
& on that basis
proceeds

6.22 having got there she knows
nothing's better   to get

rooted in that   she's
unruffled
by big troubles

6.23 yoga releases you
from the ties of pain

so persevere   practise
think positive

6.24 use your mind

drop desires   all   no exception
that come
from your will

restrain all your senses totally

6.25 शनैः शनैरुपरमेद्बुद्ध्या धृतिगृहीतया |
आत्मसंस्थं मनः कृत्वा न किंचिदपि चिन्तयेत् ||

śanaiḥ śanairuparamedbuddhyā dhṛtigṛhītayā |
ātmasaṃsthaṃ manaḥ kṛtvā na kiṃcidapi cintayet ||

6.26 यतो यतो निश्चरति मनश्चञ्चलमस्थिरम् |
ततस्ततो नियम्यैतदात्मन्येव वशं नयेत् ||

yato yato niścarati manaścañcalamasthiram |
tatastato niyamyaitadātmanyeva vaśaṃ nayet ||

6.27 प्रशान्तमनसं ह्येनं योगिनं सुखमुत्तमम् |
उपैति शान्तरजसं ब्रह्मभूतमकल्मषम् ||

praśāntamanasaṃ hyenaṃ yoginaṃ sukhamuttamam |
upaiti śāntarajasaṃ brahmabhūtamakalmaṣam ||

6.28 युञ्जन्नेवं सदात्मानं योगी विगतकल्मषः |
सुखेन ब्रह्मसंस्पर्शमत्यन्तं सुखमश्नुते ||

yuñjannevaṃ sadātmānaṃ yogī vigatakalmaṣaḥ |
sukhena brahmasaṃsparśamatyantaṃ sukhamaśnute ||

6.29 सर्वभूतस्थमात्मानं सर्वभूतानि चात्मनि |
ईक्षते योगयुक्तात्मा सर्वत्र समदर्शनः ||

sarvabhūtasthamātmānaṃ sarvabhūtāni cātmani |
īkṣate yogayuktātmā sarvatra samadarśanaḥ ||

6.25 s l o w l y cease
activity

use intellect to
hold on to steadiness

fix mind on you who you really are

mustn't think
of anything else

6.26 where wanders
the restless fickle
mind

there rein in
bring back under control
to you

6.27 the calm yogi
has the best bliss
even her passion's calm
faultless
become brahman

6.28 thus always in yoga
the yogi blemish free
taps into brahman easy just like that
no end to joy!

6.29 sees her self in all beings
all beings in her self

self same everywhere

6.30 यो मां पश्यति सर्वत्र सर्वं च मयि पश्यति ।
तस्याहं न प्रणश्यामि स च मे न प्रणश्यति ॥

yo māṃ paśyati sarvatra sarvaṃ ca mayi paśyati |
tasyāhaṃ na praṇaśyāmi sa ca me na praṇaśyati ||

6.31 सर्वभूतस्थितं यो मां भजत्येकत्वमास्थितः ।
सर्वथा वर्तमानोऽपि स योगी मयि वर्तते ॥

sarvabhūtasthitaṃ yo māṃ bhajatyekatvamāsthitaḥ |
sarvathā vartamāno'pi sa yogī mayi vartate ||

6.32 आत्मौपम्येन सर्वत्र समं पश्यति योऽर्जुन ।
सुखं वा यदि वा दुःखं स योगी परमो मतः ॥

ātmaupamyena sarvatra samaṃ paśyati yo'rjuna |
sukhaṃ vā yadi vā duḥkhaṃ sa yogī paramo mataḥ ||

6.33 अर्जुन उवाच ।
योऽयं योगस्त्वया प्रोक्तः साम्येन मधुसूदन ।
एतस्याहं न पश्यामि चञ्चलत्वात्स्थितिं स्थिराम् ॥

arjuna uvāca |
yo'yaṃ yogastvayā proktaḥ sāmyena madhusūdana |
etasyāhaṃ na paśyāmi cañcalatvātsthitiṃ sthirām ||

6.34 चञ्चलं हि मनः कृष्ण प्रमाथि बलवद्दृढम् ।
तस्याहं निग्रहं मन्ये वायोरिव सुदुष्करम् ॥

cañcalaṃ hi manaḥ kṛṣṇa pramāthi balavaddṛḍham |
tasyāhaṃ nigrahaṃ manye vāyoriva suduṣkaram ||

6.35 श्रीभगवानुवाच ।
असंशयं महाबाहो मनो दुर्निग्रहं चलम् ।
अभ्यासेन तु कौन्तेय वैराग्येण च गृह्यते ॥

śrībhagavānuvāca |
asaṃśayaṃ mahābāho mano durnigrahaṃ calam |
abhyāsena tu kaunteya vairāgyeṇa ca gṛhyate ||

6.30 she who sees me for her i am
everywhere & never gone
& everything in me she is never gone
for me

6.31 anchored in unity however she is she is
in me
she serves me in all beings

6.32 she who whether up or down
by relating everything to herself
sees unity everywhere:

'super yogi'

6.33 arjuna:
this yoga you talk of
equanimity
steady staying

restless i don't see it

6.34 mind's restless
stubborn strong extreme

staying it i believe
as trying as trying
to stay wind

6.35 krishna:
o' strong-armed arjuna
no doubt the mind's moves are hard to stay
you get a grip by practice &
undifference

6.36 असंयतात्मना योगो दुष्प्राप इति मे मतिः |
वश्यात्मना तु यतता शक्योऽवाप्तुमुपायतः ||

asaṃyatātmanā yogo duṣprāpa iti me matiḥ |
vaśyātmanā tu yatatā śakyo'vāptumupāyataḥ ||

6.37 अर्जुन उवाच |
अयतिः श्रद्धयोपेतो योगाच्चलितमानसः |
अप्राप्य योगसंसिद्धिं कां गतिं कृष्ण गच्छति ||

arjuna uvāca |
ayatiḥ śraddhayopeto yogāccalitamānasaḥ |
aprāpya yogasaṃsiddhiṃ kāṃ gatiṃ kṛṣṇa gacchati ||

6.38 कच्चिन्नोभयविभ्रष्टश्छिन्नाभ्रमिव नश्यति|
अप्रतिष्ठो महाबाहो विमूढो ब्रह्मणः पथि ||

kaccinnobhayavibhraṣṭaśchinnābhramiva naśyati |
apratiṣṭho mahābāho vimūḍho brahmaṇaḥ pathi ||

6.39 एतन्मे संशयं कृष्ण छेत्तुमर्हस्यशेषतः|
त्वदन्यः संशयस्यास्य छेत्ता न ह्युपपद्यते ||

etanme saṃśayaṃ kṛṣṇa chettumarhasyaśeṣataḥ |
tvadanyaḥ saṃśayasyāsya chettā na hyupapadyate ||

6.40 श्रीभगवानुवाच |
पार्थ नैवेह नामुत्र विनाशस्तस्य विद्यते |
न हि कल्याणकृत्कश्चिद्दुर्गतिं तात गच्छति ||

śrībhagavānuvāca |
pārtha naiveha nāmutra vināśastasya vidyate |
na hi kalyāṇakṛtkaściddurgatiṃ tāta gacchati ||

6.36 hard to get if you're self uncontrolled

can do if you're self controlled
if you systematically
try

6.37 arjuna:
she who has faith
but no discipline

mind strayed from yoga
success in yoga unfound

where does she go krishna

6.38 a dropout in both worlds
anchorless
confused on the way
of brahman
does she vanish like a torn cloud

6.39 only you can clear my doubt krishna
totally

there's none
other than you

6.40 krishna:
arjuna
she who does good things
isn't lost in this world or that
doesn't end up badly

6.41 प्राप्य पुण्यकृतां लोकानुषित्वा शाश्वती: समा:|
शुचीनां श्रीमतां गेहे योगभ्रष्टोऽभिजायते ||

prāpya puṇyakṛtāṃ lokānuṣitvā śāśvatīḥ samāḥ |
śucīnāṃ śrīmatāṃ gehe yogabhraṣṭo'bhijāyate ||

6.42 अथवा योगिनामेव कुले भवति धीमताम्|
एतद्धि दुर्लभतरं लोके जन्म यदीदृशम् ||

athavā yogināmeva kule bhavati dhīmatām |
etaddhi durlabhataraṃ loke janma yadīdṛśam ||

6.43 तत्र तं बुद्धिसंयोगं लभते पौर्वदेहिकम् |
यतते च ततो भूय: संसिद्धौ कुरुनन्दन ||

tatra taṃ buddhisaṃyogaṃ labhate paurvadehikam |
yatate ca tato bhūyaḥ saṃsiddhau kurunandana ||

6.44 पूर्वाभ्यासेन तेनैव ह्रियते ह्यवशोऽपि स:|
जिज्ञासुरपि योगस्य शब्दब्रह्मातिवर्तते ||

pūrvābhyāsena tenaiva hriyate hyavaśo'pi saḥ |
jijñāsurapi yogasya śabdabrahmātivartate ||

6.41 the interrupted yogi

gets to the worlds of do-gooders
lives there for ages is
born again in a
home of the holyfamous

6.42 or in a family
of wise yogis

this kind of birth
not easy to get
in this world

6.43 & there reconnects
to wisdom
of previous life

from there she
tries again
for success o' arjuna son of the kuru clan

6.44 she's driven
by previous practice
as if without will

is curious
about yoga

& goes beyond
just vedic recitations

6.45 प्रयत्नाद्यतमानस्तु योगी संशुद्धकिल्बिषः |
अनेकजन्मसंसिद्धस्ततो याति परां गतिम् ||

prayatnādyatamānastu yogī saṃśuddhakilbiṣaḥ |
anekajanmasaṃsiddhastato yāti parāṃ gatim ||

6.46 तपस्विभ्योऽधिकोयोगी ज्ञानिभ्योऽपिमतोऽधिकः |
कर्मिभ्यश्चाधिकोयोगी तस्माद्योगीभवार्जुन ||

tapasvibhyo'dhikoyogī jñānibhyo'pimato'dhikaḥ |
karmibhyaścādhikoyogī tasmādyogībhavārjuna ||

6.47 योगिनामपि सर्वेषां मद्गतेनान्तरात्मना |
श्रद्धावान्भजते यो मां स मे युक्ततमो मतः ||

yogināmapi sarveṣāṃ madgatenāntarātmanā |
śraddhāvānbhajate yo māṃ sa me yuktatamo mataḥ ||

7.1 श्रीभगवानुवाच |
मय्यासक्तमनाः पार्थ योगं युञ्जन्मदाश्रयः |
असंशयं समग्रं मां यथा ज्ञास्यसि तच्छृणु ||

śrībhagavānuvāca |
mayyāsaktamanāḥ pārtha yogaṃ yuñjanmadāśrayaḥ |
asaṃśayaṃ samagraṃ māṃ yathā jñāsyasi tacchṛṇu ||

7.2 ज्ञानं तेऽहं सविज्ञानमिदं वक्ष्याम्यशेषतः |
यज्ज्ञात्वा नेह भूयोऽन्यज्ज्ञातव्यमवशिष्यते ||

jñānaṃ te'haṃ savijñānamidaṃ vakṣyāmyaśeṣataḥ |
yajjñātvā neha bhūyo'nyajjñātavyamavaśiṣyate ||

6.45 by trying by controlling
the mind
the yogi's cleansed of faults

perfected across births
then goes
to the goal

6.46 a yogi's better than an ascetic
scholar
ritualist
yogi be! arjuna

6.47 & of all yogis she

whose very core whose heart
goes out to me

who devoted serves me
is most connected to me

7.1 hear how
me on your mind
practising yoga
trusting me without doubt
you'll totally know me

7.2 to you i'll give
knowledge + understanding

of that which
when you know

nothing
will remain
to be known

7.3 मनुष्याणां सहस्रेषु कश्चिद्यतति सिद्धये |
यततामपि सिद्धानां कश्चिन्मां वेत्ति तत्त्वत: ||

manuṣyāṇāṃ sahasreṣu kaścidyatati siddhaye |
yatatāmapi siddhānāṃ kaścinmāṃ vetti tattvataḥ ||

7.4 भूमिरापोऽनलो वायु: खं मनो बुद्धिरेव च |
अहंकार इतीयं मे भिन्ना प्रकृतिरष्टधा ||

bhūmirāpo'nalo vāyuḥ khaṃ mano buddhireva ca |
ahaṃkāra itīyaṃ me bhinnā prakṛtiraṣṭadhā ||

7.5 अपरेयमितस्त्वन्यां प्रकृतिं विद्धि मे पराम् |
जीवभूतां महाबाहो ययेदं धार्यते जगत् ||

apareyamitastvanyāṃ prakṛtiṃ viddhi me parām |
jīvabhūtāṃ mahābāho yayedaṃ dhāryate jagat ||

7.3 not even one in a thousand people
tries to be perfect

of those who try
& those who achieve

barely anyone
knows me truly

7.4 eight parts to
my manifest nature

earth water fire wind
ether (energy field)
mind intellect
ego

7.5 & that's not a big deal

my other nature is
the ultimate it
supports the forms of life is the

7.6 एतद्योनीनि भूतानि सर्वाणीत्युपधारय |
अहं कृत्स्नस्य जगत: प्रभव: प्रलयस्तथा ||

etadyonīni bhūtāni sarvāṇītyupadhāraya |
ahaṃ kṛtsnasya jagataḥ prabhavaḥ pralayastathā ||

7.7 मत्त: परतरं नान्यत्किंचिदस्ति धनंजय |
मयि सर्वमिदं प्रोतं सूत्रे मणिगणा इव ||

mattaḥ parataraṃ nānyatkiṃcidasti dhanaṃjaya |
mayi sarvamidaṃ protaṃ sūtre maṇigaṇā iva ||

7.8 रसोऽहमप्सु कौन्तेय प्रभास्मि शशिसूर्ययो: |
प्रणव: सर्ववेदेषु शब्द: खे पौरुषं नृषु ||

raso'hamapsu kaunteya prabhāsmi śaśisūryayoḥ |
praṇavaḥ sarvavedeṣu śabdaḥ khe pauruṣaṃ nṛṣu ||

7.9 पुण्यो गन्ध: पृथिव्यां च तेजश्चास्मि विभावसौ |
जीवनं सर्वभूतेषु तपश्चास्मि तपस्विषु ||

puṇyo gandhaḥ pṛthivyāṃ ca tejaścāsmi vibhāvasau |
jīvanaṃ sarvabhūteṣu tapaścāsmi tapasviṣu ||

7.10 बीजं मां सर्वभूतानां विद्धि पार्थ सनातनम् |
बुद्धिर्बुद्धिमतामस्मि तेजस्तेजस्विनामहम् ||

bījaṃ māṃ sarvabhūtānāṃ viddhi pārtha sanātanam |
buddhirbuddhimatāmasmi tejastejasvināmaham ||

7.11 बलं बलवतां चाहं कामरागविवर्जितम् |
धर्माविरुद्धो भूतेषु कामोऽस्मि भरतर्षभ ||

balaṃ balavatāṃ cāhaṃ kāmarāgavivarjitam |
dharmāviruddho bhūteṣu kāmo'smi bharatarṣabha ||

7.6–7.11 womb of beings

everyone! get that

I AM

the origin
the end of
the entire universe

there's no thing higher

it's all strung on me
pearls on a string

water's flavour light in moon sun om in all vedas
sound in etheric space

spunk in humans
the nice fragrance on earth
sun's brilliance
life in all living
penance in ascetics

know me ancient timeless seed
intelligence of the intelligent
radiance of the radiant

strength of the strong
who are desire & passionfree
the love in beings
that isn't inappropriate

7.12 ये चैव सात्त्विका भावा राजसास्तामसाश्च ये |
मत्त एवेति तान्विद्धि न त्वहं तेषु ते मयि ||

ye caiva sāttvikā bhāvā rājasāstāmasāśca ye |
matta eveti tānviddhi na tvahaṃ teṣu te mayi ||

7.13 त्रिभिर्गुणमयैर्भावैरेभिः सर्वमिदं जगत् |
मोहितं नाभिजानाति मामेभ्यः परमव्ययम् ||

tribhirguṇamayairbhāvairebhiḥ sarvamidaṃ jagat |
mohitaṃ nābhijānāti māmebhyaḥ paramavyayam ||

7.14 दैवी ह्येषा गुणमयी मम माया दुरत्यया |
मामेव ये प्रपद्यन्ते मायामेतां तरन्ति ते ||

daivī hyeṣā guṇamayī mama māyā duratyayā |
māmeva ye prapadyante māyāmetāṃ taranti te ||

7.12 (& the three qualities gunas)
    sattva (clarity)
    rajas (passion)
    tamas (inertia)
they're from me

i'm not in them
they're in me

7.13 the whole world is
made of these three

    so it's fooled
    under their influence

doesn't quite know i am
                    beyond these

                    constant

7.14 this   my
divine play   made of gunas

my mystery   magic   maya
    hard to fathom

    only those who
hang on to me
get past maya

7.15 न मां दुष्कृतिनो मूढाः प्रपद्यन्ते नराधमाः |
माययापहृतज्ञाना आसुरं भावमाश्रिताः ||

na māṃ duṣkṛtino mūḍhāḥ prapadyante narādhamāḥ |
māyayāpahṛtajñānā āsuraṃ bhāvamāśritāḥ ||

7.16 चतुर्विधा भजन्ते मां जनाः सुकृतिनोऽर्जुन |
आर्तो जिज्ञासुरर्थार्थी ज्ञानी च भरतर्षभ ||

caturvidhā bhajante māṃ janāḥ sukṛtino'rjuna |
ārto jijñāsurarthārthī jñānī ca bharatarṣabha ||

7.17 तेषां ज्ञानी नित्ययुक्त एकभक्तिर्विशिष्यते |
प्रियो हि ज्ञानिनोऽत्यर्थमहं स च मम प्रियः ||

teṣāṃ jñānī nityayukta ekabhaktirviśiṣyate |
priyo hi jñānino'tyarthamahaṃ sa ca mama priyaḥ ||

7.18 उदाराः सर्व एवैते ज्ञानी त्वात्मैव मे मतम् |
आस्थितः स हि युक्तात्मा मामेवानुत्तमां गतिम् ||

udārāḥ sarva evaite jñānī tvātmaiva me matam |
āsthitaḥ sa hi yuktātmā māmevānuttamāṃ gatim ||

7.19 बहूनां जन्मनामन्ते ज्ञानवान्मां प्रपद्यते |
वासुदेवः सर्वमिति स महात्मा सुदुर्लभः ||

bahūnāṃ janmanāmante jñānavānmāṃ prapadyate |
vāsudevaḥ sarvamiti sa mahātmā sudurlabhaḥ ||

7.15 fools   wrongdoers
the meanest
don't seek me

wisdom warped
by maya

their lifestyle
demonic

7.16 four kinds of rightdoers
worship me

the suffering
seekers of knowledge / success
& the wise

7.17 among them the wise
always attuned   i love her   &
noted for singular devotion   she loves me

7.18 they're all fine but
the wise one is   thought of as
my quintessence

united she
sticks with me   the ultimate goal

7.19 at the end of many lives
the wise one   one so good   is hard to find
turns to me:
'krishna's everything'

7.20 कामैस्तैस्तैर्हृतज्ञाना: प्रपद्यन्तेऽन्यदेवता: |
तं तं नियममास्थाय प्रकृत्या नियता: स्वया ||

kāmaistaistairhṛtajñānāḥ prapadyante'nyadevatāḥ |
taṃ taṃ niyamamāsthāya prakṛtyā niyatāḥ svayā ||

7.21 यो यो यां यां तनुं भक्त: श्रद्धयार्चितुमिच्छति |
तस्य तस्याचलां श्रद्धां तामेव विदधाम्यहम् ||

yo yo yāṃ yāṃ tanuṃ bhaktaḥ śraddhayārcitumicchati |
tasya tasyācalāṃ śraddhāṃ tāmeva vidadhāmyaham ||

7.22 स तया श्रद्धया युक्तस्तस्याराधनमीहते |
लभते च तत: कामान्मयैव विहितान्हितान् ||

sa tayā śraddhayā yuktastasyārādhanamīhate |
labhate ca tataḥ kāmānmayaivaḥ vihitānhitān ||

7.23 अन्तवत्तु फलं तेषां तद्भवत्यल्पमेधसाम् |
देवान्देवयजो यान्ति मद्भक्ता यान्ति मामपि ||

antavattu phalaṃ teṣāṃ tadbhavatyalpamedhasām |
devāndevayajo yānti madbhaktā yānti māmapi ||

7.24 अव्यक्तं व्यक्तिमापन्नं मन्यन्ते मामबुद्धय: |
परं भावमजानन्तो ममाव्ययमनुत्तमम् ||

avyaktaṃ vyaktimāpannaṃ manyante māmabuddhayaḥ |
paraṃ bhāvamajānanto mamāvyayamanuttamam ||

7.20 people go to other deities
with this & that wish
this & that ritual

they're limited
by their own nature

7.21 it is i who grant
unshakeable faith to

whoever prefers   to revere
whatever deity

7.22 it is i who give her
what she wants

when she worships
with this faith

7.23 but limited are the gains
for little brains

those who worship deities
go to deities

my devotees come to me   only

7.24 the unintelligent believe i   formless
am obvious

without knowing my ultimate state
    constant
    supreme.

7.25 नाहं प्रकाशः सर्वस्य योगमायासमावृतः |
मूढोऽयं नाभिजानाति लोको मामजमव्ययम् ||

nāhaṃ prakāśaḥ sarvasya yogamāyāsamāvṛtaḥ |
mūḍho'yaṃ nābhijānāti loko māmajamavyayam ||

7.26 वेदाहं समतीतानि वर्तमानानि चार्जुन |
भविष्याणि च भूतानि मां तु वेद न कश्चन ||

vedāhaṃ samatītāni vartamānāni cārjuna |
bhaviṣyāṇi ca bhūtāni māṃ tu veda na kaścana ||

7.27 इच्छाद्वेषसमुत्थेन द्वन्द्वमोहेन भारत |
सर्वभूतानि सम्मोहं सर्गे यान्ति परंतप ||

icchādveṣasamutthena dvandvamohena bhārata |
sarvabhūtāni sammohaṃ sarge yānti paraṃtapa ||

7.28 येषां त्वन्तगतं पापं जनानां पुण्यकर्मणाम् |
ते द्वन्द्वमोहनिर्मुक्ता भजन्ते मां दृढव्रताः ||

yeṣāṃ tvantagataṃ pāpaṃ janānāṃ puṇyakarmaṇām |
te dvandvamohanirmuktā bhajante māṃ dṛḍhavratāḥ ||

7.29 जरामरणमोक्षाय मामाश्रित्य यतन्ति ये |
ते ब्रह्म तद्विदुः कृत्स्नमध्यात्मं कर्म चाखिलम् ||

jarāmaraṇamokṣāya māmāśritya yatanti ye |
te brahma tadviduḥ kṛtsnamadhyātmaṃ karma cākhilam ||

7.25 i am   not visible to everyone
      masked by my mystic powers

the world   fool
doesn't realize
i am   birthless
          constant   undying

7.26 i know those who have gone
                   who are now
                   & will be

no one knows me

7.27 due to
duality delusion
      desire   aversion

all
fall   into
when they are born

7.28 but those with good deeds
                   errors at an end
freed from dualities

adore me with firm vows

7.29 those who count on me
for liberation from old age & death

they know it all   brahman
                      action &
                      the highest self

7.30 साधिभूताधिदैवं मां साधियज्ञं च ये विदुः |
प्रयाणकालेऽपि च मां ते विदुर्युक्तचेतसः ||

sādhibhūtādhidaivaṃ māṃ sādhiyajñaṃ ca ye viduḥ |
prayāṇakāle'pi ca māṃ te viduryuktacetasaḥ ||

8.1 अर्जुन उवाच |
किं तद्ब्रह्म किमध्यात्मं किं कर्म पुरुषोत्तम |
अधिभूतं च किं प्रोक्तमधिदैवं किमुच्यते ||

arjuna uvāca |
kiṃ tadbrahma kimadhyātmaṃ kiṃ karma puruṣottama |
adhibhūtaṃ ca kiṃ proktamadhidaivaṃ kimucyate ||

8.2 अधियज्ञः कथं कोऽत्र देहेऽस्मिन्मधुसूदन |
प्रयाणकाले च कथं ज्ञेयोऽसि नियतात्मभिः ||

adhiyajñaḥ kathaṃ ko'tra dehe'sminmadhusūdana |
prayāṇakāle ca kathaṃ jñeyo'si niyatātmabhiḥ ||

8.3 श्रीभगवानुवाच |
अक्षरं ब्रह्म परमं स्वभावोऽध्यात्ममुच्यते |
भूतभावोद्भवकरो विसर्गः कर्मसंज्ञितः ||

śrībhagavānuvāca |
akṣaraṃ brahma paramaṃ svabhāvo'dhyātmamucyate |
bhūtabhāvodbhavakaro visargaḥ karmasaṃjñitaḥ ||

7.30 they who know
i am
the divine fundamental being
the manifest
the fundamental yajna

even when it's time
to leave (to 'die')

they have presence of mind
(for) they know me

8.1 arjuna:
huh what exactly is this brahman
o' supreme
ultimate me
karma action
manifest
divine fundamental

8.2 fundamental sacrifice
where in this body how
& how at the time of death
can you be known
by these oh-so-self-controlled types

8.3 krishna:
'brahman' is undying ultimate

'the ultimate self' is who you really are

creation is action / procreation karma

gives rise to existence beingness

8.4 अधिभूतं क्षरो भाव: पुरुषश्चाधिदैवतम् |
अधियज्ञोऽहमेवात्र देहे देहभृतां वर ||

adhibhūtaṃ kṣaro bhāvaḥ puruṣaścādhidaivatam |
adhiyajño'hamevātra dehe dehabhṛtāṃ vara ||

8.5 अन्तकाले च मामेव स्मरन्मुक्त्वा कलेवरम् |
य: प्रयाति स मद्भावं याति नास्त्यत्र संशय: ||

antakāle ca māmeva smaranmuktvā kalevaram |
yaḥ prayāti sa madbhāvaṃ yāti nāstyatra saṃśayaḥ ||

8.6 यं यं वापि स्मरन्भावं त्यजत्यन्ते कलेवरम् |
तं तमेवैति कौन्तेय सदा तद्भावभावित: ||

yaṃ yaṃ vāpi smaranbhāvaṃ tyajatyante kalevaram |
taṃ tamevaiti kaunteya sadā tadbhāvabhāvitaḥ ||

8.7 तस्मात्सर्वेषु कालेषु मामनुस्मर युध्य च |
मय्यर्पितमनोबुद्धिर्मामेवैष्यस्यसंशयम् ||

tasmātsarveṣu kāleṣu māmanusmara yudhya ca |
mayyarpitamanobuddhirmāmevaiṣyasyasaṃśayam ||

8.8 अभ्यासयोगयुक्तेन चेतसा नान्यगामिना |
परमं पुरुषं दिव्यं याति पार्थानुचिन्तयन् ||

abhyāsayogayuktena cetasā nānyagāminā |
paramaṃ puruṣaṃ divyaṃ yāti pārthānucintayan ||

8.9 कविं पुराणमनुशासितारमणोरणीयांसमनुस्मरेद्य: |
सर्वस्य धातारमचिन्त्यरूपमादित्यवर्णं तमस: परस्तात् ||

kaviṃ purāṇamanuśāsitāraṃ
aṇoraṇīyāṃsamanusmaredyaḥ |
sarvasya dhātāramacintyarūpaṃ
ādityavarṇaṃ tamasaḥ parastāt ||

8.4 manifest is what dies

divine fundamental is the ultimate being me

i am the fundamental yajna in the body
your body arjuna

8.5 she who at the end when
out of body
contemplates me
goes to my state
of being no doubt

8.6 &
what she contemplates
is what she attains

8.7 so
think of me always & fight
offering your mind & thought
to me you'll reach me no doubt

8.8 mind focused by yoga practice
undistracted

contemplates the ultimate being
& makes it there

8.9 she who recalls the firstpoet
governor
who anchors all
subtler than atom
of unimaginable form
suncomplexion
beyond darkness

8.10 प्रयाणकाले मनसाचलेन भक्त्या युक्तो योगबलेन चैव |
भ्रुवोर्मध्ये प्राणमावेश्य सम्यक् स तं परं पुरुषमुपैति दिव्यम् ||

prayāṇakāle manasācalena
bhaktyā yukto yogabalena caiva |
bhruvormadhye prāṇamāveśya
samyak sa taṃ paraṃ puruṣamupaiti divyam ||

8.11 यदक्षरं वेदविदो वदन्ति विशन्ति यद्यतयो वीतरागाः |
यदिच्छन्तो ब्रह्मचर्यं चरन्ति तत्ते पदं संग्रहेण प्रवक्ष्ये ||

yadakṣaraṃ vedavido vadanti
viśanti yadyatayo vītarāgāḥ |
yadicchanto brahmacaryaṃ caranti
tatte padaṃ saṃgraheṇa pravakṣye ||

8.12 सर्वद्वाराणि संयम्य मनो हृदि निरुध्य च |
मूर्ध्न्याधायात्मनः प्राणमास्थितो योगधारणाम् ||

sarvadvārāṇi saṃyamya mano hṛdi nirudhya ca |
mūrdhnyādhāyātmanaḥ prāṇamāsthito yogadhāraṇām ||

8.13 ओमित्येकाक्षरं ब्रह्म व्याहरन्मामनुस्मरन् |
यः प्रयाति त्यजन्देहं स याति परमां गतिम् ||

omityekākṣaraṃ brahma vyāharanmāmanusmaran |
yaḥ prayāti tyajandehaṃ sa yāti paramāṃ gatim ||

8.14 अनन्यचेताः सततं यो मां स्मरति नित्यशः |
तस्याहं सुलभः पार्थ नित्ययुक्तस्य योगिनः ||

ananyacetāḥ satataṃ yo māṃ smarati nityaśaḥ |
tasyāhaṃ sulabhaḥ pārtha nityayuktasya yoginaḥ ||

8.15 मामुपेत्य पुनर्जन्म दुःखालयमशाश्वतम् |
नाप्नुवन्ति महात्मानः संसिद्धिं परमां गताः ||

māmupetya punarjanma duḥkhālayamaśāśvatam |
nāpnuvanti mahātmānaḥ saṃsiddhiṃ paramāṃ gatāḥ ||

8.10 when it's time to move on   mind steady
charged with devotion & yogapower
life energy entering nicely
between the brows
goes to the ultimate being

8.11 i'll give you a quick brief about this path
that the veda-savvy call undying
that passionfree ascetics embark on
that those who want follow celibacy

8.12–8.13 she who
all body-gates under control
(nine, remember)
mind arrested in the heart's intense feeling

life energy at the top of the head
in steady focused yoga
utters the one syllabic om
contemplates me

giving up the body goes
to the ultimate place

8.14 for the ever-yoked yogi
ever remembering me
mind never elsewhere
i'm easy

8.15 great perfected beings
who come to me
don't go to that sad transient place: rebirth

8.16 आब्रह्मभुवनाल्लोकाः पुनरावर्तिनोऽर्जुन |
मामुपेत्य तु कौन्तेय पुनर्जन्म न विद्यते ||

ābrahmabhuvanāllokāḥ punarāvartino'rjuna |
māmupetya tu kaunteya punarjanma na vidyate ||

8.17 सहस्रयुगपर्यन्तमहर्यद्ब्रह्मणो विदुः |
रात्रिं युगसहस्रान्तां तेऽहोरात्रविदो जनाः ||

sahasrayugaparyantamaharyadbrahmaṇo viduḥ |
rātriṃ yugasahasrāntāṃ te'horātravido janāḥ ||

8.18 अव्यक्ताद्व्यक्तयः सर्वाः प्रभवन्त्यहरागमे |
रात्र्यागमे प्रलीयन्ते तत्रैवाव्यक्तसंज्ञके ||

avyaktādvyaktayaḥ sarvāḥ prabhavantyaharāgame |
rātryāgame pralīyante tatraivāvyaktasaṃjñake ||

8.19 भूतग्रामः स एवायं भूत्वा भूत्वा प्रलीयते |
रात्र्यागमेऽवशः पार्थ प्रभवत्यहरागमे ||

bhūtagrāmaḥ sa evāyaṃ bhūtvā bhūtvā pralīyate |
rātryāgame'vaśaḥ pārtha prabhavatyaharāgame ||

8.20 परस्तस्मात्तु भावोऽन्योऽव्यक्तोऽव्यक्तात्सनातनः |
यः स सर्वेषु भूतेषु नश्यत्सु न विनश्यति ||

parastasmāttu bhāvo'nyo'vyakto'vyaktātsanātanaḥ |
yaḥ sa sarveṣu bhūteṣu naśyatsu na vinaśyati ||

8.21 अव्यक्तोऽक्षर इत्युक्तस्तमाहुः परमां गतिम् |
यं प्राप्य न निवर्तन्ते तद्धाम परमं मम ||

avyakto'kṣara ityuktastamāhuḥ paramāṃ gatim |
yaṃ prāpya na nivartante taddhāma paramaṃ mama ||

8.16 there's rebirth in all the created worlds
under brahma (the creator)
but once you reach me there's none

8.17 brahma's day = 1,000 ages
brahma's night = 1,000 ages
(an age = over 4 million earth years)

those who know that
know what day & night really mean

8.18 all the manifest came from an unmanifest
at the start of this day

at the start of this night they'll
dissolve 'unmanifest' again

8.19 these hordes of beings having been again&again
dissolve can't help it
when it's night

& come to be again
when it's day

8.20 but there's another unmanifest
beyond this unmanifest

when all beings
dissolve it doesn't

8.21 called the undying
the ultimate destination

once there
you're not coming back it's my
home

8.22 पुरुषः स परः पार्थ भक्त्या लभ्यस्त्वनन्यया |
यस्यान्तःस्थानि भूतानि येन सर्वमिदं ततम् ||

puruṣaḥ sa paraḥ pārtha bhaktyā labhyastvananyayā |
yasyāntaḥsthāni bhūtāni yena sarvamidaṃ tatam ||

8.23 यत्र काले त्वनावृत्तिमावृत्तिं चैव योगिनः |
प्रयाता यान्ति तं कालं वक्ष्यामि भरतर्षभ ||

yatra kāle tvanāvṛttimāvṛttiṃ caiva yoginaḥ |
prayātā yānti taṃ kālaṃ vakṣyāmi bharatarṣabha ||

8.24 अग्निर्ज्योतिरहः शुक्लः षण्मासा उत्तरायणम् |
तत्र प्रयाता गच्छन्ति ब्रह्म ब्रह्मविदो जनाः ||

agnirjotirahaḥ śuklaḥ ṣaṇmāsā uttarāyaṇam |
tatra prayātā gacchanti brahma brahmavido janāḥ ||

8.25 धूमो रात्रिस्तथा कृष्णः षण्मासा दक्षिणायनम् |
तत्र चान्द्रमसं ज्योतिर्योगी प्राप्य निवर्तते ||

dhūmo rātristathā kṛṣṇaḥ ṣaṇmāsā dakṣiṇāyanam |
tatra cāndramasaṃ jyotiryogī prāpya nivartate ||

8.26 शुक्लकृष्णे गती ह्येते जगतः शाश्वते मते |
एकया यात्यनावृत्तिमन्ययावर्तते पुनः ||

śuklakṛṣṇe gatī hyete jagataḥ śāśvate mate |
ekayā yātyanāvṛttimanyayāvartate punaḥ ||

8.27 नैते सृती पार्थ जानन्योगी मुह्यति कश्चन |
तस्मात्सर्वेषु कालेषु योगयुक्तो भवार्जुन ||

naite sṛtī pārtha jānanyogī muhyati kaścana |
tasmātsarveṣu kāleṣu yogayukto bhavārjuna ||

8.22 this is the ultimate divine being
anchors all beings &
permeates the universe
reached
by devotion no other way

8.23 i'll tell about a
departure time that tells
if a yogi will be
reborn or not

8.24–8.26

when the sun's	when the sun's
in the north	in the south
when it's bright daylight	when it's smoke dark night
when the moon's waxing	when the moon's waning
those who know brahman	the yogi goes to moonlight
go to brahman	& is reborn
no rebirth	
the path of light	the path of darkness

these are considered given

8.27 the yogi knows
isn't confused

always be steady arjuna
in yoga

8.28 वेदेषु यज्ञेषु तपःसु चैव दानेषु यत्पुण्यफलं प्रदिष्टम् |
अत्येति तत्सर्वमिदं विदित्वा योगी परं स्थानमुपैति चाद्यम् ||

vedeṣu yajñeṣu tapaḥsu caiva
dāneṣu yatpuṇyaphalaṃ pradiṣṭam |
atyeti tatsarvamidaṃ viditvā
yogī paraṃ sthānamupaiti cādyam ||

9.1 श्रीभगवानुवाच |
इदं तु ते गुह्यतमं प्रवक्ष्याम्यनसूयवे |
ज्ञानं विज्ञानसहितं यज्ज्ञात्वा मोक्ष्यसेऽशुभात् ||

śrībhagavānuvāca |
idaṃ tu te guhyatamaṃ pravakṣyāmyanasūyave |
jñānaṃ vijñānasahitaṃ yajjñātvā mokṣyase'śubhāt ||

9.2 राजविद्या राजगुह्यं पवित्रमिदमुत्तमम् |
प्रत्यक्षावगमं धर्म्यं सुसुखं कर्तुमव्ययम् ||

rājavidyā rājaguhyaṃ pavitramidamuttamam |
pratyakṣāvagamaṃ dharmyaṃ susukhaṃ kartumavyayam ||

9.3 अश्रद्दधानाः पुरुषा धर्मस्यास्य परंतप |
अप्राप्य मां निवर्तन्ते मृत्युसंसारवर्त्मनि ||

aśraddadhānāḥ puruṣā dharmasyāsya paraṃtapa |
aprāpya māṃ nivartante mṛtyusaṃsāravartmani ||

9.4 मया ततमिदं सर्वं जगदव्यक्तमूर्तिना |
मत्स्थानि सर्वभूतानि न चाहं तेष्ववस्थितः ||

mayā tatamidaṃ sarvaṃ jagadavyaktamūrtinā |
matsthāni sarvabhūtāni na cāhaṃ teṣvavasthitaḥ ||

9.5 न च मत्स्थानि भूतानि पश्य मे योगमैश्वरम् |
भूतभृन्न च भूतस्थो ममात्मा भूतभावनः ||

na ca matsthāni bhūtāni paśya me yogamaiśvaram |
bhūtabhṛnna ca bhūtastho mamātmā bhūtabhāvanaḥ ||

8.28 knowing all this
the yogi goes beyond

the (limited) uses of
vedas yajnas penances
charity

goes to the ultimate
the original place

9.1–9.2 you're uncynical so
i'll tell you

a knowledge + understanding

a top secret high science pure best
evident easy irreducible

a law (spiritual)
to release you from error

9.3 those who have no faith in this
don't make it to me

they're reborn
to death the way of the world

9.4–9.5 my unmanifest
permeates the universe

all beings are anchored on me not i on them
& yet not in me i am
their cause
sustenance
independent
see my awesome power!

9.6 यथाकाशस्थितो नित्यं वायुः सर्वत्रगो महान् |
तथा सर्वाणि भूतानि मत्स्थानीत्युपधारय ||

yathākāśasthito nityaṃ vāyuḥ sarvatrago mahān |
tathā sarvāṇi bhūtāni matsthānītyupadhāraya ||

9.7 सर्वभूतानि कौन्तेय प्रकृतिं यान्ति मामिकाम् |
कल्पक्षये पुनस्तानि कल्पादौ विसृजाम्यहम् ||

sarvabhūtāni kaunteya prakṛtiṃ yānti māmikām |
kalpakṣaye punastāni kalpādau visṛjāmyaham ||

9.8 प्रकृतिं स्वामवष्टभ्य विसृजामि पुनः पुनः |
भूतग्राममिमं कृत्स्नमवशं प्रकृतेर्वशात् ||

prakṛtiṃ svāmavaṣṭabhya visṛjāmi punaḥ punaḥ |
bhūtagrāmamimaṃ kṛtsnamavaśaṃ prakṛtervaśāt ||

9.9 न च मां तानि कर्माणि निबध्नन्ति धनंजय |
उदासीनवदासीनमसक्तं तेषु कर्मसु ||

na ca māṃ tāni karmāṇi nibadhnanti dhanaṃjaya |
udāsīnavadāsīnamasaktaṃ teṣu karmasu ||

9.10 मयाध्यक्षेण प्रकृतिः सूयते सचराचरम् |
हेतुनानेन कौन्तेय जगद्विपरिवर्तते ||

mayādhyakṣeṇa prakṛtiḥ sūyate sacarācaram |
hetunānena kaunteya jagadviparivartate ||

9.6 as wind vast blows everywhere but
always fixed
to the sky

on me
all beings rely

imagine!

9.7–9.8 at the end of the day a brahma day
all beings go back into my matter

at the beginning of a new day
i turn to nature my material

& come up again&again
with these hordes of beings automatic
shaped by
nature

9.9 nor do these activities
tie me down

coolly detached i sit

9.10 i keep an eye over
matternature who conceives
animate inanimate
that's how the universe turns

9.11 अवजानन्ति मां मूढा मानुषीं तनुमाश्रितम् |
परं भावमजानन्तो मम भूतमहेश्वरम् ||

avajānanti māṃ mūḍhā mānuṣīṃ tanumāśritam |
paraṃ bhāvamajānanto mama bhūtamaheśvaram ||

9.12 मोघाशा मोघकर्माणो मोघज्ञाना विचेतसः |
राक्षसीमासुरीं चैव प्रकृतिं मोहिनीं श्रिताः ||

moghāśā moghakarmāṇo moghajñānā vicetasaḥ |
rākṣasīmāsurīṃ caiva prakṛtiṃ mohinīṃ śritāḥ ||

9.13 महात्मानस्तु मां पार्थ दैवीं प्रकृतिमाश्रिताः |
भजन्त्यनन्यमनसो ज्ञात्वा भूतादिमव्ययम् ||

mahātmānastu māṃ pārtha daivīṃ prakṛtimāśritāḥ |
bhajantyananyamanaso jñātvā bhūtādimavyayam ||

9.14 सततं कीर्तयन्तो मां यतन्तश्च दृढव्रताः |
नमस्यन्तश्च मां भक्त्या नित्ययुक्ता उपासते ||

satataṃ kīrtayanto māṃ yatantaśca dṛḍhavratāḥ |
namasyantaśca māṃ bhaktyā nityayuktā upāsate ||

9.15 ज्ञानयज्ञेन चाप्यन्ये यजन्तो मामुपासते |
एकत्वेन पृथक्त्वेन बहुधा विश्वतोमुखम् ||

jñānayajñena cāpyanye yajanto māmupāsate |
ekatvena pṛthaktvena bahudhā viśvatomukham ||

9.11–9.12 fools give no cred

↓ to my human form

thoughtless   not knowing my
hopeless   true state
activities pointless   mighty god
knowledge useless   of all beings
demonic

it's their nature to be fooled

9.13–9.14 great beings
live in divine nature

undistracted   they know me   the everlasting one
they serve me   as the origin of beings
always
sing my praises
greet me
adore me   with devotion

always reined in
with firm vows they keep trying

9.15 & others
by the yajna of knowledge

worship me   who knows all
as one
as many

9.16 अहं क्रतुरहं यज्ञः स्वधाहमहमौषधम् |
मन्त्रोऽहमहमेवाज्यमहमग्निरहं हुतम् ||

ahaṃ kraturahaṃ yajñaḥ svadhāhamahamauṣadham |
mantro'hamahamevājyamahamagniraham hutam ||

9.17 पिताहमस्य जगतो माता धाता पितामहः |
वेद्यं पवित्रमोङ्कार ऋक्साम यजुरेव च ||

pitāhamasya jagato mātā dhātā pitāmahaḥ |
vedyaṃ pavitramoṃkāra ṛksāma yajureva ca ||

9.18 गतिर्भर्ता प्रभुः साक्षी निवासः शरणं सुहृत् |
प्रभवः प्रलयः स्थानं निधानं बीजमव्ययम् ||

gatirbhartā prabhuḥ sākṣī nivāsaḥ śaraṇaṃ suhṛt |
prabhavaḥ pralayaḥ sthānaṃ nidhānaṃ bījamavyayam ||

9.19 तपाम्यहमहं वर्षं निगृह्णाम्युत्सृजामि च |
अमृतं चैव मृत्युश्च सदसच्चाहमर्जुन ||

tapāmyahamahaṃ varṣaṃ nigṛhṇāmyutsṛjāmi ca |
amṛtaṃ caiva mṛtyuśca sadasaccāhamarjuna ||

9.20 त्रैविद्या मां सोमपाः पूतपापा यज्ञैरिष्ट्वा स्वर्गतिं प्रार्थयन्ते |
ते पुण्यमासाद्य सुरेन्द्रलोकम् अश्नन्ति दिव्यान्दिवि देवभोगान् ||

traividyā māṃ somapāḥ pūtapāpā
yajñairiṣṭvā svargatiṃ prārthayante |
te puṇyamāsādya surendralokaṃ
aśnanti divyāndivi devabhogān ||

9.21 ते तं भुक्त्वा स्वर्गलोकं विशालं क्षीणे पुण्ये मर्त्यलोकं विशन्ति |
एवं त्रयीधर्ममनुप्रपन्ना गतागतं कामकामा लभन्ते ||

te taṃ bhuktvā svargalokaṃ viśālaṃ
kṣīṇe puṇye martyalokaṃ viśanti |
evaṃ trayīdharmamanuprapannā
gatāgataṃ kāmakāmā labhante ||

9.16–9.19 I the yajna fire chant ritual offertory butter herb oblation

father of the universe mother founder grandpa pure om
three vedas to be known

destination carrier witness resthouse divinity refuge
friend origin end maintenance treasury seed
everlasting

i heat rain refrain exude am death immortality
i am & i am not

9.20–9.21 those who
know three vedas
drink nectar
adore me &
errors purified
by yajna they seek
heaven destination

to the world of the gods they go   heaven
enjoy joys divine

then
running out of credit they
return to the world of mortals

it's the law of the vedas
followed

back & forth
wanting & getting

9.22 अनन्याश्चिन्तयन्तो मां ये जनाः पर्युपासते |
तेषां नित्याभियुक्तानां योगक्षेमं वहाम्यहम् ||

ananyāścintayanto māṃ ye janāḥ paryupāsate |
teṣāṃ nityābhiyuktānāṃ yogakṣemaṃ vahāmyaham ||

9.23 येऽप्यन्यदेवता भक्ता यजन्ते श्रद्धयान्विताः |
तेऽपि मामेव कौन्तेय यजन्त्यविधिपूर्वकम् ||

ye'pyanyadevatā bhaktā yajante śraddhayānvitāḥ |
te'pi māmeva kaunteya yajantyavidhipūrvakam ||

9.24 अहं हि सर्वयज्ञानां भोक्ता च प्रभुरेव च |
न तु मामभिजानन्ति तत्त्वेनातश्च्यवन्ति ते ||

ahaṃ hi sarvayajñānāṃ bhoktā ca prabhureva ca |
na tu māmabhijānanti tattvenātaścyavanti te ||

9.25 यान्ति देवव्रता देवान्पितॄन्यान्ति पितृव्रताः |
भूतानि यान्ति भूतेज्या यान्ति मद्याजिनोऽपि माम् ||

yānti devavratā devānpitṛnyānti pitṛvratāḥ |
bhūtāni yānti bhūtejyā yānti madyājino'pi mām ||

9.26 पत्रं पुष्पं फलं तोयं यो मे भक्त्या प्रयच्छति |
तदहं भक्त्युपहृतमश्नामि प्रयतात्मनः ||

patraṃ puṣpaṃ phalaṃ toyaṃ yo me bhaktyā prayacchati |
tadahaṃ bhaktyupahṛtamaśnāmi prayatātmanaḥ ||

9.22 but for those who think of me   no other
who worship me
& for the disciplined among them

i personally
bring them what they don't have
preserve what they do

9.23 even those who adore other deities
with dedication devotion
        although on a tangent
really adore me

9.24 it is i who relish   eat at
all yajnas

they don't recognize me   truly
so they fail   they

9.25 who honour deities go to deities
who honour ancestors go to ancestors
who honour spirits go to spirits
who honour me come to me

9.26 she who offers
steady devotion
        a flower
        a fruit
        some water
        a leaf (a page!)
pure love
        i eat

9.27 यत्करोषि यदश्नासि यज्जुहोषि ददासि यत् |
यत्तपस्यसि कौन्तेय तत्कुरुष्व मदर्पणम् ||

yatkaroṣi yadaśnāsi yajjuhoṣi dadāsi yat |
yattapasyasi kaunteya tatkuruṣva madarpaṇam ||

9.28 शुभाशुभफलैरेवं मोक्ष्यसे कर्मबन्धनैः |
संन्यासयोगयुक्तात्मा विमुक्तो मामुपैष्यसि ||

śubhāśubhaphalairevaṃ mokṣyase karmabandhanaiḥ |
saṃnyāsayogayuktātmā vimukto māmupaiṣyasi ||

9.29 समोऽहं सर्वभूतेषु न मे द्वेष्योऽस्ति न प्रियः |
ये भजन्ति तु मां भक्त्या मयि ते तेषु चाप्यहम् ||

samo'haṃ sarvabhūteṣu na me dveṣyo'sti na priyaḥ |
ye bhajanti tu māṃ bhaktyā mayi te teṣu cāpyaham ||

9.30 अपिचेत्सुदुराचारो भजते मामनन्यभाक् |
साधुरेव स मन्तव्यः सम्यग्व्यवसितो हि सः ||

apicetsudurācāro bhajate māmananyabhāk |
sādhureva sa mantavyaḥ samyagvyavasito hi saḥ ||

9.31 क्षिप्रं भवति धर्मात्मा शश्वच्छान्तिं निगच्छति |
कौन्तेय प्रतिजानीहि न मे भक्तः प्रणश्यति ||

kṣipraṃ bhavati dharmātmā śaśvacchāntiṃ nigacchati |
kaunteya pratijānīhi na me bhaktaḥ praṇaśyati ||

9.27 whatever you do   give   eat   offer
whatever your austerity

offer it to me

9.28 be disciplined
renounce

you'll be freed
from good & bad   fruits of actions
& come to me

9.29 i'm the same to all
no favourites / hatreds
but (it's just that)

those who worship
me with devotion

they are in me
i am in them

9.30–9.31 oh even the bad   if she worships me & no other
is considered   good   well done
for she
soon becomes good
& peaceful

know this!
not a single one
of my devotees
is lost

9.32 मां हि पार्थ व्यपाश्रित्य येऽपि स्युः पापयोनयः |
स्त्रियो वैश्यास्तथा शूद्रास्तेऽपि यान्ति परां गतिम् ||

māṃ hi pārtha vyapāśritya ye'pi syuḥ pāpayonayaḥ |
striyo vaiśyāstathā śūdrāste'pi yānti parāṃ gatim ||

9.33 किं पुनर्ब्राह्मणाः पुण्या भक्ता राजर्षयस्तथा |
अनित्यमसुखं लोकमिमं प्राप्य भजस्व माम् ||

kiṃ punarbrāhmaṇāḥ puṇyā bhaktā rājarṣayastathā |
anityamasukhaṃ lokamimaṃ prāpya bhajasva mām ||

9.34 मन्मना भव मद्भक्तो मद्याजी मां नमस्कुरु |
मामेवैष्यसि युक्त्वैवमात्मानं मत्परायणः ||

manmanā bhava madbhakto madyājī māṃ namaskuru |
māmevaiṣyasi yuktvaivamātmānaṃ matparāyaṇaḥ ||

10.1 श्रीभगवानुवाच |
भूय एव महाबाहो शृणु मे परमं वचः |
यत्तेऽहं प्रीयमाणाय वक्ष्यामि हितकाम्यया ||

śrībhagavānuvāca |
bhūya eva mahābāho śṛṇu me paramaṃ vacaḥ |
yatte'haṃ prīyamāṇāya vakṣyāmi hitakāmyayā ||

10.2 न मे विदुः सुरगणाः प्रभवं न महर्षयः |
अहमादिर्हि देवानां महर्षीणां च सर्वशः ||

na me viduḥ suragaṇāḥ prabhavaṃ na maharṣayaḥ |
ahamādirhi devānāṃ maharṣīṇāṃ ca sarvaśaḥ ||

9.32–9.34 all women
vaishyas
shudras
people born to lawless mothers
who rely on me
reach the ultimate destination

compare how easy then
for a pure brahmin
or devoted sage

it's a sad transient world
put your mind on me adore me worship me

tuned up you'll
come to me
your goal

10.1 my dear arjuna
i want your welfare so

again listen i'll say
the last word on this

10.2 even sages & deities
have no clue don't know my
i am their   origin

10.3 यो मामजमनादिं च वेत्ति लोकमहेश्वरम् |
असम्मूढः स मर्त्येषु सर्वपापैः प्रमुच्यते ||

yo māmajamanādiṃ ca vetti lokamaheśvaram |
asaṃmūḍhaḥ sa martyeṣu sarvapāpaiḥ pramucyate ||

10.4 बुद्धिर्ज्ञानमसम्मोहः क्षमा सत्यं दमः शमः |
सुखं दुःखं भवोऽभवो भयं चाभयमेव च ||

buddhirjñānamasaṃmohaḥ kṣamā satyaṃ damaḥ śamaḥ |
sukhaṃ duḥkhaṃ bhavo'bhavo bhayaṃ cābhayameva ca ||

10.5 अहिंसा समता तुष्टिस्तपो दानं यशोऽयशः |
भवन्ति भावा भूतानां मत्त एव पृथग्विधाः ||

ahiṃsā samatā tuṣṭistapo dānaṃ yaśo'yaśaḥ |
bhavanti bhāvā bhūtānāṃ matta eva pṛthagvidhāḥ ||

10.6 महर्षयः सप्त पूर्वे चत्वारो मनवस्तथा |
मद्भावा मानसा जाता येषां लोक इमाः प्रजाः ||

maharṣayaḥ sapta pūrve catvāro manavastathā |
madbhāvā mānasā jātā yeṣāṃ loka imāḥ prajāḥ ||

10.7 एतां विभूतिं योगं च मम यो वेत्ति तत्त्वतः |
सोऽविकम्पेन योगेन युज्यते नात्र संशयः ||

etāṃ vibhūtiṃ yogaṃ ca mama yo vetti tattvataḥ |
so'vikampena yogena yujyate nātra saṃśayaḥ ||

10.8 अहं सर्वस्य प्रभवो मत्तः सर्वं प्रवर्तते |
इति मत्वा भजन्ते मां बुधा भावसमन्विताः ||

ahaṃ sarvasya prabhavo mattaḥ sarvaṃ pravartate |
iti matvā bhajante māṃ budhā bhāvasamanvitāḥ ||

10.3 originless
birthless
i
mighty deity   of the world

among mortals
she who knows this is
unconfused
freed from all
errors

10.4–10.5 intelligence / wisdom / clarity / endurance / self restraint / happiness / sadness / equanimity / contentment / truth / peace / nonviolence / austerity / charity / fear / fearlessness / fame / notoriety /
/ be ing / unbe ing /
all   beings'
these states of being
are my many ways

10.6 the seven sages from way back
the four manus   from whom these beings
of this world came to be
came from my mind

10.7 she who knows this truth
my manifestation   achievement
is attuned
via steady yoga   no doubt

10.8 full of feeling   i am the origin of
the intelligent   everything
worship me so   proceeds from me

10.9 मच्चित्ता मद्गतप्राणा बोधयन्तः परस्परम् |
कथयन्तश्च मां नित्यं तुष्यन्ति च रमन्ति च ||

maccittā madgataprāṇā bodhayantaḥ parasparam |
kathayantaśca māṃ nityaṃ tuṣyanti ca ramanti ca ||

10.10 तेषां सततयुक्तानां भजतां प्रीतिपूर्वकम् |
ददामि बुद्धियोगं तं येन मामुपयान्ति ते ||

teṣāṃ satatayuktānāṃ bhajatāṃ prītipūrvakam |
dadāmi buddhiyogaṃ taṃ yena māmupayānti te ||

10.11 तेषामेवानुकम्पार्थमहमज्ञानजं तमः |
नाशयाम्यात्मभावस्थो ज्ञानदीपेन भास्वता ||

teṣāmevānukampārthamahamajñānajaṃ tamaḥ |
nāśayāmyātmabhāvastho jñānadīpena bhāsvatā ||

10.9 with me on their mind
life energy focused on me
enjoying   being content

chatting about me
enlightening each other   about me

10.10 & those who   among them
always disciplined
worship me   with love

i give them the intelligence
they use
to come to me

10.11 i   empathizing with them
from within them
remove the darkness   that comes from ignorance
with the lamp of knowledge

10.12 अर्जुन उवाच |
परं ब्रह्म परं धाम पवित्रं परमं भवान् |
पुरुषं शाश्वतं दिव्यमादिदेवमजं विभुम् ||

arjuna uvāca |
paraṃ brahma paraṃ dhāma pavitraṃ paramaṃ bhavān |
puruṣaṃ śāśvataṃ divyamādidevamajaṃ vibhum ||

10.13 आहुस्त्वामृषय: सर्वे देवर्षिर्नारदस्तथा |
असितो देवलो व्यास: स्वयं चैव ब्रवीषि मे ||

āhustvāmṛṣayaḥ sarve devarṣirnāradastathā |
asito devalo vyāsaḥ svayaṃ caiva bravīṣi me ||

10.14 सर्वमेतदृतं मन्ये यन्मां वदसि केशव |
न हि ते भगवन्व्यक्तिं विदुर्देवा न दानवा: ||

sarvametadṛtaṃ manye yanmāṃ vadasi keśava |
na hi te bhagavanvyaktiṃ vidurdevā na dānavāḥ ||

10.15 स्वयमेवात्मनात्मानं वेत्थ त्वं पुरुषोत्तम |
भूतभावन भूतेश देवदेव जगत्पते ||

svayamevātmanātmānaṃ vettha tvaṃ puruṣottama |
bhūtabhāvana bhūteśa devadeva jagatpate ||

10.16 वक्तुमर्हस्यशेषेण दिव्या ह्यात्मविभूतय: |
याभिर्विभूतिभिर्लोकानिमांस्त्वं व्याप्य तिष्ठसि ||

vaktumarhasyaśeṣeṇa divyā hyātmavibhūtayaḥ |
yābhirvibhūtibhirlokānimāṃstvaṃ vyāpya tiṣṭhasi ||

10.17 कथं विद्यामहं योगिंस्त्वां सदा परिचिन्तयन् |
केषु केषु च भावेषु चिन्त्योऽसि भगवन्मया ||

kathaṃ vidyāmahaṃ yogiṃstvāṃ sadā paricintayan |
keṣu keṣu ca bhāveṣu cintyo'si bhagavanmayā ||

10.18 विस्तरेणात्मनो योगं विभूतिं च जनार्दन |
भूय: कथय तृप्तिर्हि शृण्वतो नास्ति मेऽमृतम् ||

vistareṇātmano yogaṃ vibhūtiṃ ca janārdana |
bhūyaḥ kathaya tṛptirhi śṛṇvato nāsti me'mṛtam ||

10.12–10.18

arjuna:

O'

uber brahman final destination utter purity eternal divine person original deity birthless omnipresent

that's what they say all the sages divine
sage narada & asita devala vyasa & you say so yourself

i believe
it is
all true

what you say krishna for sure neither the deities nor the demons know your manifestation
you're your own evidence

best man source of everyone's welfare deity of all beings deity of deities master of the universe

you've got to reveal your divine your manifestations how do you do it permeating the worlds and yet located in it

how can i know you o' yogi o' krishna by thinking of you constantly (i suppose but) in what states how o' god how
am i to imagine you

tell me more about yourself your power & manifestation speak again your words are nectar i haven't had enough

10.19 श्रीभगवानुवाच |
हन्त ते कथयिष्यामि दिव्या ह्यात्मविभूतयः |
प्राधान्यतः कुरुश्रेष्ठ नास्त्यन्तो विस्तरस्य मे ||

śrībhagavānuvāca |
hanta te kathayiṣyāmi divyā hyātmavibhūtayaḥ |
prādhānyataḥ kuruśreṣṭha nāstyanto vistarasya me ||

10.20 अहमात्मा गुडाकेश सर्वभूताशयस्थितः |
अहमादिश्च मध्यं च भूतानामन्त एव च ||

ahamātmā guḍākeśa sarvabhūtāśayasthitaḥ |
ahamādiśca madhyaṃ ca bhūtānāmanta eva ca ||

10.21 आदित्यानामहं विष्णुर्ज्योतिषां रविरंशुमान् |
मरीचिर्मरुतामस्मि नक्षत्राणामहं शशी ||

ādityānāmahaṃ viṣṇurjyotiṣāṃ raviraṃśumān |
marīcirmarutāmasmi nakṣatrāṇāmahaṃ śaśī ||

10.22 वेदानां सामवेदोऽस्मि देवानामस्मि वासवः |
इन्द्रियाणां मनश्चास्मि भूतानामस्मि चेतना ||

vedānāṃ sāmavedo'smi devānāmasmi vāsavaḥ |
indriyāṇāṃ manaścāsmi bhūtānāmasmi cetanā ||

10.23 रुद्राणां शङ्करश्चास्मि वित्तेशो यक्षरक्षसाम् |
वसूनां पावकश्चास्मि मेरुः शिखरिणामहम् ||

rudrāṇāṃ śaṅkaraścāsmi vitteśo yakṣarakṣasām |
vasūnāṃ pāvakaścāsmi meruḥ śikhariṇāmaham ||

10.24 पुरोधसां च मुख्यं मां विद्धि पार्थ बृहस्पतिम् |
सेनानीनामहं स्कन्दः सरसामस्मि सागरः ||

purodhasāṃ ca mukhyaṃ māṃ viddhi pārtha bṛhaspatim |
senānīnāmahaṃ skandaḥ sarasāmasmi sāgaraḥ ||

10.25 महर्षीणां भृगुरहं गिरामस्म्येकमक्षरम् |
यज्ञानां जपयज्ञोऽस्मि स्थावराणां हिमालयः ||

maharṣīṇāṃ bhṛgurahaṃ girāmasmyekamakṣaram |
yajñānāṃ japayajño'smi sthāvarāṇāṃ himālayaḥ ||

10.19 krishna:

on with it then   i'll tell you
my divine manifestations
but only the main ones for arjuna
there's no end to my spread

10.20 I AM the YOU
in the heart of all beings
i am the beginning i am the middle & the end i am

10.21–10.32 vishnu among adityas
sun among lights
marichi among maruts
moon among the night constellations
sama veda among vedas
vasava among deities
mind among senses
awareness among beings
shiva among rudras
kubera among yakshas & rakshasas
pavaka among the vasus
meru among mountains
head priest
priest of the deities
skanda among army chiefs
ocean among water bodies
brighu among sages
om among sounds
chant among yajnas
among the immovable the himalayas
holy fig among the trees
narada among divine sages
chitraratha among gandharvas
kapila among achiever yogis

10.26 अश्वत्थ: सर्ववृक्षाणां देवर्षीणां च नारदः |
गन्धर्वाणां चित्ररथ: सिद्धानां कपिलो मुनि: ||

aśvatthaḥ sarvavṛkṣāṇāṃ devarṣīṇāṃ ca nāradaḥ |
gandharvāṇāṃ citrarathaḥ siddhānāṃ kapilo muniḥ ||

10.27 उच्चै:श्रवसमश्वानां विद्धि माममृतोद्भवम् |
ऐरावतं गजेन्द्राणां नराणां च नराधिपम् ||

uccaiḥśravasamaśvānāṃ viddhi māmamṛtodbhavam |
airāvataṃ gajendrāṇāṃ narāṇāṃ ca narādhipam ||

10.28 आयुधानामहं वज्रं धेनूनामस्मि कामधुक् |
प्रजनश्चास्मि कन्दर्प: सर्पाणामस्मि वासुकि: ||

āyudhānāmahaṃ vajraṃ dhenūnāmasmi kāmadhuk |
prajanaścāsmi kandarpaḥ sarpāṇāmasmi vāsukiḥ ||

10.29 अनन्तश्चास्मि नागानां वरुणो यादसामहम् |
पितृणामर्यमा चास्मि यम: संयमतामहम् ||

anantaścāsmi nāgānāṃ varuṇo yādasāmaham |
pitṛṇāmaryamā cāsmi yamaḥ saṃyamatāmaham ||

10.30 प्रह्लादश्चास्मि दैत्यानां काल: कलयतामहम् |
मृगाणां च मृगेन्द्रोऽहं वैनतेयश्च पक्षिणाम् ||

prahlādaścāsmi daityānāṃ kālaḥ kalayatāmaham |
mṛgāṇāṃ ca mṛgendro'haṃ vainateyaśca pakṣiṇām ||

10.31 पवन: पवतामस्मि राम: शस्त्रभृतामहम् |
झषाणां मकरश्चास्मि स्रोतसामस्मि जाह्नवी ||

pavanaḥ pavatāmasmi rāmaḥ śastrabhṛtāmaham |
jhaṣāṇāṃ makaraścāsmi srotasāmasmi jāhnavī ||

10.32 सर्गाणामादिरन्तश्च मध्यं चैवाहमर्जुन |
अध्यात्मविद्या विद्यानां वाद: प्रवदतामहम् ||

sargāṇāmādirantaśca madhyaṃ caivāhamarjuna |
adhyātmavidyā vidyānāṃ vādaḥ pravadatāmaham ||

born from nectar (in oceanchurn)
ucchaishravas among horses
airavat among king elephants
king among people
thunderbolt among weapons
wish-fulfilling cow among cows
kandarpa the begetter
vasuki among serpents
ananta among the naga snakes
varuna among water beings
aryaman among ancestors
death among controllers
prahlada among daityas
time among calculators
king of beasts among beasts
vainateya among birds
wind among purifiers
rama among weapon wielders
makara among sea ferocities
ganga among rivers

i am
the beginning   the middle   & the end
of creations

the logic among debaters
knowledge among knowledges: self knowledge

10.33 अक्षराणामकारोऽस्मि द्वन्द्वः सामासिकस्य च |
अहमेवाक्षयः कालो धाताहं विश्वतोमुखः ||

akṣarāṇāmakāro'smi dvandvaḥ sāmāsikasya ca |
ahamevākṣayaḥ kālo dhātāhaṃ viśvatomukhaḥ ||

10.34 मृत्युः सर्वहरश्चाहमुद्भवश्च भविष्यताम् |
कीर्तिः श्रीर्वाक्च नारीणां स्मृतिर्मेधा धृतिः क्षमा ||

mṛtyuḥ sarvaharaścāhamudbhavaśca bhaviṣyatām |
kīrtiḥ śrīrvākca nārīṇāṃ smṛtirmedhā dhṛtiḥ kṣamā ||

10.35 बृहत्साम तथा साम्नां गायत्री छन्दसामहम् |
मासानां मार्गशीर्षोऽहमृतूनां कुसुमाकरः ||

bṛhatsāma tathā sāmnāṃ gāyatrī chandasāmaham |
māsānāṃ mārgaśīrṣo'hamṛtūnāṃ kusumākaraḥ ||

10.36 द्यूतं छलयतामस्मि तेजस्तेजस्विनामहम् |
जयोऽस्मि व्यवसायोऽस्मि सत्त्वं सत्त्ववतामहम् ||

dyutaṃ chalayatāmasmi tejastejasvināmaham |
jayo'smi vyavasāyo'smi sattvaṃ sattvavatāmaham ||

10.37 वृष्णीनां वासुदेवोऽस्मि पाण्डवानां धनंजयः |
मुनीनामप्यहं व्यासः कवीनामुशना कविः ||

vṛṣṇīnāṃ vāsudevo'smi pāṇḍavānāṃ dhanaṃjayaḥ |
munīnāmapyahaṃ vyāsaḥ kavīnāmuśanā kaviḥ ||

10.38 दण्डो दमयतामस्मि नीतिरस्मि जिगीषताम् |
मौनं चैवास्मि गुह्यानां ज्ञानं ज्ञानवतामहम् ||

daṇḍo damayatāmasmi nītirasmi jigīṣatām |
maunaṃ caivāsmi guhyānāṃ jñānaṃ jñānavatāmaham ||

10.33–10.38 ‘A’ among alphabets
combination in compound words

only i
am infinite time
creator omniscient
i am death   all-destructive
source of what will be
among femininities:
fame speech beauty
wisdom endurance memory
& constancy

brihatsama among sama chants
gayatri among metres
(cool) november among months
flowery spring among seasons
gambling of the dishonest
radiance of the radiant
victory
effort
good’s goodness
vasudeva among vrishnis

& i am you arjuna among pandavas

among sages vyasa
among poets ushanas
clout of rulers
advice for those who want to win
silence among secrets
knowledge of the knowledgeable

10.39 यच्चापि सर्वभूतानां बीजं तदहमर्जुन |
न तदस्ति विना यत्स्यान्मया भूतं चराचरम् ||

yaccāpi sarvabhūtānāṃ bījaṃ tadahamarjuna |
na tadasti vinā yatsyānmayā bhūtaṃ carācaram ||

10.40 नान्तोऽस्ति मम दिव्यानां विभूतीनां परंतप |
एष तूद्देशत: प्रोक्तो विभूतेर्विस्तरो मया ||

nānto'sti mama divyānāṃ vibhūtīnāṃ paraṃtapa |
eṣa tūddeśataḥ prokto vibhūtervistaro mayā ||

10.41 यद्यद्विभूतिमत्सत्त्वं श्रीमदूर्जितमेव वा |
तत्तदेवावगच्छ त्वं मम तेजोंऽशसंभवम् ||

yadyadvibhūtimatsattvaṃ śrīmadūrjitameva vā |
tattadevāvagaccha tvaṃ mama tejoṃ'śasaṃbhavam ||

10.42 अथवा बहुनैतेन किं ज्ञातेन तवार्जुन |
विष्टभ्याहमिदं कृत्स्नमेकांशेन स्थितो जगत् ||

athavā bahunaitena kiṃ jñātena tavārjuna |
viṣṭabhyāhamidaṃ kṛtsnamekāṃśena sthito jagat ||

10.39 i am the seed of all beings
animate inanimate
without me nothing could be

10.40 there's no end
to my manifestations
divinity

all these examples
extent
of my manifestations

10.41 in every instance
whatever's powerful glorious lively
is a part of my glory

10.42 but what's the point of
so much knowledge arjuna

i support the universe
with so little of my self

11.1 अर्जुन उवाच |
मदनुग्रहाय परमं गुह्यमध्यात्मसंज्ञितम् |
यत्त्वयोक्तं वचस्तेन मोहोऽयं विगतो मम ||

arjuna uvāca |
madanugrahāya paramaṃ guhyamadhyātmasaṃjñitam |
yattvayoktaṃ vacastena moho'yaṃ vigato mama ||

11.2 भवाप्ययौ हि भूतानां श्रुतौ विस्तरशो मया |
त्वत्तः कमलपत्राक्ष माहात्म्यमपि चाव्ययम् ||

bhavāpyayau hi bhūtānāṃ śrutau vistaraśo mayā |
tvattaḥ kamalapatrākṣa māhātmyamapi cāvyayam ||

11.3 एवमेतद्यथात्थ त्वमात्मानं परमेश्वर |
द्रष्टुमिच्छामि ते रूपमैश्वरं पुरुषोत्तम ||

evametadyathāttha tvamātmānaṃ parameśvara |
draṣṭumicchāmi te rūpamaiśvaraṃ puruṣottama ||

11.4 मन्यसे यदि तच्छक्यं मया द्रष्टुमिति प्रभो |
योगेश्वर ततो मे त्वं दर्शयात्मानमव्ययम् ||

manyase yadi tacchakyaṃ mayā draṣṭumiti prabho |
yogeśvara tato me tvaṃ darśayātmānamavyayam ||

11.5 श्रीभगवानुवाच |
पश्य मे पार्थ रूपाणि शतशोऽथ सहस्रशः |
नानाविधानि दिव्यानि नानावर्णाकृतीनि च ||

śrībhagavānuvāca |
paśya me pārtha rūpāṇi śataśo'tha sahasraśaḥ |
nānāvidhāni divyāni nānāvarṇākṛtīni ca ||

11.6 पश्यादित्यान्वसून्रुद्रानश्विनौ मरुतस्तथा |
बहून्यदृष्टपूर्वाणि पश्याश्चर्याणि भारत ||

paśyādityānvasūnrudrānaśvinau marutastathā |
bahūnyadṛṣṭapūrvāṇi paśyāścaryāṇi bhārata ||

11.1 arjuna:

my confusion's gone
you've kindly
told me the secret
spiritual

11.2 i heard in detail from you krishna
irreducible awesomeness
how beings come to be
and unbe

11.3 so this what you describe krishna
i'd like to see

your divine form

11.4 if you believe i can (withstand it)
krishna please
show me
your infinite

11.5 krishna:

see my divine forms arjuna
hundreds or rather thousands

all sorts of
colours & shapes

11.6 see

the (celestials) vasus adityas
maruts rudras & ashvins

how many
wow never seen before

11.7 इहैकस्थं जगत्कृत्स्नं पश्याद्य सचराचरम् |
मम देहे गुडाकेश यच्चान्यद्द्रष्टुमिच्छसि ||

ihaikasthaṃ jagatkṛtsnaṃ paśyādya sacarācaram |
mama dehe guḍākeśa yaccānyaddraṣṭumicchasi ||

11.8 न तु मां शक्यसे द्रष्टुमनेनैव स्वचक्षुषा |
दिव्यं ददामि ते चक्षुः पश्य मे योगमैश्वरम् ||

na tu māṃ śakyase draṣṭumanenaiva svacakṣuṣā |
divyaṃ dadāmi te cakṣuḥ paśya me yogamaiśvaram ||

11.9 संजय उवाच |
एवमुक्त्वा ततो राजन्महायोगेश्वरो हरिः |
दर्शयामास पार्थाय परमं रूपमैश्वरम् ||

saṃjaya uvāca |
evamuktvā tato rājanmahāyogeśvaro hariḥ |
darśayāmāsa pārthāya paramaṃ rūpamaiśvaram ||

11.10 अनेकवक्त्रनयनमनेकाद्भुतदर्शनम् |
अनेकदिव्याभरणं दिव्यानेकोद्यतायुधम् ||

anekavaktranayanamanekādbhutadarśanam |
anekadivyābharaṇaṃ divyānekodyatāyudham ||

11.11 दिव्यमाल्याम्बरधरं दिव्यगन्धानुलेपनम् |
सर्वाश्चर्यमयं देवमनन्तं विश्वतोमुखम् ||

divyamālyāmbaradharaṃ divyagandhānulepanam |
sarvāścaryamayaṃ devamanantaṃ viśvatomukham ||

11.12 दिवि सूर्यसहस्रस्य भवेद्युगपदुत्थिता |
यदि भाः सदृशी सा स्याद्भासस्तस्य महात्मनः ||

divi sūryasahasrasya bhavedyugapadutthitā |
yadi bhāḥ sadṛśī sā syādbhāsastasya mahātmanaḥ ||

11.7 here arjuna
see now with me

the entire universe
in my body

animate inanimate
& whatever else you want to see

11.8 oh you're unable
to see me with your eyes

ok i give you
a divine eye
now see
my divine power

11.9 sanjaya (to dhritarashtra):
& then vishnu the powerful (krishna)
showed his ultimate divine form to arjuna

11.10 myriad mouths eyes
divine jewellery
raised weaponry
what a sight

11.11 in divine garlands & clothes
perfumes & balms
infinite
omniscient   facing all directions
at once ah   all wondrous

11.12 if   all of a sudden   a thousand suns rise
together in the sky
imagine that
that   the brilliance of this awesome one

11.13 तत्रैकस्थं जगत्कृत्स्नं प्रविभक्तमनेकधा |
अपश्यद्देवदेवस्य शरीरे पाण्डवस्तदा ||

tatraikastham̩ jagatkr̥tsnam̩ pravibhaktamanekadhā |
apaśyaddevadevasya śarīre pāṇḍavastadā ||

11.14 ततः स विस्मयाविष्टो हृष्टरोमा धनंजयः |
प्रणम्य शिरसा देवं कृताञ्जलिरभाषत ||

tataḥ sa vismayāviṣṭo hr̥ṣṭaromā dhanaṃjayaḥ |
praṇamya śirasā devaṃ kr̥tāñjalirabhāṣata ||

11.15 अर्जुन उवाच |
पश्यामि देवांस्तव देव देहे सर्वांस्तथा भूतविशेषसङ्घान् |
ब्रह्माणमीशं कमलासनस्थं ऋषींश्च सर्वानुरगांश्च दिव्यान् ||

arjuna uvāca |
paśyāmi devāṃstava deva dehe
sarvāṃstathā bhūtaviśeṣasaṅghān |
brahmāṇamīśaṃ kamalāsanasthaṃ
r̥ṣīṃśca sarvānuragāṃśca divyān ||

11.16 अनेकबाहूदरवक्त्रनेत्रं पश्यामि त्वां सर्वतोऽनन्तरूपम् |
नान्तं न मध्यं न पुनस्तवादिं पश्यामि विश्वेश्वर विश्वरूप ||

anekabāhūdaravaktranetraṃ
paśyāmi tvāṃ sarvato'nantarūpam |
nāntaṃ na madhyaṃ na punastavādiṃ
paśyāmi viśveśvara viśvarūpa ||

11.13 there with krishna
arjuna saw
in the body
of the god of gods
a diverse one universe

11.14 arjuna
overcome by surprise
goosebumps
bowing his head
said reverentially

11.15 omigod i see in your body deities
a gathering of all sorts of beings
brahma seated on a lotus
divine serpents & all the sages

11.16 i see you everywhere infinite form
myriad eyes arms bellies faces

no end no middle no beginning

i see the deity of the universe
the universe its form

11.17 किरीटिनं गदिनं चक्रिणं च तेजोराशिं सर्वतो दीप्तिमन्तम् |
पश्यामि त्वां दुर्निरीक्ष्यं समन्ताद् दीप्तानलार्कद्युतिमप्रमेयम् ||

kirīṭinaṃ gadinaṃ cakriṇaṃ ca
tejorāśiṃ sarvato dīptimantam |
paśyāmi tvāṃ durnirīkṣyaṃ samantād
dīptānalārkadyutimaprameyam ||

11.18 त्वमक्षरं परमं वेदितव्यं त्वमस्य विश्वस्य परं निधानम् |
त्वमव्ययः शाश्वतधर्मगोप्ता सनातनस्त्वं पुरुषो मतो मे ||

tvamakṣaraṃ paramaṃ veditavyaṃ
tvamasya viśvasya paraṃ nidhānam |
tvamavyayaḥ śāśvatadharmagoptā
sanātanastvaṃ puruṣo mato me ||

11.19 अनादि मध्यान्तं अनन्तवीर्यं अनन्तबाहुं शशिसूर्यनेत्रम् |
पश्यामि त्वां दीप्तहुताशवक्त्रं स्वतेजसा विश्वमिदं तपन्तम ||

anādi madhyāntam anantavīryam
anantabāhuṃ śaśisūryanetram |
paśyāmi tvāṃ dīptahutāśavaktraṃ
svatejasā viśvamidaṃ tapantam ||

11.17 i see you so hard to see
in totality

with a crown club discus

blazes

sun fire radiance

infinite

mass of light

shining everywhere

11.18 i get it you are the highest goal of knowledge
the deepest anchor of the world

everlasting undying
defender of eternal law

the original one

11.19 i see you without beginning middle end

infinite arms
infinite strength

your eyes the sun & moon
your mouth a blazing pyre

by your brilliance
the universe afire

11.20 द्यावापृथिव्योरिदमन्तरं हि व्याप्तं त्वयैकेन दिशश्च सर्वाः |
दृष्ट्वाद्भुतं रूपमुग्रं तवेदं लोकत्रयं प्रव्यथितं महात्मन् ||

dyāvāpṛthivyoridamantaraṃ hi
vyāptaṃ tvayaikena diśaśca sarvāḥ |
dṛṣṭvādbhutaṃ rūpamugraṃ tavedaṃ
lokatrayaṃ pravyathitaṃ mahātman ||

11.21 अमी हि त्वां सुरसङ्घा विशन्ति केचिद्भीताः प्राञ्जलयो गृणन्ति |
स्वस्तीत्युक्त्वा महर्षिसिद्धसङ्घाः स्तुवन्ति त्वां स्तुतिभिः पुष्कलाभिः ||

amī hi tvāṃ surasaṅghā viśanti
kecidbhītāḥ prāñjalayo gṛṇanti |
svastītyuktvā maharṣisiddhasaṅghāḥ
stuvanti tvāṃ stutibhiḥ puṣkalābhiḥ ||

11.22 रुद्रादित्या वसवो ये च साध्या विश्वेऽश्विनौ मरुतश्चोष्मपाश्च |
गन्धर्वयक्षासुरसिद्धसङ्घा वीक्षन्ते त्वां विस्मिताश्चैव सर्वे ||

rudrādityā vasavo ye ca sādhyā
viśve'śvinau marutaścoṣmapāśca |
gandharvayakṣāsurasiddhasaṅghā
vīkṣante tvāṃ vismitāścaiva sarve ||

11.23 रूपं महत्ते बहुवक्त्रनेत्रं महाबाहो बहुबाहूरुपादम् |
बहूदरं बहुदंष्ट्राकरालं दृष्ट्वा लोकाः प्रव्यथितास्तथाऽहम् ||

rūpaṃ mahatte bahuvaktranetraṃ
mahābāho bahubāhūrupādam |
bahūdaraṃ bahudaṃṣṭrākarālaṃ
dṛṣṭvā lokāḥ pravyathitāstathā'ham ||

11.20 in all directions you o'
solo you fill the whole
between heaven & earth

the three worlds (earth heaven & inbetween)
shudder
at this a terrible marvel
form

11.21 there hordes of deities
(i see) going into you they're
terrified they
praise you
make reverent signs

hordes of great
accomplished sages
they say hello they
praise you profusely in hymns

11.22 they the adityas the rudras vasus & sadhyas
see all the deities of the universe
you the ashvins the maruts the ancestors
hordes of gandharvas yakshas demons
& the accomplished

& they're all bewildered

11.23 seeing your myriad
mouths eyes arms thighs feet
bellies & gory teeth

the worlds shudder &
so do i

11.24 नभःस्पृशं दीप्तमनेकवर्णं व्यात्ताननं दीप्तविशालनेत्रम् |
दृष्ट्वा हि त्वां प्रव्यथितान्तरात्मा धृतिं न विन्दामि शमं च विष्णो ||

nabhaḥspṛśaṃ dīptamanekavarṇaṃ
vyāttānanaṃ dīptaviśālanetram |
dṛṣṭvā hi tvāṃ pravyathitāntarātmā
dhṛtiṃ na vindāmi śamaṃ ca viṣṇo ||

11.25 दंष्ट्राकरालानि च ते मुखानि दृष्ट्वैव कालानलसन्निभानि |
दिशो न जाने न लभे च शर्म प्रसीद देवेश जगन्निवास ||

daṃṣṭrākarālāni ca te mukhāni
dṛṣṭvaiva kālānalasannibhāni |
diśo na jāne na labhe ca śarma
prasīda deveśa jagannivāsa ||

11.26 अमी च त्वां धृतराष्ट्रस्य पुत्राः सर्वे सहैवावनिपालसङ्घैः |
भीष्मो द्रोणः सूतपुत्रस्तथासौ सहास्मदीयैरपि योधमुख्यैः ||

amī ca tvāṃ dhṛtarāṣṭrasya putrāḥ
sarve sahaivāvanipālasaṅghaiḥ |
bhīṣmo droṇaḥ sūtaputrastathāsau
sahāsmadīyairapi yodhamukhyaiḥ ||

11.27 वक्त्राणि ते त्वरमाणा विशन्ति दंष्ट्राकरालानि भयानकानि |
केचिद्विलग्ना दशनान्तरेषु संदृश्यन्ते चूर्णितैरुत्तमाङ्गैः ||

vaktrāṇi te tvaramāṇā viśanti
daṃṣṭrākarālāni bhayānakāni |
kecidvilagnā daśanāntareṣu
saṃdṛśyante cūrṇitairuttamāṅgaiḥ ||

11.24 seeing you a blaze a spectrum
touching the sky

mouth agape fiery
expansive eyes o' vishnu

i tremble within i find no calm
i can't stand it

11.25 seeing your mouths your gory tusks like
the end of time blaze

i don't know where i am
i can't find a place
have mercy!
deity of deities
home of the universe

11.26 there all of dhritarashtra's sons with
(i see) hordes of kings
bhishma drona karna
& our main warriors too

11.27 they rush into your mouths
tusks gory scary
some caught between your teeth
ugh! see crushed heads

11.28 यथा नदीनां बहवोऽम्बुवेगा: समुद्रमेवाभिमुखा द्रवन्ति |
तथा तवामी नरलोकवीरा विशन्ति वक्त्राण्यभिविज्वलन्ति ||

yathā nadīnāṃ bahavo'mbuvegāḥ
samudramevābhimukhā dravanti |
tathā tavāmī naralokavīrā
viśanti vaktrāṇyabhivijvalanti ||

11.29 यथा प्रदीप्तं ज्वलनं पतङ्गा विशन्ति नाशाय समृद्धवेगा: |
तथैव नाशाय विशन्ति लोका: तवापि वक्त्राणि समृद्धवेगा: ||

yathā pradīptaṃ jvalanaṃ pataṅgā
viśanti nāśāya samṛddhavegāḥ |
tathaiva nāśāya viśanti lokāḥ
tavāpi vaktrāṇi samṛddhavegāḥ ||

11.30 लेलिह्यसे ग्रसमान: समन्तात् लोकान्समग्रान्वदनैर्ज्वलद्भि: |
तेजोभिरापूर्य जगत्समग्रं भासस्तवोग्रा: प्रतपन्ति विष्णो ||

lelihyase grasamānaḥ samantāt
lokānsamagrānvadanairjvaladbhiḥ |
tejobhirāpūrya jagatsamagraṃ
bhāsastavogrāḥ pratapanti viṣṇo ||

11.31 आख्याहि मे को भवानुग्ररूपो नमोऽस्तु ते देववर प्रसीद |
विज्ञातुमिच्छामि भवन्तमाद्यं न हि प्रजानामि तव प्रवृत्तिम् ||

ākhyāhi me ko bhavānugrarūpo
namo'stu te devavara prasīda |
vijñātumicchāmi bhavantamādyaṃ
na hi prajānāmi tava pravṛttim ||

11.28 the heroes of the human world
enter your mouths blazing
as river currents
run to the ocean

11.29 the worlds hurry into your mouths
to be destroyed
frenzied moths
to flame

11.30 all around you devour you lick
all the worlds
with your fiery mouths

(while) your brilliance fills
the worlds
your rays consume them

11.31 tell me who you are sir
o' so ferocious
saluts to you
o' best of deities
mercy

i want to know original one
about your ways
i have no clue

11.32 श्रीभगवानुवाच |
कालोऽस्मि लोकक्षयकृत्प्रवृद्धो लोकान्समाहर्तुमिह प्रवृत्तः |
ऋतेऽपि त्वां न भविष्यन्ति सर्वे येऽवस्थिताः प्रत्यनीकेषु योधाः ||

śrībhagavānuvāca |
kālo'smi lokakṣayakṛtpravṛddho
lokānsamāhartumiha pravṛttaḥ |
ṛte'pi tvāṃ na bhaviṣyanti sarve
ye'vasthitāḥ pratyanīkeṣu yodhāḥ ||

11.33 तस्मात्त्वमुत्तिष्ठ यशो लभस्व जित्वा शत्रून्भुङ्क्ष्व राज्यंसमृद्धम् |
मयैवैते निहताः पूर्वमेव निमित्तमात्रं भव सव्यसाचिन् ||

tasmāttvamuttiṣṭha yaśo labhasva
jitvā śatrūnbhuṅkṣva rājyaṃsamṛddham |
mayaivaite nihatāḥ pūrvameva
nimittamātraṃ bhava savyasācin ||

11.34 द्रोणं च भीष्मं च जयद्रथं च कर्णं तथान्यानपि योधवीरान् |
मया हतांस्त्वं जहि मा व्यथिष्ठा युध्यस्व जेतासि रणे सपत्नान् ||

droṇaṃ ca bhīṣmaṃ ca jayadrathaṃ ca
karṇaṃ tathānyānapi yodhavīrān |
mayā hatāṃstvaṃ jahi mā vyathiṣṭhā
yudhyasva jetāsi raṇe sapatnān ||

11.35 संजय उवाच |
एतच्छ्रुत्वा वचनं केशवस्य कृताञ्जलिर्वेपमानः किरीटी |
नमस्कृत्वा भूय एवाह कृष्णं सगद्गदं भीतभीतः प्रणम्य ||

saṃjaya uvāca |
etacchrutvā vacanaṃ keśavasya
kṛtāñjalirvepamānaḥ kirīṭī |
namaskṛtvā bhūya evāha kṛṣṇaṃ
sagadgadaṃ bhītabhītaḥ praṇamya ||

11.32 krishna:
i am time the force
that does the world in

i've come to annihilate
the worlds

even without you (killing them)
they positioned on the opposite side
will not be

11.33 so stand up get some cred
conquer enemies then enjoy the office

they've been killed by me already
you just be arjuna
an instrument

11.34 drona bhishma jayadrata karna
& other war heroes
have been killed by me so
kill don't flounder
fight you'll conquer the enemies
in the war

11.35 sanjaya (to dhritarashtra):
hearing krishna's words a shaken arjuna reverential
handsfolding fearful bowed stammered again

11.36 अर्जुन उवाच |
स्थाने हृषीकेश तव प्रकीर्त्या जगत्प्रहृष्यत्यनुरज्यते च |
रक्षांसि भीतानि दिशो द्रवन्ति सर्वे नमस्यन्ति च सिद्धसङ्घाः ||

arjuna uvāca |
sthāne hṛṣīkeśa tava prakīrtyā
jagatprahṛṣyatyanurajyate ca |
rakṣāṃsi bhītāni diśo dravanti
sarve namasyanti ca siddhasaṅghāḥ ||

11.37 कस्माच्च ते न नमेरन्महात्मन् गरीयसे ब्रह्मणोऽप्यादिकर्त्रे |
अनन्त देवेश जगन्निवास त्वमक्षरं सदसत्तत्परं यत् ||

kasmācca te na nameranmahātman
garīyase brahmaṇo'pyādikartre |
ananta deveśa jagannivāsa
tvamakṣaraṃ sadasattatparaṃ yat ||

11.38 त्वमादिदेवः पुरुषः पुराणः त्वमस्य विश्वस्य परं निधानम् |
वेत्तासि वेद्यं च परं च धाम त्वया ततं विश्वमनन्तरूप ||

tvamādidevaḥ puruṣaḥ purāṇaḥ
tvamasya viśvasya paraṃ nidhānam |
vettāsi vedyaṃ ca paraṃ ca dhāma
tvayā tataṃ viśvamanantarūpa ||

11.39 वायुर्यमोऽग्निर्वरुणः शशाङ्कः प्रजापतिस्त्वं प्रपितामहश्च |
नमो नमस्तेऽस्तु सहस्रकृत्वः पुनश्च भूयोऽपि नमो नमस्ते ||

vāyuryamo'gnirvaruṇaḥ śaśāṅkaḥ
prajāpatistvaṃ prapitāmahaśca |
namo namaste'stu sahasrakṛtvaḥ
punaśca bhūyo'pi namo namaste ||

11.36 arjuna:

it's appropriate
the universe celebrates
& enjoys your fame

demons   scared run
          here & there
& the perfected bow to you

11.37 & why shouldn't they
  you're the original creator
  greater than brahma

deity of deities
infinite
home of the universe   you're undying
  what is   what isn't   & beyond

11.38 you're
first deity the ancient one
this universe's deepest anchor

the knower
the to-be-known the final destination

your infinite form   permeates
the universe

11.39 you are   the deities
wind death fire water moon

prajapati first ancestor

salaam to you a thousand times
&again   salaam   salaam

11.40 नमः पुरस्तादथ पृष्ठतस्ते नमोऽस्तु ते सर्वत एव सर्व |
अनन्तवीर्यामितविक्रमस्त्वं सर्वं समाप्नोषि ततोऽसि सर्वः ||

namaḥ purastādatha pṛṣṭhataste
namo'stu te sarvata eva sarva |
anantavīryāmitavikramastvaṃ
sarvaṃ samāpnoṣi tato'si sarvaḥ ||

11.41 सखेति मत्वा प्रसभं यदुक्तं हे कृष्ण हे यादव हे सखेति |
अजानता महिमानं तवेदं मया प्रमादात्प्रणयेन वापि ||

sakheti matvā prasabhaṃ yaduktaṃ
he kṛṣṇa he yādava he sakheti |
ajānatā mahimānaṃ tavedaṃ
mayā pramādātpraṇayena vāpi ||

11.42 यच्चावहासार्थमसत्कृतोऽसि विहारशय्यासनभोजनेषु |
एकोऽथवाप्यच्युत तत्समक्षं तत्क्षामये त्वामहमप्रमेयम् ||

yaccāvahāsārthamasatkṛto'si
vihāraśayyāsanabhojaneṣu |
eko'thavāpyacyuta tatsamakṣaṃ
tatkṣāmaye tvāmahamaprameyam ||

11.43 पितासि लोकस्य चराचरस्य त्वमस्य पूज्यश्च गुरुर्गरीयान् |
न त्वत्समोऽस्त्यभ्यधिकः कुतोऽन्यो लोकत्रयेऽप्यप्रतिमप्रभाव ||

pitāsi lokasya carācarasya
tvamasya pūjyaśca gururgarīyān |
na tvatsamo'styabhyadhikaḥ kuto'nyo
lokatraye'pyapratimaprabhāva ||

11.40 salaam from the front from the back
from all sides surround salaam (o' omnipresent)
(to) endless boundless valour & force
you are the end of everything
so you are everything

11.41 from ignorance of your power
tipsiness
or fondness
i've been rash
said whatnot 'hey krishna
hey yaduboy hey buddy'

thought you (just) friend

11.42 if for jokes' sake when we went out
i've treated you or lay back
disrespectfully or sat around or ate
in privacy or good lord
in front of others

i beg pardon o' unfathomable

11.43 you're the father of the world
of the animate inanimate
its worshipped
weighty teacher

there's nothing like you in the three worlds
so how could there be
anything better than you
o' of incomparable glory

11.44 तस्मात्प्रणम्य प्रणिधाय कायं प्रसादये त्वामहमीशमीड्यम् |
पितेव पुत्रस्य सखेव सख्युः प्रियः प्रियायार्हसि देव सोढुम् ||

tasmātpraṇamya praṇidhāya kāyaṃ
prasādaye tvāmahamīśamīḍyam |
piteva putrasya sakheva sakhyuḥ
priyaḥ priyāyārhasi deva soḍhum ||

11.45 अदृष्टपूर्वं हृषितोऽस्मि दृष्ट्वा भयेन च प्रव्यथितं मनो मे |
तदेव मे दर्शय देवरूपं प्रसीद देवेश जगन्निवास ||

adṛṣṭapūrvaṃ hṛṣito'smi dṛṣṭvā
bhayena ca pravyathitaṃ mano me |
tadeva me darśaya devarūpaṃ
prasīda deveśa jagannivāsa ||

11.46 किरीटिनं गदिनं चक्रहस्तं इच्छामि त्वां द्रष्टुमहं तथैव |
तेनैव रूपेण चतुर्भुजेन सहस्रबाहो भव विश्वमूर्ते ||

kirīṭinaṃ gadinaṃ cakrahastaṃ
icchāmi tvāṃ draṣṭumahaṃ tathaiva |
tenaiva rūpeṇa caturbhujena
sahasrabāho bhava viśvamūrte ||

11.47 श्रीभगवानुवाच |
मया प्रसन्नेन तवार्जुनेदं रूपं परं दर्शितमात्मयोगात् |
तेजोमयं विश्वमनन्तमाद्यं यन्मे त्वदन्येन न दृष्टपूर्वम् ||

śrībhagavānuvāca |
mayā prasannena tavārjunedaṃ
rūpaṃ paraṃ darśitamātmayogāt |
tejomayaṃ viśvamanantamādyaṃ
yanme tvadanyena na dṛṣṭapūrvam ||

11.44 so i salute i prostrate
be generous o' laudable god
bear with me as father to son
friend to friend
lover to beloved

11.45–11.46 i'm happy enough seeing
the previously unseen

(but) my mind's in panic shaken
have mercy

o' god of gods
o' home of the universe
o' god show me that form

with a crown
a club
discus in hand

i want to see you only like that
o' universe of forms
o' thousand-armed become
four-armed

11.47 god:
pleased with you
this ultimate form an endless brilliant
original universe
was displayed
by my power

that hasn't been seen by anyone else before

11.48 न वेदयज्ञाध्ययनैर्न दानैर्न च क्रियाभिर्न तपोभिरुग्रैः |
एवंरूपः शक्य अहं नृलोके द्रष्टुं त्वदन्येन कुरुप्रवीर ||

na vedayajñādhyayanairna dānaiḥ
na ca kriyābhirna tapobhirugraiḥ |
evaṃrūpaḥ śakya ahaṃ nṛloke
draṣṭuṃ tvadanyena kurupravīra ||

11.49 मा ते व्यथा मा च विमूढभावो दृष्ट्वा रूपं घोरमीदृङ्ममेदम् |
व्यपेतभी: प्रीतमना: पुनस्त्वं तदेव मे रूपमिदं प्रपश्य ||

mā te vyathā mā ca vimūḍhabhāvo
dṛṣṭvā rūpaṃ ghoramīdṛṅmamedam |
vyapetabhīḥ prītamanāḥ punastvaṃ
tadeva me rūpamidaṃ prapaśya ||

11.50 संजय उवाच |
इत्यर्जुनं वासुदेवस्तथोक्त्वा स्वकं रूपं दर्शयामास भूयः |
आश्वासयामास च भीतमेनं भूत्वा पुन: सौम्यवपुर्महात्मा ||

saṃjaya uvāca |
ityarjunaṃ vāsudevastathoktvā
svakaṃ rūpaṃ darśayāmāsa bhūyaḥ |
āśvāsayāmāsa ca bhītamenaṃ
bhūtvā punaḥ saumyavapurmahātmā ||

11.51 अर्जुन उवाच |
दृष्ट्वेदं मानुषं रूपं तव सौम्यं जनार्दन |
इदानीमस्मि संवृत्त: सचेता: प्रकृतिं गत: ||

arjuna uvāca |
dṛṣṭvedaṃ mānuṣaṃ rūpaṃ tava saumyaṃ janārdana |
idānīmasmi saṃvṛttaḥ sacetāḥ prakṛtiṃ gataḥ ||

11.48 i can't be seen in this form
by anyone other than by you arjuna
o' hero of the kurus
in the human world
whether via veda yajna & study
or charity or rituals
or severe austerities

11.49 don't be miserable
don't feel confused
cheer up again
be fearfree

having seen my terrible form
see my form's this!

11.50 sanjaya to dhritarashtra:
having said so to arjuna
krishna showed his human form
again nice & mild
let terrified arjuna breathe again

11.51 arjuna:
seeing this your gentle human form
i'm relaxed now my
mind's back to normal

11.52 श्रीभगवानुवाच |
सुदुर्दर्शमिदं रूपं दृष्टवानसि यन्मम |
देवा अप्यस्य रूपस्य नित्यं दर्शनकाङ्क्षिणः ||

śrībhagavānuvāca |
sudurdarśamidaṃ rūpaṃ dṛṣṭvānasi yanmama |
devā apyasya rūpasya nityaṃ darśanakāṅkṣiṇaḥ ||

11.53 नाहं वेदैर्न तपसा न दानेन न चेज्यया |
शक्य एवंविधो द्रष्टुं दृष्टवानसि मां यथा ||

nāhaṃ vedairna tapasā na dānena na cejyayā |
śakya evaṃvidho draṣṭuṃ dṛṣṭavānasi māṃ yathā ||

11.54 भक्त्या त्वनन्यया शक्य अहमेवंविधोऽर्जुन |
ज्ञातुं द्रष्टुं च तत्त्वेन प्रवेष्टुं च परंतप ||

bhaktyā tvananyayā śakya ahamevaṃvidho'rjuna |
jñātuṃ draṣṭuṃ ca tattvena praveṣṭuṃ ca paraṃtapa ||

11.55 मत्कर्मकृन्मत्परमो मद्भक्तः सङ्गवर्जितः |
निर्वैरः सर्वभूतेषु यः स मामेति पाण्डव ||

matkarmakṛnmatparamo madbhaktaḥ saṅgavarjitaḥ |
nirvairaḥ sarvabhūteṣu yaḥ sa māmeti pāṇḍava ||

12.1 अर्जुन उवाच |
एवं सततयुक्ता ये भक्तास्त्वां पर्युपासते |
ये चाप्यक्षरमव्यक्तं तेषां के योगवित्तमाः ||

arjuna uvāca |
evaṃ satatayuktā ye bhaktāstvāṃ paryupāsate |
ye cāpyakṣaramavyaktaṃ teṣāṃ ke yogavittamāḥ ||

11.52 what you've seen   this form
is hard to get to see
even the deities want to

11.53 the way you've seen me
(normally) impossible
    via vedas or austerity
    rituals or charity

11.54 only by singleminded devotion
can i   my truth
be known seen
entered

11.55   arjuna
she who

devoted
sees me as supreme
does my work
    free from
    attachment & hatred
    to all beings
reaches me

12.1 arjuna: between

devotees   always attuned
who worship your person
    &
those who (go for)
the eternal impersonal

who knows yoga better?

12.2 श्रीभगवानुवाच |
मय्यावेश्य मनो ये मां नित्ययुक्ता उपासते |
श्रद्धया परयोपेतास्ते मे युक्ततमा मताः ||

śrībhagavānuvāca |
mayyāveśya mano ye māṃ nityayuktā upāsate |
śraddhayā parayopetāste me yuktatamā matāḥ ||

12.3 ये त्वक्षरमनिर्देश्यमव्यक्तं पर्युपासते |
सर्वत्रगमचिंत्यंच कूटस्थमचलंध्रुवम् ||

ye tvakṣaramanirdeśyamavyaktaṃ paryupāsate |
sarvatragamaciṃtyaṃca kūṭasthaṃacalaṃdhruvam ||

12.4 सन्नियम्येन्द्रियग्रामं सर्वत्र समबुद्धयः |
ते प्राप्नुवन्ति मामेव सर्वभूतहिते रताः ||

saṃniyamyendriyagrāmaṃ sarvatra samabuddhayaḥ |
te prāpnuvanti māmeva sarvabhūtahite ratāḥ ||

12.5 क्लेशोऽधिकतरस्तेषामव्यक्तासक्तचेतसाम् |
अव्यक्ताहि गतिर्दुःखं देहवद्भिरवाप्यते ||

kleśo'dhikatarasteṣāmavyaktāsaktacetasām ||
avyaktāhi gatirduḥkhaṃ dehavadbhiravāpyate ||

12.6 ये तु सर्वाणि कर्माणि मयि संन्यस्य मत्परः |
अनन्येनैव योगेन मां ध्यायन्त उपासते ||

ye tu sarvāṇi karmāṇi mayi saṃnyasya matparaḥ |
ananyenaiva yogena māṃ dhyāyanta upāsate ||

12.7 तेषामहं समुद्धर्ता मृत्युसंसारसागरात् |
भवामि नचिरात्पार्थ मय्यावेशितचेतसाम् ||

teṣāmahaṃ samuddhartā mṛtyusaṃsārasāgarāt |
bhavāmi nacirātpārtha mayyāveśitacetasām ||

12.2 krishna:

those who   mind lost in me
worship   always attuned

blessed with superlative faith
they're the most linked i think (but)

12.3–12.4 those who meditate
on me   as the

eternal indeterminate unmanifest omnipresent
unthinkable fixed immovable constant

controlling senses
equable everywhere
glad in the welfare of all beings

they too reach me (though)

12.5 it's harder for them
attached to the unmanifest impersonal

(for) the unembodied is reached
with difficulty by the bodied

12.6–12.7 offering all work to me supreme
with singleminded yoga those who
think of me
worship me whose
thoughts are lost in me

before long   i uplift them
from the ocean
of recurring 'death'

12.8 मय्येव मन आधत्स्व मयि बुद्धिं निवेशय |
निवसिष्यसि मय्येव अत ऊर्ध्वं न संशयः ||

mayyeva mana ādhatsva mayi buddhiṃ niveśaya |
nivasiṣyasi mayyeva ata ūrdhvaṃ na saṃśayaḥ ||

12.9 अथचित्तं समाधातुं न शक्नोषि मयि स्थिरम् |
अभ्यासयोगेन ततो मामिच्छाप्तुं धनंजय ||

athacittaṃ samādhātuṃ na śaknoṣi mayi sthiram |
abhyāsayogena tato māmicchāptuṃ dhanaṃjaya ||

12.10 अभ्यासेऽप्यसमर्थोऽसि मत्कर्मपरमो भव |
मदर्थमपि कर्माणि कुर्वन्सिद्धिमवाप्स्यसि ||

abhyāse'pyasamartho'si matkarmaparamo bhava |
madarthamapi karmāṇi kurvansiddhimavāpsyasi ||

12.11 अथैतदप्यशक्तोऽसि कर्तुं मद्योगमाश्रितः |
सर्वकर्मफलत्यागं ततः कुरु यतात्मवान् ||

athaitadapyaśakto'si kartuṃ madyogamāśritaḥ |
sarvakarmaphalatyāgaṃ tataḥ kuru yatātmavān ||

12.12 श्रेयो हि ज्ञानमभ्यासाज्ज्ञानाद्ध्यानं विशिष्यते |
ध्यानात्कर्मफलत्यागस्त्यागाच्छान्तिरनन्तरम् ||

śreyo hi jñānamabhyāsājjñānāddhyānaṃ viśiṣyate |
dhyānātkarmaphalatyāgastyāgācchāntiranantaram ||

12.8 put your mind only on me
make your thoughts enter me   you'll
live in me   from now on   there's
no doubt about that

12.9–12.10 but if you're incapable
of fixing mind on me
practise yoga   to reach me

& if you're no good at that
be keen do my work

do things for my sake you'll be
successful

12.11 & if you're powerless to do that too
seek refuge in my power

renounce the results of your actions
& work with self restraint

12.12 wisdom's better than practice (but)
meditation's better than wisdom

& better than meditation
renunciation of results of activities

renunciation → peace   at once

12.13 अद्वेष्टा सर्वभूतानां मैत्रः करुण एव च |
निर्ममो निरहंकारः समदुःखसुखः क्षमी ||

adveṣṭā sarvabhūtānāṃ maitraḥ karuṇa eva ca |
nirmamo nirahaṃkāraḥ samaduḥkhasukhaḥ kṣamī ||

12.14 संतुष्टः सततं योगी यतात्मा दृढनिश्चयः |
मय्यर्पितमनोबुद्धिर्यो मद्भक्तः स मे प्रियः ||

saṃtuṣṭaḥ satataṃ yogī yatātmā dṛḍhaniścayaḥ |
mayyarpitamanobuddhiryo madbhaktaḥ sa me priyaḥ ||

12.15 यस्मान्नोद्विजते लोको लोकान्नोद्विजते च यः |
हर्षामर्षभयोद्वेगैर्मुक्तो यः स च मे प्रियः ||

yasmānnodvijate loko lokānnodvijate ca yaḥ |
harṣāmarṣabhayodvegairmukto yaḥ sa ca me priyaḥ ||

12.16 अनपेक्षः शुचिर्दक्ष उदासीनो गतव्यथः |
सर्वारम्भपरित्यागी यो मद्भक्तः स मे प्रियः ||

anapekṣaḥ śucirdakṣa udāsīno gatavyathaḥ |
sarvārambhaparityāgī yo madbhaktaḥ sa me priyaḥ ||

12.17 यो न हृष्यति न द्वेष्टि न शोचति न काङ्क्षति |
शुभाशुभपरित्यागी भक्तिमान्यः स मे प्रियः ||

yo na hṛṣyati na dveṣṭi na śocati na kāṅkṣati |
śubhāśubhaparityāgī bhaktimānyaḥ sa me priyaḥ ||

12.18 समः शत्रौ च मित्रे च तथा मानापमानयोः |
शीतोष्णसुखदुःखेषु समः सङ्गविवर्जितः ||

samaḥ śatrau ca mitre ca tathā mānāpamānayoḥ |
śītoṣṇasukhaduḥkheṣu samaḥ saṅgavivarjitaḥ ||

12.19 तुल्यनिन्दास्तुतिर्मौनी संतुष्टो येन केनचित् |
अनिकेतः स्थिरमतिर्भक्तिमान्मे प्रियो नरः ||

tulyanindāstutirmaunī saṃtuṣṭo yena kenacit |
aniketaḥ sthiramatirbhaktimānme priyo naraḥ ||

12.13–12.20 she who's devoted

& friendly patient compassionate
without hatred for all
free from 'this is mine' & 'i'm the doer'
same in happiness & sadness
always content self-restrained determined
mind & thoughts offered to me
doesn't hate the world & vice versa
free from excitement impatience fear distress
impartial pure capable detached unanxious
renouncing all ventures
doesn't celebrate or hate   mourn or crave
renounces + & -
friend = foe   honour = disgrace
praise = blame
cold = heat   pleasure = pain
free from attachment   content with anything
silent
steady   nonmaterialistic

meditates on this knowledge   nectar
holds faith
& is keen
on me supreme

is my love   i repeat!

12.20 ये तु धर्म्यामृतमिदं यथोक्तं पर्युपासते |
श्रद्दधाना मत्परमा भक्तास्तेऽतीव मे प्रियाः ||

ye tu dharmyāmṛtamidaṃ yathoktaṃ paryupāsate |
śraddadhānā matparamā bhaktāste'tīva me priyāḥ ||

13.0 अर्जुन उवाच |
प्रकृतिं पुरुषं चैव क्षेत्रं क्षेत्रज्ञमेव च |
एतद्वेदितुमिच्छामि ज्ञानं ज्ञेयं च केशव ||

arjuna uvāca |
prakṛtiṃ puruṣaṃ caiva kṣetraṃ kṣetrajñameva ca |
etadveditumicchāmi jñānaṃ jñeyaṃ ca keśava ||

13.1 श्रीभगवानुवाच |
इदं शरीरं कौन्तेय क्षेत्रमित्यभिधीयते |
एतद्यो वेत्ति तं प्राहुः क्षेत्रज्ञ इति तद्विदः ||

śrībhagavānuvāca |
idaṃ śarīraṃ kaunteya kṣetramityabhidhīyate |
etadyo vetti taṃ prāhuḥ kṣetrajña iti tadvidaḥ ||

13.2 क्षेत्रज्ञं चापि मां विद्धि सर्वक्षेत्रेषु भारत |
क्षेत्रक्षेत्रज्ञयोर्ज्ञानं यत्तज्ज्ञानं मतं मम ||

kṣetrajñaṃ cāpi māṃ viddhi sarvakṣetreṣu bhārata |
kṣetrakṣetrajñayorjñānaṃ yattajjñānaṃ mataṃ mama ||

13.3 तत्क्षेत्रं यच्च यादृक्च यद्विकारि यतश्च यत् |
स च यो यत्प्रभावश्च तत्समासेन मे शृणु ||

tatkṣetraṃ yacca yādṛkca yadvikāri yataśca yat |
sa ca yo yatprabhāvaśca tatsamāsena me śṛṇu ||

13.0 arjuna:

what's prakriti — nature matter energy manifestation

what's purusha — will spirit person doer

field — & who knows it

knowledge — & who knows it

this i want to know

13.1 krishna:

body = field &
realizer = knower
so scholars say

13.2 in every body
the knower is me

so true knowledge i believe
is knowledge of both
field & knower

13.3 hear from me
in summary:

field: what exactly
what sort
how & why it changes

who's the knower
& what are his powers

13.4 ऋषिभिर्बहुधा गीतं छन्दोभिर्विविधैः पृथक् |
ब्रह्मसूत्रपदैश्चैव हेतुमद्भिर्विनिश्चितैः ||

ṛṣibhirbahudhā gītaṃ chandobhirvividhaiḥ pṛthak |
brahmasūtrapadaiścaiva hetumadbhirviniścitaiḥ ||

13.5 महाभूतान्यहंकारो बुद्धिरव्यक्तमेव च |
इन्द्रियाणि दशैकं च पञ्च चेन्द्रियगोचराः ||

mahābhūtānyahaṃkāro buddhiravyaktameva ca |
indriyāṇi daśaikaṃ ca paṃca cendriyagocarāḥ ||

13.6 इच्छा द्वेषः सुखं दुःखं संघातश्चेतना धृतिः |
एतत्क्षेत्रं समासेन सविकारमुदाहृतम् ||

icchā dveṣaḥ sukhaṃ duḥkhaṃ saṃghātaścetanā dhṛtiḥ |
etatkṣetraṃ samāsena savikāramudāhṛtam ||

13.7 अमानित्वमदम्भित्वमहिंसा क्षान्तिरार्जवम् |
आचार्योपासनं शौचं स्थैर्यमात्मविनिग्रहः ||

amānitvamadambhitvamahiṃsā kṣāntirārjavam |
ācāryopāsanaṃ śaucaṃ sthairyamātmavinigrahaḥ ||

13.4 sung by sages
in many well-reasoned definitive
ways
hymns brahmasutras

13.5–13.6 the field of change
is this in brief

the elements (earth water fire air ether)
ego the 'i am the doer' idea
intellect
including the unmanifest (subconscious)

sense apparatus
ten + one (ear eye tongue skin nose
hands feet mouth anus genital
mind)
sense places
five (sound touch colour taste smell)

attraction repulsion
pleasure pain

the organism altogether

awareness will

13.7 & true knowledge
is this:

absence of pride hypocrisy
nonviolence patience rightness
attention to the teacher
selfcontrol purity constancy

13.8 इन्द्रियार्थेषु वैराग्यमनहंकार एव च |
जन्ममृत्युजराव्याधिदुःखदोषानुदर्शनम् ||

indriyārtheṣu vairāgyamanahaṃkāra eva ca |
janmamṛtyujarāvyādhiduḥkhadoṣānudarśanam ||

13.9 असक्तिरनभिष्वङ्गः पुत्रदारगृहादिषु |
नित्यं च समचित्तत्वमिष्टानिष्टोपपत्तिषु ||

asaktiranabhiṣvaṅgaḥ putradāragṛhādiṣu |
nityaṃ ca samacittatvamiṣṭāniṣṭopapattiṣu ||

13.10 मयि चानन्ययोगेन भक्तिरव्यभिचारिणी |
विविक्तदेशसेवित्वमरतिर्जनसंसदि ||

mayi cānanyayogena bhaktiravyabhicāriṇī |
viviktadeśasevitvamaratirjanasaṃsadi ||

13.11 अध्यात्मज्ञाननित्यत्वं तत्वज्ञानार्थदर्शनम् |
एतज्ज्ञानमिति प्रोक्तमज्ञानं यदतोऽन्यथा ||

adhyātmajñānanityatvaṃ tattvajñānārthadarśanam |
etajjñānamiti proktamajñānaṃ yadato'nyathā ||

13.12 ज्ञेयं यत्तत्प्रवक्ष्यामि यज्ज्ञात्वामृतमश्नुते |
अनादिमत्परं ब्रह्म न सत्तन्नासदुच्यते ||

jñeyaṃ yattatpravakṣyāmi yajjñātvāmṛtamaśnute |
anādimatparaṃ brahma na sattannāsaducyate ||

13.13 सर्वतः पाणिपादं तत्सर्वतोऽक्षिशिरोमुखम् |
सर्वतः श्रुतिमल्लोके सर्वमावृत्य तिष्ठति ||

sarvataḥ pāṇipādaṃ tatsarvato'kṣiśiromukham |
sarvataḥ śrutimalloke sarvamāvṛtya tiṣṭhati ||

13.8 keeping
birth death ageing sickness pain imperfections
in mind
desirelessness for sense objects
'i am the doer'-ism

13.9 detachment
unclinging to home spouse kids etcetera

level headedness
whatever happens
whether you like it or not

13.10 unwandering devotion in me united
wandering to places of sol
uncomfortable in crowds

13.11 always aware of the spiritual
seeing the purpose
of realization
everything else is ignorance

13.12 what's got to be known by which
one gets immortality i'll reveal:
it is
brahman

without beginning
the ultimate
neither 'is' nor 'isn't'

13.13 hand foot eye head face everywhere
ear everywhere
permeating everything
it stays

13.14 सर्वेन्द्रियगुणाभासं सर्वेन्द्रियविवर्जितम् |
असक्तं सर्वभृच्चैव निर्गुणं गुणभोक्तृ च ||

sarvendriyaguṇābhāsaṃ sarvendriyavivarjitam |
asaktaṃ sarvabhṛccaiva nirguṇaṃ guṇabhoktṛ ca ||

13.15 बहिरन्तश्च भूतानामचरं चरमेव च |
सूक्ष्मत्वात्तदविज्ञेयं दूरस्थं चान्तिके च तत् ||

bahirantaśca bhūtānāmacaraṃ carameva ca |
sūkṣmatvāttadavijñeyaṃ dūrasthaṃ cāntike ca tat ||

13.16 अविभक्तं च भूतेषु विभक्तमिव च स्थितम् |
भूतभर्तृ च तज्ज्ञेयं ग्रसिष्णु प्रभविष्णु च ||

avibhaktaṃ ca bhūteṣu vibhaktamiva ca sthitam |
bhūtabhartṛ ca tajjñeyaṃ grasiṣṇu prabhaviṣṇu ca ||

13.17 ज्योतिषामपि तज्ज्योतिस्तमसः परमुच्यते |
ज्ञानं ज्ञेयं ज्ञानगम्यं हृदि सर्वस्य विष्ठितम् ||

jyotiṣāmapi tajjyotistamasaḥ paramucyate |
jñānaṃ jñeyaṃ jñānagamyaṃ hṛdi sarvasya viṣṭhitam ||

13.14 apparently has the functions qualities gunas
of all the senses but it's
free from all the senses

unattached to anything yet
holds everything

qualityless yet   has no gunas but
relishes qualities experiences through gunas

13.15 in animate & inanimate beings
& out

far away so close

too subtle to be understood

13.16 one not many   but as if many
parts   beings

creator
sustainer
devourer   of beings

13.17 light beyond par
darkness beyond par

knowledge
to be known
goal of knowledge
(right here)
in every
heart

13.18 इति क्षेत्रं तथा ज्ञानं ज्ञेयं चोक्तं समासतः ।
मद्भक्त एतद्विज्ञाय मद्भावायोपपद्यते ॥

iti kṣetraṃ tathā jñānaṃ jñeyaṃ coktaṃ samāsataḥ |
madbhakta etadvijñāya madbhāvāyopapadyate ||

13.19 प्रकृतिं पुरुषं चैव विद्ध्यनादी उभावपि ।
विकारांश्च गुणांश्चैव विद्धि प्रकृतिसंभवान् ॥

prakṛtiṃ puruṣaṃ caiva viddhyanādi ubhāvapi |
vikārāṃśca guṇāṃścaiva viddhi prakṛtisaṃbhavān ||

13.20 कार्यकारणकर्तृत्वे हेतुः प्रकृतिरुच्यते ।
पुरुषः सुखदुःखानां भोक्तृत्वे हेतुरुच्यते ॥

kāryakāraṇakartṛtve hetuḥ prakṛtirucyate |
puruṣaḥ sukhaduḥkhānāṃ bhoktṛtve heturucyate ||

13.21 पुरुषः प्रकृतिस्थो हि भुङ्क्ते प्रकृतिजान्गुणान् ।
कारणं गुणसङ्गोऽस्य सदसद्योनिजन्मसु ॥

puruṣaḥ prakṛtistho hi bhuṅkte prakṛtijānguṇān |
kāraṇaṃ guṇasaṅgo'sya sadasadyonijanmasu ||

13.22 उपद्रष्टानुमन्ता च भर्ता भोक्ता महेश्वरः ।
परमात्मेति चाप्युक्तो देहेऽस्मिन्पुरुषः परः ॥

upadraṣṭānumantā ca bhartā bhoktā maheśvaraḥ |
paramātmeti cāpyukto dehe'sminpuruṣaḥ paraḥ ||

13.18 (in short) field knowledge
& what's to be known
knowing these my devotee
gets closer to becomes
me

13.19 purusha spirit person doer activator knower
& prakriti nature material field form
from which rise
transformations
& gunas
are both
beginningless

13.20 as for action-reaction-actor
prakriti's behind it
(while)
purusha
experiences causes
pleasure & pain

13.21 purusha
anchors in nature &
experiences natureborn gunas

reborn in wombs good & bad
depending on association
with gunas (rebirth depends on
the quality / company
you keep)

13.22 as witness approver
supporter enjoyer god
'ultimate you' is in this body as
ultimate purusha

13.23 य एवं वेत्ति पुरुषं प्रकृतिं च गुणैः सह |
सर्वथा वर्तमानोऽपि न स भूयोऽभिजायते ||

ya evaṃ vetti puruṣaṃ prakṛtiṃ ca guṇaiḥ saha |
sarvathā vartamāno'pi na sa bhūyo'bhijāyate ||

13.24 ध्यानेनात्मनि पश्यन्ति केचिदात्मानमात्मना |
अन्ये साङ्ख्येन योगेन कर्मयोगेन चापरे ||

dhyānenātmani paśyanti kecidātmānamātmanā |
anye sāṅkhyena yogena karmayogena cāpare ||

13.25 अन्ये त्वेवमजानन्तः श्रुत्वान्येभ्य उपासते |
तेऽपि चातितरन्त्येव मृत्युं श्रुतिपरायणाः ||

anye tvevamajānantaḥ śrutvānyebhya upāsate |
te'pi cātitarantyeva mṛtyuṃ śrutiparāyaṇāḥ ||

13.26 यावत्संजायते किंचित्सत्त्वं स्थावरजङ्गमम् |
क्षेत्रक्षेत्रज्ञसंयोगात्तद्विद्धि भरतर्षभ ||

yāvatsaṃjāyate kiṃcitsattvaṃ sthāvarajaṅgamam |
kṣetrakṣetrajñasaṃyogāttadviddhi bharatarṣabha ||

13.27 समं सर्वेषु भूतेषु तिष्ठन्तं परमेश्वरम् |
विनश्यत्स्वविनश्यन्तं यः पश्यति स पश्यति ||

samaṃ sarveṣu bhūteṣu tiṣṭhantaṃ parameśvaram
vinaśyatsvavinaśyantaṃ yaḥ paśyati sa paśyati ||

13.23 she who knows this   purusha-prakriti-gunas
no matter where
    in the lives cycle
isn't reborn

13.24 some realize themselves   who they really are
by themselves

by meditation
on themselves

some via samkhya
    reasoning

some via karma yoga
    activity

13.25 others who know no better
hear about it from others
& worship it
    they also cross 'death'
    devoted to what they've heard of

13.26 whatever is born   arjuna
    moving or still
comes from the union
    of the field & knower

13.27 god is in all beings
equally
isn't destroyed when they are

    she who can see that
    has insight

13.28 समं पश्यन्हि सर्वत्र समवस्थितमीश्वरम् |
न हिनस्त्यात्मनात्मानं ततो याति परां गतिम् ||

samaṃ paśyanhi sarvatra samavasthitamīśvaram |
na hinastyātmanātmānaṃ tato yāti parāṃ gatim ||

13.29 प्रकृत्यैव च कर्माणि क्रियमाणानि सर्वशः |
यः पश्यति तथात्मानमकर्तारं स पश्यति ||

prakṛtyaiva ca karmāṇi kriyamāṇāni sarvaśaḥ |
yaḥ paśyati tathātmānamakartāraṃ sa paśyati ||

13.30 यदा भूतपृथग्भावमेकस्थमनुपश्यति |
तत एव च विस्तारं ब्रह्म सम्पद्यते तदा ||

yadā bhūtapṛthagbhāvamekasthamanupaśyati |
tata eva ca vistāraṃ brahma saṃpadyate tadā ||

13.31 अनादित्वान्निर्गुणत्वात्परमात्मायमव्ययः |
शरीरस्थोऽपि कौन्तेय न करोति न लिप्यते ||

anāditvānnirguṇatvātparamātmāyamavyayaḥ |
śarīrastho'pi kaunteya na karoti na lipyate ||

13.32 यथा सर्वगतं सौक्ष्म्यादाकाशं नोपलिप्यते |
सर्वत्रावस्थितो देहे तथात्मा नोपलिप्यते ||

yathā sarvagataṃ saukṣmyādākāśaṃ nopalipyate |
sarvatrāvasthito dehe tathātmā nopalipyate ||

13.33 यथा प्रकाशयत्येकः कृत्स्नं लोकमिमं रविः |
क्षेत्रं क्षेत्री तथा कृत्स्नं प्रकाशयति भारत ||

yathā prakāśayatyekaḥ kṛtsnaṃ lokamimaṃ raviḥ |
kṣetraṃ kṣetrī tathā kṛtsnaṃ prakāśayati bhārata ||

13.28 seeing the same god godself everywhere
doesn't hurt others
others = herself

reaches the ultimate goal

13.29 she who realizes that all
actions are done by nature
& not by the person
really realizes

13.30 when she sees the many states
rooted on the one nature
branching out from it
then she reaches brahman

13.31 the beginningless featureless
everlasting
ultimate self ultimate you god
although in the body
doesn't act
isn't affected

13.32 like ether goes every where
nothing affects it
the true you god in your body
nothing can touch it

13.33 all it takes is one sun
the whole world's illuminated
so a knower
to an entire field

13.34 क्षेत्रक्षेत्रज्ञयोरेवमन्तरं ज्ञानचक्षुषा |
भूतप्रकृतिमोक्षं च ये विदुर्यान्ति ते परम् ||

kṣetrakṣetrajñayorevamantaraṃ jñānacakṣuṣā |
bhūtaprakṛtimokṣaṃ ca ye viduryānti te param ||

14.1 श्रीभगवानुवाच |
परं भूय: प्रवक्ष्यामि ज्ञानानां ज्ञानमुत्तमम् |
यज्ज्ञात्वा मुनय: सर्वे परां सिद्धिमितो गता: ||

śrībhagavānuvāca |
paraṃ bhūyaḥ pravakṣyāmi jñānānāṃ jñānamuttamam |
yajjñātvā munayaḥ sarve parāṃ siddhimito gatāḥ ||

14.2 इदं ज्ञानमुपाश्रित्य मम साधर्म्यमागता: |
सर्गेऽपि नोपजायन्ते प्रलये न व्यथन्ति च ||

idaṃ jñānamupāśritya mama sādharmyamāgatāḥ |
sarge'pi nopajāyante pralaye na vyathanti ca ||

14.3 मम योनिर्महद् ब्रह्म तस्मिन्गर्भं दधाम्यहम् |
संभव: सर्वभूतानां ततो भवति भारत ||

mama yonirmahad brahma tasmingarbhaṃ dadhāmyaham |
saṃbhavaḥ sarvabhūtānāṃ tato bhavati bhārata ||

14.4 सर्वयोनिषु कौन्तेय मूर्तय: संभवन्ति या: |
तासां ब्रह्म महद्योनिरहं बीजप्रद: पिता ||

sarvayoniṣu kaunteya mūrtayaḥ saṃbhavanti yāḥ |
tāsāṃ brahma mahadyoniraham bījapradaḥ pitā ||

13.34 by knowledge-eye
she who differentiates
    knower as free from field
    beings as free from matter
she goes
to the goal

14.1 i'll say even more
of the best knowledge
by which all seeekers
attain realization

14.2 assured they
got to my state they
are not born at creation
not scared at dissolution

14.3 mighty brahma
is my womb
    where i place my seed

the origin of all
beings is
right there   arjuna

14.4 for any form from any womb

brahma is womb   archetypal womb
i'm dad seed

14.5 सत्त्वं रजस्तम इति गुणाः प्रकृतिसंभवाः |
निबध्नन्ति महाबाहो देहे देहिनमव्ययम् ||

sattvaṃ rajastama iti guṇāḥ prakṛtisaṃbhavāḥ |
nibadhnanti mahābāho dehe dehinamavyayam ||

14.6 तत्र सत्त्वं निर्मलत्वात्प्रकाशकमनामयम् |
सुखसङ्गेन बध्नाति ज्ञानसङ्गेन चानघ ||

tatra sattvaṃ nirmalatvātprakāśakamanāmayam |
sukhasaṅgena badhnāti jñānasaṅgena cānagha ||

14.7 रजो रागात्मकं विद्धि तृष्णासङ्गसमुद्भवम् |
तन्निबध्नाति कौन्तेय कर्मसङ्गेन देहिनम् ||

rajo rāgātmakaṃ viddhi tṛṣṇāsaṅgasamudbhavam |
tannibadhnāti kaunteya karmasaṅgena dehinam ||

14.8 तमस्त्वज्ञानजं विद्धि मोहनं सर्वदेहिनाम् |
प्रमादालस्यनिद्राभिस्तन्निबध्नाति भारत ||

tamastvajñānajaṃ viddhi mohanaṃ sarvadehinām |
pramādālasyanidrābhistannibadhnāti bhārata ||

14.9 सत्त्वं सुखे सञ्जयति रजः कर्मणि भारत |
ज्ञानमावृत्य तु तमः प्रमादे सञ्जयत्युत ||

sattvaṃ sukhe sañjayati rajaḥ karmaṇi bhārata |
jñānamāvṛtya tu tamaḥ pramāde sañjayatyuta ||

14.10 रजस्तमश्चाभिभूय सत्त्वं भवति भारत |
रजः सत्त्वं तमश्चैव तमः सत्त्वं रजस्तथा ||

rajastamaścābhibhūya sattvaṃ bhavati bhārata |
rajaḥ sattvaṃ tamaścaiva tamaḥ sattvaṃ rajastathā ||

14.5 sattva – rajas – tamas
are gunas qualities
natureborn

tie the embodied infinite you
to the body

14.6 sattva
healthy shining purity
links you to happiness
& knowledge

14.7 rajas
passion
comes from desire & attachment
links you to action

14.8 tamas
comes from ignorance
confuses
links you to confusion
laziness sleepiness

14.9–14.10 when sattva dominates
→ happiness

when rajas dominates
→ action

when tamas dominates
hides knowledge →
→ confusion

14.11 सर्वद्वारेषु देहेऽस्मिन्प्रकाश उपजायते |
ज्ञानं यदा तदा विद्याद्विवृद्धं सत्त्वमित्युत ||

sarvadvāreṣu dehe'sminprakāśa upajāyate |
jñānaṃ yadā tadā vidyādvivṛddhaṃ sattvamityuta ||

14.12 लोभ: प्रवृत्तिरारम्भ: कर्मणामशम: स्पृहा |
रजस्येतानि जायन्ते विवृद्धे भरतर्षभ ||

lobhaḥ pravṛttirārambhaḥ karmaṇāmaśamaḥ spṛhā |
rajasyetāni jāyante vivṛddhe bharatarṣabha ||

14.13 अप्रकाशोऽप्रवृत्तिश्च प्रमादो मोह एव च |
तमस्येतानि जायन्ते विवृद्धे कुरुनन्दन ||

aprakāśo'pravṛttiśca pramādo moha eva ca |
tamasyetāni jāyante vivṛddhe kurunandana ||

14.14 यदा सत्त्वे प्रवृद्धे तु प्रलयं याति देहभृत् |
तदोत्तमविदां लोकानमलान्प्रतिपद्यते ||

yadā sattve pravṛddhe tu pralayaṃ yāti dehabhṛt |
tadottamavidāṃ lokānamalānpratipadyate ||

14.15 रजसि प्रलयं गत्वा कर्मसङ्गिषु जायते |
तथा प्रलीनस्तमसि मूढयोनिषु जायते ||

rajasi pralayaṃ gatvā karmasaṅgiṣu jāyate |
tathā pralīnastamasi mūḍhayoniṣu jāyate ||

14.16 कर्मण: सुकृतस्याहु: सात्त्विकं निर्मलं फलम् |
रजसस्तु फलं दु:खमज्ञानं तमस: फलम् ||

karmaṇaḥ sukṛtasyāhuḥ sāttvikaṃ nirmalaṃ phalam |
rajasastu phalaṃ duḥkhamajñānaṃ tamasaḥ phalam ||

14.17 सत्त्वात्संजायते ज्ञानं रजसो लोभ एव च |
प्रमादमोहौ तमसो भवतोऽज्ञानमेव च ||

sattvātsaṃjāyate jñānaṃ rajaso lobha eva ca |
pramādamohau tamaso bhavato'jñānameva ca ||

14.11–14.13 via all bodygates (nine)

when knowledge light
shines …
… sattva

greed activity
stirring lust
restlessness …
… rajas

darkness inertia
confusion …
… tamas

14.14–14.18 when a being with a body
goes through 'death'
in the influence
of sattva rajas or tamas

sattvic goes stainlessly
to the highest worlds
of knowledgeable

rajasic is reborn
in the world
of action

tamasic is reborn
in the wombs
of the fooled

the result of sattva action is pure
rajas results in pain
tamas in ignorance

14.18 ऊर्ध्वं गच्छन्ति सत्त्वस्था मध्ये तिष्ठन्ति राजसाः |
जघन्यगुणवृत्तिस्था अधो गच्छन्ति तामसाः ||

ūrdhvaṃ gacchanti sattvasthā madhye tiṣṭhanti rājasāḥ |
jaghanyaguṇavṛttisthā adho gacchanti tāmasāḥ ||

14.19 नान्यं गुणेभ्यः कर्तारं यदा द्रष्टानुपश्यति |
गुणेभ्यश्च परं वेत्ति मद्भावं सोऽधिगच्छति ||

nānyaṃ guṇebhyaḥ kartāraṃ yadā draṣṭānupaśyati |
guṇebhyaśca paraṃ vetti madbhāvaṃ so'dhigacchati ||

14.20 गुणानेतानतीत्य त्रीन्देही देहसमुद्भवान् |
जन्ममृत्युजरादुःखैर्विमुक्तोऽमृतमश्नुते ||

guṇānetānatītya trīndehī dehasamudbhavān |
janmamṛtyujarāduḥkhairvimukto'mṛtamaśnute ||

14.21 अर्जुन उवाच |
कैर्लिङ्गैस्त्रीन्गुणानेतानतीतो भवति प्रभो |
किमाचारः कथं चैतांस्त्रीन्गुणानतिवर्तते ||

arjuna uvāca |
kairliṅgaistrīnguṇānetānatīto bhavati prabho |
kimācāraḥ kathaṃ caitāṃstrīnguṇānativartate ||

14.22 श्रीभगवानुवाच |
प्रकाशं च प्रवृत्तिं च मोहमेव च पाण्डव |
न द्वेष्टि संप्रवृत्तानि न निवृत्तानि काङ्क्षति ||

śrībhagavānuvāca |
prakāśaṃ ca pravṛttiṃ ca mohameva ca pāṇḍava |
ta dveṣṭi saṃpravṛttāni na nivṛttāni kāṅkṣati ||

from sattva is born knowledge
from rajas desire
from tamas confusion ignorance

the sattvic goes up
rajasic stays in the middle
tamasic goes below

14.19 when she knows
the doer's none other than gunas
& knows what transcends them
she attains my state

14.20 when she transcends
these three gunas that cause the body

she's freed
from birth death age pain
reaches immortality

14.21 arjuna:
what is the sign of a transcended one
how does she behave
how does she transcend the three

14.22 krishna:
in knowledge activity confusion
she   doesn't hate what's there
doesn't want what's not

14.23 उदासीनवदासीनो गुणैर्यो न विचाल्यते |
गुणा वर्तन्त इत्येवं योऽवतिष्ठति नेङ्गते ||

udāsīnavadāsīno guṇairyo na vicālyate |
guṇā vartanta ityevaṃ yo'vatiṣṭhati neṅgate ||

14.24 समदुःखसुखः स्वस्थः समलोष्टाश्मकाञ्चनः |
तुल्यप्रियाप्रियो धीरस्तुल्यनिन्दात्मसंस्तुतिः ||

samaduḥkhasukhaḥ svasthaḥ samaloṣṭāśmakāñcanaḥ |
tulyapriyāpriyo dhīrastulyanindātmasaṃstutiḥ ||

14.25 मानापमानयोस्तुल्यस्तुल्यो मित्रारिपक्षयोः |
सर्वारम्भपरित्यागी गुणातीतः स उच्यते ||

mānāpamānayostulyastulyo mitrāripakṣayoḥ |
sarvārambhaparityāgī guṇātītaḥ sa ucyate ||

14.26 मां च योऽव्यभिचारेण भक्तियोगेन सेवते |
स गुणान्समतीत्यैतान्ब्रह्मभूयाय कल्पते ||

māṃ ca yo'vyabhicāreṇa bhaktiyogena sevate |
sa guṇānsamatītyaitānbrahmabhūyāya kalpate ||

14.27 ब्रह्मणो हि प्रतिष्ठाहममृतस्याव्ययस्य च |
शाश्वतस्य च धर्मस्य सुखस्यैकान्तिकस्य च ||

brahmaṇo hi pratiṣṭhāhamamṛtasyāvyayasya ca |
śāśvatasya ca dharmasya sukhasyaikāntikasya ca ||

14.23 she who
is as if detached

by (three) gunas unperturbed
steady not stirred

thinks 'oh that's them gunas
at work'

14.24–14.25 self-reliant steady renouncing all ventures
pain = pleasure
stone = gold = clay
loved = not loved

friend = foe
honour = disgrace
praise = blame

transcends gunas it is said

14.26 & she who transcending gunas
with unwandering devotion bhakti
serves me

is ready
to be
one

with brahman

14.27 i am the site
of brahman
of immortal undying eternal law unique bliss

15.1 श्रीभगवानुवाच |
ऊर्ध्वमूलमधःशाखमश्वत्थं प्राहुरव्ययम् |
छन्दांसि यस्य पर्णानि यस्तं वेद स वेदवित् ||

śrībhagavānuvāca |
ūrdhvamūlamadhaḥśākhamaśvatthaṃ prāhuravyayam |
chandāṃsi yasya parṇāni yastaṃ veda sa vedavit ||

15.2 अधश्चोर्ध्वं प्रसृतास्तस्य शाखा गुणप्रवृद्धा विषयप्रवालाः |
अधश्च मूलान्यनुसंततानि कर्मानुबन्धीनि मनुष्यलोके ||

adhaścordhvaṃ prasṛtāstasya śākhā
guṇapravṛddhā viṣayapravālāḥ |
adhaśca mūlānyanusaṃtatāni
karmānubandhīni manuṣyaloke ||

15.3 न रूपमस्येह तथोपलभ्यते नान्तो न चादिर्न च संप्रतिष्ठा |
अश्वत्थमेनं सुविरूढमूलं असङ्गशस्त्रेण दृढेन छित्त्वा ||

na rūpamasyeha tathopalabhyate
nānto na cādirna ca saṃpratiṣṭhā |
aśvatthamenaṃ suvirūḍhamūlaṃ
asaṅgaśastreṇa dṛḍhena chittvā ||

15.1 krishna:

an endless tree
the tree of life

roots above
limbs below

& its leaves they say
are vedic hymns
    she who knows this
    knows the veda

15.2 high & low
its branches flow

qualities feed it

& objects of desire
sprout there

& below
the stretching (aerial) roots
plant activities in the world of humans

15.3 you can't quite get it

its form its start its end
& foundation

a full-grown root like
this can be cut
only by the strong

with the axe: detachment

15.4 ततः पदं तत्परिमार्गितव्यं यस्मिन्गता न निवर्तन्ति भूयः |
तमेव चाद्यं पुरुषं प्रपद्ये यतः प्रवृत्तिः प्रसृता पुराणी ||

tataḥ padaṃ tatparimārgitavyaṃ
yasmingatā na nivartanti bhūyaḥ |
tameva cādyaṃ puruṣaṃ prapadye
yataḥ pravṛttiḥ prasṛtā purāṇī ||

15.5 निर्मानमोहा जितसङ्गदोषा अध्यात्मनित्या विनिवृत्तकामाः |
द्वन्द्वैर्विमुक्ताः सुखदुःखसंज्ञैः गच्छन्त्यमूढाः पदमव्ययं तत् ||

nirmānamohā jitasaṅgadoṣā
adhyātmanityā vinivṛttakāmāḥ |
dvandvairvimuktāḥ sukhaduḥkhasaṃjñaiḥ
gacchantyamūḍhāḥ padamavyayaṃ tat ||

15.6 न तद्भासयते सूर्यो न शशाङ्को न पावकः |
यद्गत्वा न निवर्तन्ते तद्धाम परमं मम ||

na tadbhāsayate sūryo na śaśāṅko na pāvakaḥ |
yadgatvā na nivartante taddhāma paramaṃ mama ||

15.7 ममैवांशो जीवलोके जीवभूतः सनातनः |
मनःषष्ठानीन्द्रियाणि प्रकृतिस्थानि कर्षति ||

mamaivāṃśo jīvaloke jīvabhūtaḥ sanātanaḥ |
manaḥṣaṣṭhānīndriyāṇi prakṛtisthāni karṣati ||

15.4 so seek detachment then! there where
those who go
don't return

(say)
'refuge i seek in the ancient spirit
that first gushed creativity'

15.5 arrogance
faults &
attachments vanquished

always in the spiritual

turning from lusts
free from pairings pleasure pain
unfooled they go
 there the everlasting place

15.6 unlit by sun
 moon
 fire

it's my place beyond

 they go there &
 don't come back

15.7 a being a mere part of me ancient
when becoming in the living world

draws six senses:
 smell taste touch sight hearing mind

from matter nature
to itself

15.8 शरीरं यदवाप्नोति यच्चाप्युत्क्रामतीश्वरः |
गृहीत्वैतानि संयाति वायुर्गन्धानिवाशयात् ||

śarīraṃ yadavāpnoti yaccāpyutkrāmatīśvaraḥ |
gṛhitvaitāni saṃyāti vāyurgandhānivāśayāt ||

15.9 श्रोत्रं चक्षुः स्पर्शनं च रसनं घ्राणमेव च |
अधिष्ठाय मनश्चायं विषयानुपसेवते ||

śrotraṃ cakṣuḥ sparśanaṃ ca rasanaṃ ghrāṇameva ca |
adhiṣṭhāya manaścāyaṃ viṣayānupasevate ||

15.10 उत्क्रामन्तं स्थितं वापि भुञ्जानं वा गुणान्वितम् |
विमूढा नानुपश्यन्ति पश्यन्ति ज्ञानचक्षुषः ||

utkrāmantaṃ sthitaṃ vāpi bhuñjānaṃ vā guṇānvitam |
vimūḍhā nānupaśyanti paśyanti jñānacakṣuṣaḥ ||

15.11 यतन्तो योगिनश्चैनं पश्यन्त्यात्मन्यवस्थितम् |
यतन्तोऽप्यकृतात्मानो नैनं पश्यन्त्यचेतसः ||

yatanto yoginaścainaṃ paśyantyātmanyavasthitam |
yatanto’pyakṛtātmāno nainaṃ paśyantyacetasaḥ ||

15.12 यदादित्यगतं तेजो जगद्भासयतेऽखिलम् |
यच्चन्द्रमसि यच्चाग्नौ तत्तेजो विद्धि मामकम् ||

yadādityagataṃ tejo jagadbhāsayate’khilam |
yaccandramasi yaccāgnau tattejo viddhi māmakam ||

15.8 when it god
takes a body
& when it ups & goes

it carries these (senses) along
as wind carries scents from a source

(so the spirit carries
its characteristics)

15.9 over hearing sight touch taste smell & mind
it presides

& objects of desire
it savours

15.10 whether it's going or staying or enjoying
or if it has qualities
only the knowing eyes see it
not the fooled

15.11 striving yogis
see it in themselves
the unready don't
even if they try

15.12 the brilliance from the sun
that illuminates the universe without stop

in the moon

in fire
note
it's mine

15.13 गामाविश्य च भूतानि धारयाम्यहमोजसा |
पुष्णामि चौषधीः सर्वाः सोमो भूत्वा रसात्मकः ||

gāmāviśya ca bhūtāni dhārayāmyahamojasā |
puṣṇāmi cauṣadhīḥ sarvāḥ somo bhūtvā rasātmakaḥ ||

15.14 अहं वैश्वानरो भूत्वा प्राणिनां देहमाश्रितः |
प्राणापानसमायुक्तः पचाम्यन्नं चतुर्विधम् ||

ahaṃ vaiśvānaro bhūtvā prāṇināṃ dehamāśritaḥ |
prāṇāpānasamāyuktaḥ pacāmyannaṃ caturvidham ||

15.15 सर्वस्य चाहं हृदि सन्निविष्टो मत्तः स्मृतिर्ज्ञानमपोहनं च |
वेदैश्च सर्वैरहमेव वेद्यो वेदान्तकृद्वेदविदेव चाहम् ||

sarvasya cāhaṃ hṛdi sanniviṣṭo
mattaḥ smṛtirjñānamapohanaṃ ca |
vedaiśca sarvairahameva vedyo
vedāntakṛdvedavideva cāham ||

15.16 द्वाविमौ पुरुषौ लोके क्षरश्चाक्षर एव च |
क्षरः सर्वाणि भूतानि कूटस्थोऽक्षर उच्यते ||

dvāvimau puruṣau loke kṣaraścākṣara eva ca |
kṣaraḥ sarvāṇi bhūtāni kūṭastho'kṣara ucyate ||

15.13 i enter the earth &
with my energy
support all beings

then as soma nectar juicy
i make all plants blossom

15.14 becoming digestive fire
i live
in the body of beings

with
inhalation   life breath
& exhalation   abdominal breath

i consume four types of food

15.15 in every heart   i am
i am memory wisdom & their negation

i am the author of the vedanta
the knower of the vedanta

in the vedas i am
all that's to be known

15.16 in this world there are two
perishable imperishable

all living beings perish

what doesn't change
is called imperishable

15.17 उत्तमः पुरुषस्त्वन्यः परमात्मेत्युदाहृतः |
यो लोकत्रयमाविश्य बिभर्त्यव्यय ईश्वरः ||

uttamaḥ puruṣastvanyaḥ paramātmetyudāhṛtaḥ |
yo lokatrayamāviśya bibhartyavyaya īśvaraḥ ||

15.18 यस्मात्क्षरमतीतोऽहमक्षरादपि चोत्तमः |
अतोऽस्मि लोके वेदे च प्रथितः पुरुषोत्तमः ||

yasmātkṣaramatīto'hamakṣarādapi cottamaḥ |
ato'smi loke vede ca prathitaḥ puruṣottamaḥ ||

15.19 यो मामेवमसम्मूढो जानाति पुरुषोत्तमम् |
स सर्वविद्भजति मां सर्वभावेन भारत ||

yo māmevamasaṃmūḍho jānāti puruṣottamam |
sa sarvavidbhajati māṃ sarvabhāvena bhārata ||

15.20 इति गुह्यतमं शास्त्रमिदमुक्तं मयानघ |
एतद्बुद्ध्वा बुद्धिमान्स्यात्कृतकृत्यश्च भारत ||

iti guhyatamaṃ śāstramidamuktaṃ mayānagha |
etadbuddhvā buddhimānsyātkṛtakṛtyaśca bhārata ||

15.17 but there's another the highest
the 'supreme'

who enters the three worlds
& supports them

15.18 because i am beyond the perishable
because i am beyond the imperishable

i am   in the world & in the vedas
known
as supreme

15.19 she who   not a fool
knows me

all-knowing
supreme

adores me
with her entire
being

15.20 this supersecret science
has been spoken by me

knowing this
one should become
enlightened
all duties done

16.1 श्रीभगवानुवाच |
अभयं सत्त्वसंशुद्धिर्ज्ञानयोगव्यवस्थितिः |
दानं दमश्च यज्ञश्च स्वाध्यायस्तप आर्जवम् ||

śrībhagavānuvāca |
abhayaṃ sattvasaṃśuddhirjñānayogavyavasthitiḥ |
dānaṃ damaśca yajñaśca svādhyāyastapa ārjavam ||

16.2 अहिंसा सत्यमक्रोधस्त्यागः शान्तिरपैशुनम् |
दया भूतेष्वलोलुप्त्वं मार्दवं ह्रीरचापलम् ||

ahiṃsā satyamakrodhastyāgaḥ śāntirapaiśunam |
dayā bhūteṣvaloluptvaṃ mārdavaṃ hrīracāpalam ||

16.3 तेजः क्षमा धृतिः शौचमद्रोहोनातिमानिता |
भवन्ति संपदं दैवीमभिजातस्य भारत ||

tejaḥ kṣamā dhṛtiḥ śaucamadrohonātimānitā |
bhavanti saṃpadaṃ daivīmabhijātasya bhārata ||

16.4 दम्भो दर्पोऽभिमानश्च क्रोधः पारुष्यमेव च |
अज्ञानं चाभिजातस्य पार्थ संपदमासुरीम् ||

dambho darpo'bhimānaśca krodhaḥ pāruṣyameva ca |
ajñānaṃ cābhijātasya pārtha saṃpadamāsurīm ||

16.5 दैवी संपद्विमोक्षाय निबन्धायासुरी मता |
मा शुचः संपदं दैवीमभिजातोऽसि पाण्डव ||

daivī saṃpadvimokṣāya nibandhāyāsurī matā |
mā śucaḥ saṃpadaṃ daivīmabhijāto'si pāṇḍava ||

16.6 द्वौ भूतसर्गौ लोकेऽस्मिन्दैव आसुर एव च |
दैवो विस्तरशः प्रोक्त आसुरं पार्थ मे शृणु ||

dvau bhūtasargau loke'smindaiva āsura eva ca |
daivo vistaraśaḥ prokta āsuraṃ pārtha me śṛṇu ||

16.1–16.4 krishna:

these are the assets
of the inherently divine

fearless allpure
set on the way of wisdom
charitable self controlled & right
does yajna self study austerities
nonviolent truthful angerless renunciate
peaceful nonslanderous compassionate
nondesirous modest gentle unfickle
radiant patient courageous
hygienic untreacherous
not overproud

& these the inherent demonic

hypocrisy egoism
anger harshness ignorance

16.5 the divine leads to liberation
demonic to bondage

don't worry
you are born
to divine destiny

16.6 (so) two types of beings in this world
divine
demonic

enough said of the divine

here's more
about the demonic

16.7 प्रवृत्तिं च निवृत्तिं च जना न विदुरासुराः |
न शौचं नापि चाचारो न सत्यं तेषु विद्यते ||

pravṛttiṃ ca nivṛttiṃ ca janā na vidurāsurāḥ |
na śaucaṃ nāpi cācāro na satyaṃ teṣu vidyate ||

16.8 असत्यमप्रतिष्ठं ते जगदाहुरनीश्वरम् |
अपरस्परसंभूतं किमन्यत्कामहैतुकम् ||

asatyamapratiṣṭhaṃ te jagadāhuranīśvaram |
aparasparasaṃbhūtaṃ kimanyatkāmahaitukam ||

16.9 एतां दृष्टिमवष्टभ्य नष्टात्मानोऽल्पबुद्धयः |
प्रभवन्त्युग्रकर्माणः क्षयाय जगतोऽहिताः ||

etāṃ dṛṣṭimavaṣṭabhya naṣṭātmāno'lpabuddhayaḥ |
prabhavantyugrakarmāṇaḥ kṣayāya jagato'hitāḥ ||

16.10 काममाश्रित्य दुष्पूरं दम्भमानमदान्विताः |
मोहाद्गृहीत्वाऽसद्ग्राहान्प्रवर्तन्तेऽशुचिव्रताः ||

kāmamāśritya duṣpūraṃ dambhamānamadānvitāḥ |
mohādgṛhītvā'sadgrāhānpravartante'śucivratāḥ ||

16.11 चिन्तामपरिमेयां च प्रलयान्तामुपाश्रिताः |
कामोपभोगपरमा एतावदिति निश्चिताः ||

cintāmaparimeyāṃ ca pralayāntāmupāśritāḥ |
kāmopabhogaparamā etāvaditi niścitāḥ ||

16.7 they don't know
when to act
& when to rest

no
purity nicety
truth   in them

16.8 shaky without truth
they say the universe
is godless
one happened without the other

    & worse   happened
    via lust!

16.9 with this view
these lost smallminded
come up
with terrible acts to
destroy the world

16.10 in desire insatiable
with arrogance hypocrisy
deluded tipsy   they carry on
hang on to lies &   impure practices

16.11 in infinite worries
unto the end
hedonists
    they're sure that's
    all there is to it

16.12 आशापाशशतैर्बद्धाः कामक्रोधपरायणाः |
ईहन्ते कामभोगार्थमन्यायेनार्थसंचयान् ||

āśāpāśaśatairbaddhāḥ kāmakrodhaparāyaṇāḥ |
īhante kāmabhogārthamanyāyenārthasaṃcayān ||

16.13 इदमद्य मया लब्धमिमं प्राप्स्ये मनोरथम् |
इदमस्तीदमपि मे भविष्यति पुनर्धनम् ||

idamadya mayā labdhamimaṃ prāpsye manoratham |
idamastīdamapi me bhaviṣyati punardhanam ||

16.14 असौ मया हतः शत्रुर्हनिष्ये चापरानपि |
ईश्वरोऽहमहं भोगी सिद्धोऽहं बलवान्सुखी ||

asau mayā hataḥ śatrurhaniṣye cāparānapi |
īśvaro'hamahaṃ bhogī siddho'haṃ balavānsukhī ||

16.15 आढ्योऽभिजनवानस्मि कोऽन्योऽस्ति सदृशो मया |
यक्ष्ये दास्यामि मोदिष्य इत्यज्ञानविमोहिताः ||

āḍhyo'bhijanavānasmi ko'nyos'ti sadṛśo mayā |
yakṣye dāsyāmi modiṣya ityajñānavimohitāḥ ||

16.16 अनेकचित्तविभ्रान्ता मोहजालसमावृताः |
प्रसक्ताः कामभोगेषु पतन्ति नरकेऽशुचौ ||

anekacittavibhrāntā mohajālasamāvṛtāḥ |
prasaktāḥ kāmabhogeṣu patanti narake'śucau ||

16.17 आत्मसंभाविताः स्तब्धा धनमानमदान्विताः |
यजन्ते नामयज्ञैस्ते दम्भेनाविधिपूर्वकम् ||

ātmasaṃbhāvitāḥ stabdhā dhanamānamadānvitāḥ |
yajante nāmayajñaiste dambhenāvidhipūrvakam ||

16.12 snared in hundreds of hope-ropes
dedicated to anger desire

they want to make money   in illegal ways
for pleasure

16.13 'this i picked up today
& this heart's desire   i will too
& this is mine   this money
& this too will be mine'

16.14 'that foe's done in   by me
      i'll get the others too
i'm god i'm debauchee
      successful powerful happy'

16.15 'i'm rich i'm classy
      no one else compares to me
yeah i'll do the rites donate enjoy'

that's how they are   misled
by ignorance

16.16 spun out by many thoughts
netted by delusion
clinging to pleasures
they fall   impure
      hell!

16.17 full of themselves diehards
high & proud on wealth
      offer namesake rituals
      with hypocrisy
                  not the correct way

16.18 अहंकारं बलं दर्पं कामं क्रोधं च संश्रिताः |
मामात्मपरदेहेषु प्रद्विषन्तोऽभ्यसूयकाः ||

ahaṃkāraṃ balaṃ darpaṃ kāmaṃ krodhaṃ ca saṃśritāḥ |
māmātmaparadeheṣu pradviṣanto'bhyasūyakāḥ ||

16.19 तानहं द्विषतः क्रूरान्संसारेषु नराधमान् |
क्षिपाम्यजस्रमशुभानासुरीष्वेव योनिषु ||

tānahaṃ dviṣataḥ krurānsaṃsāreṣu narādhamān |
kṣipāmyajasramaśubhānāsurīṣveva yoniṣu ||

16.20 आसुरीं योनिमापन्ना मूढा जन्मनि जन्मनि |
मामप्राप्यैव कौन्तेय ततो यान्त्यधमां गतिम् ||

āsurīṃ yonimāpannā mūḍhā janmani janmani |
māmaprāpyaiva kaunteya tato yāntyadhamāṃ gatim ||

16.21 त्रिविधं नरकस्येदं द्वारं नाशनमात्मनः |
कामः क्रोधस्तथा लोभस्तस्मादेतत्त्रयं त्यजेत् ||

trividhaṃ narakasyedaṃ dvāraṃ nāśanamātmanaḥ |
kāmaḥ krodhastathā lobhastasmādetattrayaṃ tyajet ||

16.22 एतैर्विमुक्तः कौन्तेय तमोद्वारैस्त्रिभिर्नरः |
आचरत्यात्मनः श्रेयस्ततो याति परां गतिम् ||

etairvimuktaḥ kaunteya tamodvāraistribhirnaraḥ |
ācaratyātmanaḥ śreyastato yāti parāṃ gatim ||

16.23 यः शास्त्रविधिमुत्सृज्य वर्तते कामकारतः |
न स सिद्धिमवाप्नोति न सुखं न परां गतिम् ||

yaḥ śāstravidhimutsṛjya vartate kāmakārataḥ |
na sa siddhimavāpnoti na sukhaṃ na parāṃ gatim ||

16.18 in a state of egoism power envy
anger desire arrogance they
hate me in their own bodies
& others'

16.19 i always throw
these bad cruel haters
the worst of all humans
in this gig
into demonic wombs

16.20 having got there
the fools birth after birth
not getting to me

they carry on to
worse places

16.21 desire anger greed
are the three gates of hell
one's destruction
one must give them up

16.22 when free from these three
gates of darkness arjuna
one does what's good
for oneself &

walks the high way

16.23 she who ignores
shastras (ancient sciences treatises of knowledge)
goes as she pleases

reaches neither perfection
nor happiness or the goal

16.24 तस्माच्छास्त्रं प्रमाणं ते कार्याकार्यव्यवस्थितौ |
ज्ञात्वा शास्त्रविधानोक्तं कर्म कर्तुमिहार्हसि ||

tasmācchāstraṃ pramāṇaṃ te kāryākāryavyavasthitau |
jñātvā śāstravidhānoktaṃ karma kartumihārhasi ||

17.1 अर्जुन उवाच |
ये शास्त्रविधिमुत्सृज्य यजन्ते श्रद्धयान्विता: |
तेषां निष्ठा तु का कृष्ण सत्त्वमाहो रजस्तम: ||

arjuna uvāca |
ye śāstravidhimutsṛjya yajante śraddhayānvitāḥ |
teṣāṃ niṣṭhā tu kā kṛṣṇa sattvamāho rajastamaḥ ||

17.2 श्रीभगवानुवाच |
त्रिविधा भवति श्रद्धा देहिनां सा स्वभावजा |
सात्त्विकी राजसी चैव तामसी चेति तां शृणु ||

śrībhagavānuvāca |
trividhā bhavati śraddhā dehināṃ sā svabhāvajā |
sāttvikī rājasī caiva tāmasī ceti tāṃ śṛṇu ||

17.3 सत्त्वानुरूपा सर्वस्य श्रद्धा भवति भारत |
श्रद्धामयोऽयं पुरुषो यो यच्छ्रद्धः स एव सः ||

sattvānurūpā sarvasya śraddhā bhavati bhārata |
śraddhāmayo'yaṃ puruṣo yo yacchraddhaḥ sa eva saḥ ||

17.4 यजन्ते सात्त्विका देवान्यक्षरक्षांसि राजसा: |
प्रेतान्भूतगणांश्चान्ये यजन्ते तामसा जना: ||

yajante sāttvikā devānyakṣarakṣāṃsi rājasāḥ |
pretānbhūtagaṇāṃścānye yajante tāmasā janāḥ ||

16.24 take shastras as your guide
figure out
what's to be done
& what not

know what the shastras say
& do your duty

17.1 arjuna:
what about those faithful
who throw out the shastras

where do they stand   are they
sattva rajas or tamas

17.2 krishna:
listen
three types of faith
come naturally
for beings   for those in bodies

sattvic   rajasic   tamasic

17.3 everyone's faith
is in line with her
nature

a person is made of faith
whatever she believes
she is

17.4 the sattvic offer to deities
the rajasic to spirits & demons
the tamasic to the departed & to ghosts

17.5 अशास्त्रविहितं घोरं तप्यन्ते ये तपो जनाः |
दम्भाहंकारसंयुक्ताः कामरागबलान्विताः ||

aśāstravihitaṃ ghoraṃ tapyante ye tapo janāḥ |
dambhāhaṃkārasaṃyuktāḥ kāmarāgabalānvitāḥ ||

17.6 कर्षयन्तः शरीरस्थं भूतग्राममचेतसः |
मां चैवान्तःशरीरस्थं तान्विद्ध्यासुरनिश्चयान् ||

karṣayantaḥ śarīrasthaṃ bhūtagrāmamacetasaḥ |
māṃ caivāntaḥśarīrasthaṃ tānviddhyāsuraniścayān ||

17.7 आहारस्त्वपि सर्वस्य त्रिविधो भवति प्रियः |
यज्ञस्तपस्तथा दानं तेषां भेदमिमं शृणु ||

āhārastvapi sarvasya trividho bhavati priyaḥ |
yajñastapastathā dānaṃ teṣāṃ bhedamimaṃ śṛṇu ||

17.8 आयुःसत्त्वबलारोग्यसुखप्रीतिविवर्धनाः |
रस्याः स्निग्धाः स्थिरा हृद्या आहाराः सात्त्विकप्रियाः ||

āyuḥsattvabalārogyasukhaprītivivardhanāḥ |
rasyāḥ snigdhāḥ sthirā hṛdyā āhārāḥ sāttvikapriyāḥ ||

17.9 कट्वम्ललवणात्युष्णतीक्ष्णरूक्षविदाहिनः |
आहारा राजसस्येष्टा दुःखशोकामयप्रदाः ||

kaṭvamlalavaṇātyuṣṇatīkṣṇarūkṣavidāhinaḥ |
āhārā rājasasyeṣṭā duḥkhaśokāmayapradāḥ ||

17.10 यातयामं गतरसं पूति पर्युषितं च यत् |
उच्छिष्टमपि चामेध्यं भोजनं तामसप्रियम् ||

yātayāmaṃ gatarasaṃ pūti paryuṣitaṃ ca yat |
ucchiṣṭamapi cāmedhyaṃ bhojanaṃ tāmasapriyam ||

17.5 those who not in line with scriptures
do harrowing
penance with egoism hypocrisy
passion power desire

17.6 thoughtless torture
of elements in their body
& me in their body

are demonic wills

17.7 besides
the food everyone likes
is three types

different in offering austerity charity

17.8 the sattvic likes
hearty smooth
substantial flavour
for truth liveliness strength health
& a happy good feeling

17.9 the rajasic wants
hot pungent sour salty
sharp dry
it causes sadness grief illness

17.10 & the tamasic likes
stale outofflavour
putrid leftovers
impure rejects

17.11 अफलाकाङ्क्षिभिर्यज्ञो विधिदृष्टो य इज्यते |
यष्टव्यमेवेति मनः समाधाय स सात्त्विकः ||

aphalākāṅkṣibhiryajño vidhidṛṣṭo ya ijyate |
yaṣṭavyameveti manaḥ samādhāya sa sāttvikaḥ ||

17.12 अभिसंधाय तु फलं दम्भार्थमपि चैव यत् |
इज्यते भरतश्रेष्ठ तं यज्ञं विद्धि राजसम् ||

abhisaṃdhāya tu phalaṃ dambhārthamapi caiva yat |
ijyate bharataśreṣṭha taṃ yajñaṃ viddhi rājasam ||

17.13 विधिहीनमसृष्टान्नं मन्त्रहीनमदक्षिणम् |
श्रद्धाविरहितं यज्ञं तामसं परिचक्षते ||

vidhihīnamasṛṣṭānnaṃ mantrahīnamadakṣiṇam |
śraddhāvirahitaṃ yajñaṃ tāmasaṃ paricakṣate ||

17.14 देवद्विजगुरुप्राज्ञपूजनं शौचमार्जवम् |
ब्रह्मचर्यमहिंसा च शारीरं तप उच्यते ||

devadvijaguruprājñapūjanaṃ śaucamārjavam |
brahmacaryamahiṃsā ca śārīraṃ tapa ucyate ||

17.15 अनुद्वेगकरं वाक्यं सत्यं प्रियहितं च यत् |
स्वाध्यायाभ्यसनं चैव वाङ्मयं तप उच्यते ||

anudvegakaraṃ vākyaṃ satyaṃ priyahitaṃ ca yat |
svādhyāyābhyasanaṃ caiva vāñmayaṃ tapa ucyate ||

17.16 मनः प्रसादः सौम्यत्वं मौनमात्मविनिग्रहः |
भावसंशुद्धिरित्येतत्तपो मानसमुच्यते ||

manaḥ prasādaḥ saumyatvaṃ maunamātmavinigrahaḥ |
bhāvasaṃśuddhirityetattapo mānasamucyate ||

17.11 yajna done correctly by
those who don't aim at gain
for offering's sake
in mind
= sattvic

17.12 when gain's in view
& the offering's a show
the yajna
= rajasic

17.13 yajna without faith protocol
food chant
gratuity
= tamasic

17.14 physical austerity:
reverence to deities
to twice-born
(brahmins vaishyas kshatriyas)
teachers & the wise
purity rightness celibacy nonviolence

17.15 verbal austerity:
words that don't cause pain
that are true & nice & mean well
& repetition of sacred texts

17.16 mental austerity:
calm gentle silent self-controlled
pure feelings

17.17 श्रद्धया परया तप्तं तपस्तत्त्रिविधं नरैः |
अफलाकाङ्क्षिभिर्युक्तैः सात्त्विकं परिचक्षते ||

śraddhayā parayā taptaṃ tapastattrividhaṃ naraiḥ |
aphalākāṅkṣibhiryuktaiḥ sāttvikaṃ paricakṣate ||

17.18 सत्कारमानपूजार्थं तपो दम्भेन चैव यत् |
क्रियते तदिह प्रोक्तं राजसं चलमध्रुवम् ||

satkāramānapūjārthaṃ tapo dambhena caiva yat |
kriyate tadiha proktaṃ rājasaṃ calamadhruvam ||

17.19 मूढग्राहेणात्मनो यत्पीडया क्रियते तपः |
परस्योत्सादनार्थं वा तत्तामसमुदाहृतम् ||

mūḍhagrāheṇātmano yatpīḍayā kriyate tapaḥ |
parasyotsādanārthaṃ vā tattāmasamudāhṛtam ||

17.20 दातव्यमिति यद्दानं दीयतेऽनुपकारिणे |
देशे काले च पात्रे च तद्दानं सात्त्विकं स्मृतम् ||

dātavyamiti yaddānaṃ dīyate'nupakāriṇe |
deśe kāle ca pātre ca taddānaṃ sāttvikaṃ smṛtam ||

17.21 यत्तु प्रत्युपकारार्थं फलमुद्दिश्य वा पुनः |
दीयते च परिक्लिष्टं तद्दानं राजसं स्मृतम् ||

yattu pratyupakārārthaṃ phalamuddiśya vā punaḥ |
dīyate ca parikliṣṭaṃ taddānaṃ rājasaṃ smṛtam ||

17.22 अदेशकाले यद्दानमपात्रेभ्यश्च दीयते |
असत्कृतमवज्ञातं तत्तामसमुदाहृतम् ||

adeśakāle yaddānamapātrebhyaśca dīyate |
asatkṛtamavajñātaṃ tattāmasamudāhṛtam ||

17.17 this triple discipline
without agenda
with high faith
= sattvic

17.18 when false
for propriety face ritual
= rajasic
unstable shifty

17.19 when it's
with foolish ideas of oneself
tormented
or to topple someone
= tamasic

17.20 a gift that's given
for giving's sake not to return a favour
at the right time & place
to the right person
= sattvic

17.21 a grudging
quid pro quo
for gain
= rajasic

17.22 at the wrong time & place
to the wrong person
with disrespect contempt
= tamasic

17.23 ॐ तत्सदिति निर्देशो ब्रह्मणस्त्रिविधः स्मृतः |
ब्राह्मणास्तेन वेदाश्च यज्ञाश्च विहिताः पुरा ||

oṃ tatsaditi nirdeśo brahmaṇastrividhaḥ smṛtaḥ |
brāhmaṇāstena vedāśca yajñāśca vihitāḥ purā ||

17.24 तस्माद् ॐ इत्युदाहृत्य यज्ञदानतपःक्रियाः |
प्रवर्तन्ते विधानोक्ताः सततं ब्रह्मवादिनाम् ||

tasmād oṃ ityudāhṛtya yajñadānatapaḥkriyāḥ |
pravartante vidhānoktāḥ satataṃ brahmavādinām ||

17.25 तदित्यनभिसंधाय फलं यज्ञतपःक्रियाः |
दानक्रियाश्च विविधाः क्रियन्ते मोक्षकाङ्क्षिभिः ||

tadityanabhisaṃdhāya phalaṃ yajñatapaḥkriyāḥ |
dānakriyāśca vividhāḥ kriyante mokṣakāṅkṣibhiḥ ||

17.26 सद्भावे साधुभावे च सदित्येतत्प्रयुज्यते |
प्रशस्ते कर्मणि तथा सच्छब्दः पार्थ युज्यते ||

sadbhāve sādhubhāve ca sadityetatprayujyate |
praśaste karmaṇi tathā sacchabdaḥ pārtha yujyate ||

17.23 om tat sat
set as the
triple chant of brahman
organized the priests vedas & yajnas
way back

17.24 om
the way to start
a yajna charity
action austerity

so say
the followers of
brahman always

17.25 tat
thus

say those who want
liberation

via yajna charity various
actions austerity
not aiming for profit

17.26 sat
i.e.
in truth
in goodness

& said
for an action worth
appreciating

17.27 यज्ञे तपसि दाने च स्थितिः सदिति चोच्यते |
कर्म चैव तदर्थीयं सदित्येवाभिधीयते ||

yajñe tapasi dāne ca sthitiḥ saditi cocyate |
karma caiva tadarthīyaṃ sadityevābhidhīyate ||

17.28 अश्रद्धया हुतं दत्तं तपस्तप्तं कृतं च यत् |
असदित्युच्यते पार्थ न च तत्प्रेत्य नो इह ||

aśraddhayā hutaṃ dattaṃ tapastaptaṃ kṛtaṃ ca yat |
asadityucyate pārtha na ca tatpretya no iha ||

18.1 अर्जुन उवाच |
संन्यासस्य महाबाहो तत्त्वमिच्छामि वेदितुम् |
त्यागस्य च हृषीकेश पृथक्केशिनिषूदन ||

arjuna uvāca |
saṃnyāsasya mahābāho tattvamicchāmi veditum |
tyāgasya ca hṛṣīkeśa pṛthakkeśiniṣūdana ||

18.2 श्रीभगवानुवाच |
काम्यानां कर्मणां न्यासं संन्यासं कवयो विदुः |
सर्वकर्मफलत्यागं प्राहुस्त्यागं विचक्षणाः ||

śrībhagavānuvāca |
kāmyānāṃ karmaṇāṃ nyāsaṃ saṃnyāsaṃ kavayo viduḥ |
sarvakarmaphalatyāgaṃ prāhustyāgaṃ vicakṣaṇāḥ ||

18.3 त्याज्यं दोषवदित्येके कर्म प्राहुर्मनीषिणः |
यज्ञदानतपःकर्म न त्याज्यमिति चापरे ||

tyājyaṃ doṣavadityeke karma prāhurmanīṣiṇaḥ |
yajñadānatapaḥkarma na tyājyamiti cāpare ||

17.27 when steady in
sacrifice discipline charity
said to be sat

related activities
said to be sat

17.28 austerity activity &
what's given
without faith
is good for nothing here & hereafter
said to be asat

18.1 arjuna:
what's the nature
of asceticism i want to know
how's renunciation
different

18.2 krishna:
asceticism is giving up
selfish activities
as poets know
& the wise declare
renunciation is giving up
fruits of action

18.3 activity's flawed say the wise
give it up

& others say no
yajna charity austerity activity
not to be given up

18.4 निश्चयं शृणु मे तत्र त्यागे भरतसत्तम |
त्यागो हि पुरुषव्याघ्र त्रिविधः सम्प्रकीर्तितः ||

niścayaṃ śṛṇu me tatra tyāge bharatasattama |
tyāgo hi puruṣavyāghra trividhaḥ samprakīrtitaḥ ||

18.5 यज्ञदानतपःकर्म न त्याज्यं कार्यमेव तत् |
यज्ञो दानं तपश्चैव पावनानि मनीषिणाम् ||

yajñadānatapaḥkarma na tyājyaṃ kāryameva tat |
yajño dānaṃ tapaścaiva pāvanāni manīṣiṇām ||

18.6 एतान्यपि तु कर्माणि सङ्गं त्यक्त्वा फलानि च |
कर्तव्यानीति मे पार्थ निश्चितं मतमुत्तमम् ||

etānyapi tu karmāṇi saṅgaṃ tyaktvā phalāni ca |
kartavyānīti me pārtha niścitaṃ matamuttamam ||

18.7 नियतस्य तु संन्यासः कर्मणो नोपपद्यते |
मोहात्तस्य परित्यागस्तामसः परिकीर्तितः ||

niyatasya tu saṃnyāsaḥ karmaṇo nopapadyate |
mohāttasya parityāgastāmasaḥ parikīrtitaḥ ||

18.8 दुःखमित्येव यत्कर्म कायक्लेशभयात्त्यजेत् |
स कृत्वा राजसं त्यागं नैव त्यागफलं लभेत् ||

duḥkhamityeva yatkarma kāyakleśabhayāttyajet |
sa kṛtvā rājasaṃ tyāgaṃ naiva tyāgaphalaṃ labhet ||

18.4 listen to the last word   mine
on this

three types
of renunciation

18.5 activity   yajna   charity   austerity
not to be given up but
to be done

they purify the wise

18.6 but   my last word
they've got to be done
minus attachment
to fruit of action

18.7 isn't right to give up
activity that's duty

when due to delusion it's
said to be
tamasic

18.8 when given up
because difficult
because fear of pain it's
rajasic

no benefit's gained

18.9 कार्यमित्येव यत्कर्म नियतं क्रियतेऽर्जुन |
सङ्गं त्यक्त्वा फलं चैव स त्यागः सात्त्विको मतः ||

kāryamityeva yatkarma niyataṃ kriyate'rjuna |
saṅgaṃ tyaktvā phalaṃ caiva sa tyāgaḥ sāttviko mataḥ ||

18.10 न द्वेष्ट्यकुशलं कर्म कुशले नानुषज्जते |
त्यागी सत्त्वसमाविष्टो मेधावी छिन्नसंशयः ||

na dveṣṭyakuśalaṃ karma kuśale nānuṣajjate |
tyāgī sattvasamāviṣṭo medhāvī chinnasaṃśayaḥ ||

18.11 न हि देहभृता शक्यं त्यक्तुं कर्माण्यशेषतः |
यस्तु कर्मफलत्यागी स त्यागीत्यभिधीयते ||

na hi dehabhṛtā śakyaṃ tyaktuṃ karmāṇyaśeṣataḥ |
yastu karmaphalatyāgī sa tyāgītyabhidhīyate ||

18.12 अनिष्टमिष्टं मिश्रं च त्रिविधं कर्मणः फलम् |
भवत्यत्यागिनां प्रेत्य न तु संन्यासिनां क्वचित् ||

aniṣṭamiṣṭaṃ miśraṃ ca trividhaṃ karmaṇaḥ phalam |
bhavatyatyāginām pretya na tu saṃnyāsinām kvacit ||

18.13 पञ्चैतानि महाबाहो कारणानि निबोध मे |
साङ्ख्ये कृतान्तें प्रोक्तानि सिद्धये सर्वकर्मणाम् ||

pañcaitāni mahābāho kāraṇāni nibodha me |
sāṅkhye kṛtānte proktāni siddhaye sarvakarmaṇām ||

18.9 when what must be done
is done   disciplined

giving up attachment gain it's
sattvic

18.10 doubts snapped off
the wise one   renunciate
is full of sattva
    doesn't stick to doing what's nice
    doesn't detest what's not

18.11 not possible
for the one who bears a body
to give up action entirely

        so
the one who gives up
    fruit of actions
is called
one who gives up   renunciate

18.12 those who do not renounce
have three results
when they depart
    bad good mixed
not so
for those who do

18.13 learn arjuna
    as samkhya says
there are five causes
for the success of all actions

18.14 अधिष्ठानं तथा कर्ता करणं च पृथग्विधम् |
विविधाश्च पृथक्चेष्टा दैवं चैवात्र पञ्चमम् ||

adhiṣṭhānaṃ tathā kartā karaṇaṃ ca pṛthagvidham |
vividhāśca pṛthakceṣṭā daivaṃ caivātra pañcamam ||

18.15 शरीरवाङ्मनोभिर्यत्कर्म प्रारभते नरः |
न्याय्यं वा विपरीतं वा पञ्चैते तस्य हेतवः ||

śarīravāṅmanobhiryatkarma prārabhate naraḥ |
nyāyyaṃ vā viparītaṃ vā pañcaite tasya hetavaḥ ||

18.16 तत्रैवं सति कर्तारमात्मानं केवलं तु यः |
पश्यत्यकृतबुद्धित्वान्न स पश्यति दुर्मतिः ||

tatraivaṃ sati kartāramātmānaṃ kevalaṃ tu yaḥ |
paśyatyakṛtabuddhitvānna sa paśyati durmatiḥ ||

18.17 यस्य नाहंकृतो भावो बुद्धिर्यस्य न लिप्यते |
हत्वाऽपि स इमाँल्लोकान्न हन्ति न निबध्यते ||

yasya nāhaṃkṛto bhāvo buddhiryasya na lipyate |
hatvā'pi sa imāṃllokānna hanti na nibadhyate ||

18.18 ज्ञानं ज्ञेयं परिज्ञाता त्रिविधा कर्मचोदना |
करणं कर्म कर्तेति त्रिविधः कर्मसंग्रहः ||

jñānaṃ jñeyaṃ parijñātā trividhā karmacodanā |
karaṇaṃ karma karteti trividhaḥ karmasaṃgrahaḥ ||

18.14 body site of action
doer agent
organs instruments
activities
& divine grace

18.15 whatever one does
whether lawful or contrary
with body speech or mind
it's because of these five

18.16 this being so
she who sees only herself
as the doer
doesn't get it in half-baked understanding
the dimwit

18.17 she whose attitude
not egoistic

intellect
not unclear

even if she kills these people worlds
doesn't really
isn't bound

18.18 what's known
what's to-be-known
& the one who knows
cause action

& action
is made of
act
actor
instrument

18.19 ज्ञानं कर्म च कर्ता च त्रिधैव गुणभेदत: |
प्रोच्यते गुणसङ्ख्याने यथावच्छृणु तान्यपि ||

jñānaṃ karma ca kartā ca tridhaiva guṇabhedataḥ |
procyate guṇasaṅkhyāne yathāvacchṛṇu tānyapi ||

18.20 सर्वभूतेषु येनैकं भावमव्ययमीक्षते |
अविभक्तं विभक्तेषु तज्ज्ञानं विद्धि सात्त्विकम् ||

sarvabhūteṣu yenaikaṃ bhāvamavyayamīkṣate |
avibhaktaṃ vibhakteṣu tajjñānaṃ viddhi sāttvikam ||

18.21 पृथक्त्वेन तु यज्ज्ञानं नानाभावान्पृथग्विधान् |
वेत्ति सर्वेषु भूतेषु तज्ज्ञानं विद्धि राजसम् ||

pṛthaktvena tu yajjñānaṃ nānābhāvānpṛthagvidhān |
vetti sarveṣu bhūteṣu tajjñānaṃ viddhi rājasam ||

18.22 यत्तु कृत्स्नवदेकस्मिन्कार्ये सक्तमहैतुकम् |
अतत्त्वार्थवदल्पं च तत्तामसमुदाहृतम् ||

yattu kṛtsnavadekasminkārye saktamahaitukam |
atattvārthavadalpaṃ ca tattāmasamudāhṛtam ||

18.23 नियतं सङ्गरहितमरागद्वेषत: कृतम् |
अफलप्रेप्सुना कर्म यत्तत्सात्त्विकमुच्यते ||

niyataṃ saṅgarahitamarāgadveṣataḥ kṛtam |
aphalaprepsunā karma yattatsāttvikamucyate ||

18.24 यत्तुकामेप्सुना कर्म साहंकारेण वा पुन: |
क्रियते बहुलायासं तद्राजसमुदाहृतम् ||

yattu kāmepsunā karma sāhaṃkāreṇa vā punaḥ |
kriyate bahulāyāsaṃ tadrājasamudāhṛtam ||

18.19 knowledge
action
actor
    according to samkhya
are of three types

18.20 by sattvic knowledge
one knows   one eternal
                   in all beings
unity in diversity

18.21 by rajasic knowledge
one knows   one by one
many beings

18.22 by tamasic knowledge
one's attached
to what's to be done
                   pointless petty
not why

18.23 sattvic action is
disciplined
    free   from attachment
    without desire hatred
    without wanting gain

18.24 rajasic action is
selfish
    egoistic
    strenuous

18.25 अनुबन्धं क्षयं हिंसामनपेक्ष्य च पौरुषम् |
मोहादारभ्यते कर्म यतत्तामसमुच्यते ||

anubandhaṃ kṣayaṃ hiṃsāmanapekṣya ca pauruṣam |
mohādārabhyate karma yatattāmasamucyate ||

18.26 मुक्तसङ्गोऽनहंवादी धृत्युत्साहसमन्वितः |
सिद्ध्यसिद्ध्योर्निर्विकारः कर्ता सात्त्विक उच्यते ||

muktasaṅgo'nahaṃvādī dhṛtyutsāhasamanvitaḥ |
siddhyasiddhyornirvikāraḥ kartā sāttvika ucyate ||

18.27 रागी कर्मफलप्रेप्सुर्लुब्धो हिंसात्मकोऽशुचिः |
हर्षशोकान्वितः कर्ता राजसः परिकीर्तितः ||

rāgī karmaphalaprepsurlubdho hiṃsātmako'śuciḥ |
harṣaśokānvitaḥ kartā rājasaḥ parikīrtitaḥ ||

18.28 अयुक्तः प्राकृतः स्तब्धः शठो नैष्कृतिकोऽलसः |
विषादी दीर्घसूत्री च कर्ता तामस उच्यते ||

ayuktaḥ prākṛtaḥ stabdhaḥ śaṭho naiṣkṛtiko'lasaḥ |
viṣādī dīrghasūtrī ca kartā tāmasa ucyate ||

18.29 बुद्धेर्भेदं धृतेश्चैव गुणतस्त्रिविधं शृणु |
प्रोच्यमानमशेषेण पृथक्त्वेन धनंजय ||

buddherbhedaṃ dhṛteścaiva guṇatastrividhaṃ śṛṇu |
procyamānamaśeṣeṇa pṛthaktvena dhanaṃjaya ||

18.25 tamasic action
started in delusion
regardless of consequence
harm loss
& of one's own competence

18.26 the sattvic doer is free
from attachment
doesn't talk about herself
steadfast
enthusiastic
unchanging
in success & failure

18.27 the rajasic doer
passionate greedy
wants gain
by nature violent
impure
all joy or grief

18.28 the tamasic doer
undisciplined deceitful lazy procrastinator
stubborn depressive wicked show-off

18.29 now for the fine distinctions
of intelligence
& will
as per the gunas the qualities
here's a full primer
hear

18.30 प्रवृत्तिं च निवृत्तिं च कार्याकार्ये भयाभये |
बन्धं मोक्षं च या वेत्ति बुद्धिः सा पार्थ सात्त्विकी ||

pravṛttiṃ ca nivṛttiṃ ca kāryākārye bhayābhaye |
bandhaṃ mokṣaṃ ca yā vetti buddhiḥ sā pārtha sāttvikī ||

18.31 यया धर्ममधर्मं च कार्यं चाकार्यमेव च |
अयथावत्प्रजानाति बुद्धिः सा पार्थ राजसी ||

yayā dharmamadharmaṃ ca kāryaṃ cākāryameva ca |
ayathāvatprajānāti buddhiḥ sā pārtha rājasī ||

18.32 अधर्मं धर्ममिति या मन्यते तमसावृता |
सर्वार्थान्विपरीतांश्च बुद्धिः सा पार्थ तामसी ||

adharmaṃ dharmamiti yā manyate tamasāvṛtā |
sarvārthānviparītāṃśca buddhiḥ sā pārtha tāmasī ||

18.33 धृत्या यया धारयते मनःप्राणेन्द्रियक्रियाः |
योगेनाव्यभिचारिण्या धृतिः सा पार्थ सात्त्विकी ||

dhṛtyā yayā dhārayate manaḥprāṇendriyakriyāḥ |
yogenāvyabhicāriṇyā dhṛtiḥ sā pārtha sāttvikī ||

18.34 यया तु धर्मकामार्थान्धृत्या धारयतेऽर्जुन |
प्रसङ्गेन फलाकाङ्क्षी धृतिः सा पार्थ राजसी ||

yayā tu dharmakāmārthāndhṛtyā dhārayate'rjuna |
prasaṅgena phalākāṅkṣī dhṛtiḥ sā pārtha rājasī ||

18.35 यया स्वप्नं भयं शोकं विषादं मदमेव च |
न विमुञ्चति दुर्मेधा धृतिः सा पार्थ तामसी ||

yayā svapnaṃ bhayaṃ śokaṃ viṣādaṃ madameva ca |
na vimuñcati durmedhā dhṛtiḥ sā pārtha tāmasī ||

18.30 sattvic intelligence understands
freedom   bondage
when to act   when to not
what to do   what to fear
what to not

18.31 rajasic intelligence confounds
right with wrong
what to do with what not

18.32 tamasic intelligence
    steeped in darkness
thinks wrong right
    & everything contrary

18.33 a sattvic will
holds mind breath of life
    & the actions of senses
    via yoga
unwavering

18.34 a rajasic will
stays firm   for pleasure money righteousness
    but selfish
    attached

18.35 the tamasic will
stubborn
    can't give up
    sleep fear grief pride depression
dullhead!

18.36 सुखं त्विदानीं त्रिविधं शृणु मे भरतर्षभ |
अभ्यासाद्रमते यत्र दु:खान्तं च निगच्छति ||

sukhaṃ tvidānīṃ trividhaṃ śṛṇu me bharatarṣabha |
abhyāsādramate yatra duḥkhāntaṃ ca nigacchati ||

18.37 यत्तदग्रे विषमिव परिणामेऽमृतोपमम् |
तत्सुखं सात्त्विकं प्रोक्तमात्मबुद्धिप्रसादजम् ||

yattadagre viṣamiva pariṇāme'mṛtopamam |
tatsukhaṃ sāttvikaṃ proktamātmabuddhiprasādajam ||

18.38 विषयेन्द्रियसंयोगाद्यत्तदग्रेऽमृतोपमम् |
परिणामे विषमिव तत्सुखं राजसं स्मृतम् ||

viṣayendriyasaṃyogādyattadagre'mṛtopamam |
pariṇāme viṣamiva tatsukhaṃ rājasaṃ smṛtam ||

18.39 यदग्रे चानुबन्धे च सुखं मोहनमात्मन: |
निद्रालस्यप्रमादोत्थं तत्तामसमुदाहृतम् ||

yadagre cānubandhe ca sukhaṃ mohanamātmanaḥ |
nidrālasyapramādotthaṃ tattāmasamudāhṛtam ||

18.40 न तदस्ति पृथिव्यां वा दिवि देवेषु वा पुन: |
सत्त्वं प्रकृतिजैर्मुक्तं यदेभि: स्यात्त्रिभिर्गुणै: ||

na tadasti pṛthivyāṃ vā divi deveṣu vā punaḥ |
sattvaṃ prakṛtijairmuktaṃ yadebhiḥ syāttribhirguṇaiḥ ||

18.41 ब्राह्मणक्षत्रियविशां शूद्राणां च परंतप |
कर्माणि प्रविभक्तानि स्वभावप्रभवैर्गुणै: ||

brāhmaṇakṣatriyaviśāṃ śūdrāṇāṃ ca paraṃtapa |
karmāṇi pravibhaktāni svabhāvaprabhavairguṇaiḥ ||

18.36 now hear about happinesses three
one enjoys by practice
& goes to
the end of sorrow

18.37 what seems like poison at first
is like nectar in the end

this happiness sattvic said to come
from self insight
& clarity

18.38 the meeting of
senses & objects seems
like nectar at first but later
poisonlike that's rajasic happiness

18.39 tamasic happiness
    deludes at first
    & in outcome
it comes from sleep laziness negligence

18.40 there isn't one being born to matter nature
    on earth or among
    the deities in 'heaven'
who's free
from these three gunas sattvic rajasic tamasic

18.41 the work
of the four varnas
    (brahmin kshatriya vaishya shudra)
is assigned
by their gunas their innate nature

18.42 शमो दमस्तप: शौचं क्षान्तिरार्जवमेव च |
ज्ञानं विज्ञानमास्तिक्यं ब्रह्मकर्म स्वभावजम् ||

śamo damastapaḥ śaucaṃ kṣāntirārjavameva ca |
jñānaṃ vijñānamāstikyaṃ brahmakarma svabhāvajam ||

18.43 शौर्यं तेजो धृतिर्दाक्ष्यं युद्धे चाप्यपलायनम् |
दानमीश्वरभावश्च क्षात्रं कर्म स्वभावजम् ||

śauryaṃ tejo dhṛtirdākṣyaṃ yuddhe cāpyapalāyanam |
dānamīśvarabhāvaśca kṣātraṃ karma svabhāvajam ||

18.44 कृषिगौरक्ष्यवाणिज्यं वैश्यकर्म स्वभावजम् |
परिचर्यात्मकं कर्म शूद्रस्यापि स्वभावजम् ||

kṛṣigaurakṣyavāṇijyaṃ vaiśyakarma svabhāvajam |
paricaryātmakaṃ karma śūdrasyāpi svabhāvajam ||

18.45 स्वे स्वे कर्मण्यभिरत: संसिद्धिं लभते नर: |
स्वकर्मनिरत: सिद्धिं यथा विन्दति तच्छृणु ||

sve sve karmaṇyabhirataḥ saṃsiddhiṃ labhate naraḥ |
svakarmaṇirataḥ siddhiṃ yathā vindati tacchṛṇu ||

18.42 by nature
the work of a brahmin is
peace control austerity purity patience rightness
knowledge wisdom faith

18.43 heroism pageantry will skill
charity grandeur
& not deserting in war

by nature
the work of the kshatriya

18.44 farming shepherding trade
by nature the vaishya's

& by nature
service
the work of the shudra

18.45 when each is delighted in her own
work reaches perfection

so hear how one finds
perfection in one's own

18.46 यत: प्रवृत्तिर्भूतानां येन सर्वमिदं ततम् |
स्वकर्मणा तमभ्यर्च्य सिद्धिं विन्दति मानव: ||

yataḥ pravṛttirbhūtānāṃ yena sarvamidaṃ tatam |
svakarmaṇā tamabhyarcya siddhiṃ vindati mānavaḥ ||

18.47 श्रेयान्स्वधर्मो विगुण: परधर्मात्स्वनुष्ठितात् |
स्वभावनियतं कर्म कुर्वन्नाप्नोति किल्बिषम् ||

śreyānsvadharmo viguṇaḥ paradharmātsvanuṣṭhitāt |
svabhāvaniyataṃ karma kurvannāpnoti kilbiṣam ||

18.48 सहजं कर्म कौन्तेय सदोषमपि न त्यजेत् |
सर्वारम्भा हि दोषेण धूमेनाग्निरिवावृता: ||

sahajaṃ karma kaunteya sadoṣamapi na tyajet |
sarvārambhā hi doṣeṇa dhūmenāgnirivāvṛtāḥ ||

18.49 असक्तबुद्धि: सर्वत्र जितात्मा विगतस्पृह: |
नैष्कर्म्यसिद्धिं परमां संन्यासेनाधिगच्छति ||

asaktabuddhiḥ sarvatra jitātmā vigataspṛhaḥ |
naiṣkarmyasiddhiṃ paramāṃ saṃnyāsenādhigacchati ||

18.50 सिद्धिं प्राप्तो यथा ब्रह्म तथाप्नोति निबोध मे |
समासेनैव कौन्तेय निष्ठा ज्ञानस्य या परा ||

siddhiṃ prāpto yathā brahma tathāpnoti nibodha me |
samāsenaiva kaunteya niṣṭhā jñānasya yā parā ||

18.46 by dedicating one's work
to the origin of beings
by whom the universe is permeated
one reaches perfection

18.47 better to play one's own role unremarkable
than another's role well

working in line with innate nature
one isn't culpable

18.48 mustn't give up
work you're born with
even when it's not nice
(& anyway) all missions are clouded by flaws
as fire by smoke

18.49 one achieves
ideal actionlessness by
renunciation
self mastery
desirelessness
& an always detached
intelligence

18.50 after perfection how
does one attain brahman
the highest state
knowledge
here's a brief

18.51 बुद्ध्या विशुद्धया युक्तो धृत्यात्मानं नियम्य च |
शब्दादीन्विषयांस्त्यक्त्वा रागद्वेषौ व्युदस्य च ||

buddhyā viśuddhayā yukto dhṛtyātmānaṃ niyamya ca |
śabdādīnviṣayāṃstyaktvā rāgadveṣau vyudasya ca ||

18.52 विविक्तसेवी लघ्वाशी यतवाक्कायमानसः |
ध्यानयोगपरो नित्यं वैराग्यं समुपाश्रितः ||

viviktasevī laghvāśī yatavākkāyamānasaḥ |
dhyānayogaparo nityaṃ vairāgyaṃ samupāśritaḥ ||

18.53 अहंकारं बलं दर्पं कामं क्रोधं परिग्रहम् |
विमुच्य निर्ममः शान्तो ब्रह्मभूयाय कल्पते ||

ahaṃkāraṃ balaṃ darpaṃ kāmaṃ krodhaṃ parigraham |
vimucya nirmamaḥ śānto brahmabhūyāya kalpate ||

18.54 ब्रह्मभूतः प्रसन्नात्मा न शोचति न काङ्क्षति |
समः सर्वेषु भूतेषु मद्भक्तिं लभते पराम् ||

brahmabhūtaḥ prasannātmā na śocati na kāṅkṣati |
samaḥ sarveṣu bhūteṣu madbhaktiṃ labhate parām ||

18.55 भक्त्या मामभिजानाति यावान्यश्चास्मि तत्त्वतः |
ततो मां तत्त्वतो ज्ञात्वा विशते तदनन्तरम् ||

bhaktyā māmabhijānāti yāvānyaścāsmi tattvataḥ |
tato māṃ tattvato jñātvā viśate tadanantaram ||

18.56 सर्वकर्माण्यपि सदा कुर्वाणो मद्व्यपाश्रयः |
मत्प्रसादादवाप्नोति शाश्वतं पदमव्ययम् ||

sarvakarmāṇyapi sadā kurvāṇo madvyapāśrayaḥ |
matprasādādavāpnoti śāśvataṃ padamavyayam ||

18.51–18.53 by pure intelligence attuned
determined controlled
giving up egoism aggression
arrogance desire anger
possessiveness attraction repulsion
sound & other sense objects
living alone eating lightly
controlling speech mind body
relying on detachment
peaceful unselfish
always in yoga the highest

one gets fit for oneness
with brahman

18.54 one with brahman
soothed neither mourns nor wants

to all beings equal
to me most devoted

18.55 through devotion
aware who i am
what i am
& knowing my reality
at once enters me

18.56 relying on me
for all work always
she reaches by my grace
eternal infinite place

18.57 चेतसा सर्वकर्माणि मयि संन्यस्य मत्परः |
बुद्धियोगमुपाश्रित्य मच्चित्तः सततं भव ||

cetasā sarvakarmāṇi mayi saṃnyasya matparaḥ |
buddhiyogamupāśritya maccittaḥ satataṃ bhava ||

18.58 मच्चित्तः सर्वदुर्गाणि मत्प्रसादात्तरिष्यसि |
अथ चेत्वमहंकारान्न श्रोष्यसि विनङ्क्ष्यसि ||

maccittaḥ sarvadurgāṇi matprasādāttariṣyasi |
atha cettvamahaṃkārānna śroṣyasi vinaṅkṣyasi ||

18.59 यदहंकारमाश्रित्य न योत्स्य इति मन्यसे |
मिथ्यैष व्यवसायस्ते प्रकृतिस्त्वां नियोक्ष्यति ||

yadahaṃkāramāśritya na yotsya iti manyase |
mithyaiṣa vyavasāyaste prakṛtistvāṃ niyokṣyati ||

18.60 स्वभावजेन कौन्तेय निबद्धः स्वेन कर्मणा |
कर्तुं नेच्छसि यन्मोहात्करिष्यस्यवशोऽपि तत् ||

svabhāvajena kaunteya nibaddhaḥ svena karmaṇā |
kartuṃ necchasi yanmohātkariṣyasyavaśo'pi tat ||

18.61 ईश्वरः सर्वभूतानां हृद्देशेऽर्जुन तिष्ठति |
भ्रामयन्सर्वभूतानि यन्त्रारूढानि मायया ||

īśvaraḥ sarvabhūtānāṃ hṛddeśe'rjuna tiṣṭhati |
bhrāmayansarvabhūtāni yantrārūḍhāni māyayā ||

18.62 तमेव शरणं गच्छ सर्वभावेन भारत |
तत्प्रसादात्परां शान्तिं स्थानं प्राप्स्यसि शाश्वतम् ||

tameva śaraṇaṃ gaccha sarvabhāvena bhārata |
tatprasādātparāṃ śāntiṃ sthānaṃ prāpsyasi śāśvatam ||

18.57 mentally give it all up
over to me supreme
take refuge in wisdom as yoga
mind on me constantly be

18.58 you'll cross the hard times by my grace
but if egoistic you
you don't listen you're
finished

18.59 if you think
'i'm-the-doer so
i won't fight'
your idea's in vain for
your nature will push you

18.60 you're bound to your duty your destiny
by your innate nature

what you don't wish
to do you will
do against your will
in delusion

18.61 god lives in the heart of all beings
& by maya power illusion
makes them move as if
strung on a gizmo

18.62 go to god only
with your entire being
from that grace you'll find
a most peaceful place for ever

18.63 इति ते ज्ञानमाख्यातं गुह्याद्गुह्यतरं मया |
विमृश्यैतदशेषेण यथेच्छसि तथा कुरु ||

iti te jñānamākhyātaṃ guhyādguhyataraṃ mayā |
vimṛśyaitadaśeṣeṇa yathecchasi tathā kuru ||

18.64 सर्वगुह्यतमं भूयः शृणु मे परमं वचः |
इष्टोऽसि मे दृढमिति ततो वक्ष्यामि ते हितम् ||

sarvaguhyatamaṃ bhūyaḥ śṛṇu me paramaṃ vacaḥ |
iṣṭo'si me dṛḍhamiti tato vakṣyāmi te hitam ||

18.65 मन्मना भव मद्भक्तो मद्याजी मां नमस्कुरु |
मामेवैष्यसि सत्यं ते प्रतिजाने प्रियोऽसि मे ||

manmanā bhava madbhakto madyājī māṃ namaskuru |
māmevaiṣyasi satyaṃ te pratijāne priyo'si me ||

18.66 सर्वधर्मान्परित्यज्य मामेकं शरणं व्रज |
अहं त्वां सर्वपापेभ्यो मोक्षयिष्यामि मा शुचः ||

sarvadharmānparityajya māmekaṃ śaraṇaṃ vraja |
ahaṃ tvāṃ sarvapāpebhyo mokṣayiṣyāmi mā śucaḥ ||

18.63 thus

knowledge
secret of secrets
has been explained to you

think it over
all of it

then do as you wish

18.64 & most secret of all again
my last word
listen again

you are loved for sure
by me

so i'll speak
for your good

18.65 heart be full of me
be devoted to me
do the rites for me
do homage to me you'll

come to me
i promise truly
you are
my love

18.66 give up all paths
trust me only

i'll free you from all sins
don't worry

18.67 इदं ते नातपस्काय नाभक्ताय कदाचन |
न चाशुश्रूषवे वाच्यं न च मां योऽभ्यसूयति ||

idaṃ te nātapaskāya nābhaktāya kadācana |
na cāśuśrūṣave vācyaṃ na ca māṃ yo'bhyasūyati ||

18.68 य इदं परमं गुह्यं मद्भक्तेष्वभिधास्यति |
भक्तिं मयि परां कृत्वा मामेवैष्यत्यसंशयः ||

ya idaṃ paramaṃ guhyaṃ madbhakteṣvabhidhāsyati |
bhaktiṃ mayi parāṃ kṛtvā māmevaiṣyatyasaṃśayaḥ ||

18.69 न च तस्मान्मनुष्येषु कश्चिन्मे प्रियकृत्तमः |
भविता न च मे तस्मादन्यः प्रियतरो भुवि ||

na ca tasmānmanuṣyeṣu kaścinme priyakṛttamaḥ |
bhavitā na ca me tasmādanyaḥ priyataro bhuvi ||

18.70 अध्येष्यते च य इमं धर्म्यं संवादमावयोः |
ज्ञानयज्ञेन तेनाहमिष्टः स्यामिति मे मतिः ||

adhyeṣyate ca ya imaṃ dharmyaṃ saṃvādamāvayoḥ |
jñānayajñena tenāhamiṣṭaḥ syāmiti me matiḥ ||

18.71 श्रद्धावाननसूयश्च शृणुयादपि यो नरः |
सोऽपि मुक्तः शुभाँल्लोकान्प्राप्नुयात्पुण्यकर्मणाम् ||

śraddhāvānanasūyaśca śṛṇuyādapi yo naraḥ |
so'pi muktaḥ śubhāṃllokānprāpnuyātpuṇyakarmaṇām ||

18.67 this (gita)   must not be told
to one without austerity   faith
who doesn't want to hear it
& who speaks ill of me

18.68 she who lays out
this utter secret
to my devotees
the highest act of devotion
will come to me without doubt

18.69 & no one
does more loving
service than her

& no one
will be more beloved
to me than her

18.70 she who studies this
nice dialogue of ours

i'll be loved
by her knowledge-yajna
that's my take

18.71 even she who merely hears it
full of faith uncynical
is freed
& goes to happy worlds
of those with pure actions

18.72 कच्चिदेतच्छ्रुतं पार्थ त्वयैकाग्रेण चेतसा |
कच्चिदज्ञानसम्मोहः प्रनष्टस्ते धनंजय ||

kaccidetacchrutaṃ pārtha tvayaikāgreṇa cetasā
kaccidajñānasaṃmohaḥ pranaṣṭaste dhanaṃjaya

18.73 अर्जुन उवाच |
नष्टो मोहः स्मृतिर्लब्धा त्वत्प्रसादान्मयाच्युत |
स्थितोऽस्मि गतसंदेहः करिष्ये वचनं तव ||

arjuna uvāca |
naṣṭo mohaḥ smṛtirlabdhā tvatprasādānmayācyuta |
sthito'smi gatasaṃdehaḥ kariṣye vacanaṃ tava ||

18.74 संजय उवाच |
इत्यहं वासुदेवस्य पार्थस्य च महात्मनः |
संवादमिममश्रौषमद्भुतं रोमहर्षणम् ||

saṃjaya uvāca |
ityahaṃ vāsudevasya pārthasya ca mahātmanaḥ |
saṃvādamimamaśrauṣamadbhutaṃ romaharṣaṇam ||

18.75 व्यासप्रसादाच्छ्रुतवानेतद्गुह्यमहं परम् |
योगं योगेश्वरात्कृष्णात्साक्षात्कथयतः स्वयम् ||

vyāsaprasādācchrutavānetadguhyamahaṃ param |
yogaṃ yogeśvarātkṛṣṇātsākṣātkathayataḥ svayam ||

18.72 has all this
been heard by you   arjuna
with a focused mind

has your ignorance & confusion
been destroyed

18.73 arjuna:
lost delusion
gained wisdom memory
by your grace   o' unchanging krishna

i stand corrected doubts gone
i will do as you say

18.74 sanjaya:
this
wonderful dialogue
krishna & arjuna's
is what i heard

so rare it makes
one's hair stands on end

18.75 by the grace of vyasa (author of mahabharata in which this gita is)
i've heard this utter secret
which krishna himself
said

18.76 राजन्संस्मृत्य संस्मृत्य संवादमिममद्भुतम् |
केशवार्जुनयोः पुण्यं हृष्यामि च मुहुर्मुहुः ||

rājansaṃsmṛtya saṃsmṛtya saṃvādamimamadbhutam |
keśavārjunayoḥ puṇyaṃ hṛṣyāmi ca muhurmuhuḥ ||

18.77 तच्च संस्मृत्य संस्मृत्य रूपमत्यद्भुतं हरेः |
विस्मयो मे महान्राजन्हृष्यामि च पुनः पुनः ||

tacca saṃsmṛtya saṃsmṛtya rūpamatyadbhutaṃ hareḥ |
vismayo me mahānrājanhṛṣyāmi ca punaḥ punaḥ ||

18.78 यत्र योगेश्वरः कृष्णो यत्र पार्थो धनुर्धरः |
तत्र श्रीर्विजयो भूतिर्ध्रुवा नीतिर्मतिर्मम

yatra yogeśvaraḥ kṛṣṇo yatra pārtho dhanurdharaḥ |
tatra śrīrvijayo bhūtirdhruvā nītirmatirmama

18.76 o' king dhritarashtra
again&again i
remember this
sacred wonderful dialogue
between krishna & arjuna

again&again
i feel happy

18.77 again&again i
remember krishna's very wonderful form
& again&again
i feel happy
o' king my
astonishment is great

18.78 i believe
wherever there is krishna the master of yoga
wherever there is arjuna the archer
there will be

beauty
victory
prosperity

steady righteousness

ABOUT THE TRANSLATOR

MANI RAO is the author of eleven poetry books, including *Sing to Me*, *Ghostmasters* and *Echolocation*. Her books in translation from Sanskrit include *Saundarya Lahari* and *Kalidasa for the 21st Century Reader*. She did immersive fieldwork among tantric communities in Andhra–Telangana for *Living Mantra: Mantra, Deity and Visionary Experience Today*. Rao has an MFA in Creative Writing and a PhD in Religious Studies. She lives in Bangalore and Puttaparthi.

HarperCollins *Publishers* India

At HarperCollins India, we believe in telling the best stories and finding the widest readership for our books in every format possible. We started publishing in 1992; a great deal has changed since then, but what has remained constant is the passion with which our authors write their books, the love with which readers receive them, and the sheer joy and excitement that we as publishers feel in being a part of the publishing process.

Over the years, we've had the pleasure of publishing some of the finest writing from the subcontinent and around the world, including several award-winning titles and some of the biggest bestsellers in India's publishing history. But nothing has meant more to us than the fact that millions of people have read the books we published, and that somewhere, a book of ours might have made a difference.

As we look to the future, we go back to that one word—a word which has been a driving force for us all these years.

Read.

Harper Collins
4th
HARPER PERENNIAL
HARPER BUSINESS
HARPER BLACK
हार्पर हिन्दी
HarperCollins *Children's Books*
HARPER DESIGN
HARPER VANTAGE
Harper Sport